W9-DAT-777

CITY OF STONE

**Other Books on Jerusalem
by Meron Benvenisti**

The Crusaders in the Holy Land (1973)

Facing the Sealed Wall (1973)

Jerusalem, the Torn City (1977)

The Peace of Jerusalem (1981)

Conflicts and Contradictions (1986)

The Shepherds' War (1989)

Hallowed Ground (1990)

CITY OF STONE
The Hidden History of Jerusalem

Meron Benvenisti

Translated by Maxine Kaufman Nunn

UNIVERSITY OF CALIFORNIA PRESS

Berkeley   Los Angeles   London

#3455342]

University of California Press
Berkeley and Los Angeles, California

University of California Press, Ltd.
London, England

© 1996 by
The Regents of the University of California
First Paperback Printing 1998

Library of Congress Cataloging-in-Publication Data

Benvenisti, Meron, 1934–
    City of stone : the hidden history of Jerusalem / Meron Benvenisti
    : translated by Maxine Kaufman Nunn
        p.   cm.
    Includes index.
    ISBN 0-520-20521-9 (alk. paper); 0-520-207688 (pbk; alk. paper)
        1. Jerusalem--History.   2. Jerusalem--Ethnic relations.   3. Jewish
    -Arab relations.   I. Title.
    DS109.9.B48   1996
    956.94'42--dc20   96-14965
                                                                   CIP
Printed in the United States of America

9 8 7 6 5 4 3 2 1

The paper used in this publication meets the minimum
requirements of American National Standard for
Information Sciences—Permanence of Paper for Printed
Library Materials, ANSI Z39.48-1984.

CONTENTS

LIST OF ILLUSTRATIONS

FIGURES

MAPS

CHAPTER ONE

THE QUARRY OF HISTORY

On Monday, September 4, 1995—the ninth day of the month of Elul in the year A.H. 5755 (according to the Jewish calendar)—the Israeli prime minister Yitzhak Rabin officially opened the celebrations marking the 3,000th anniversary of the establishment of Jerusalem as capital of the Kingdom of Israel. Lasting fifteen months, the festivities focused on the founder of the House of David, who conquered the Jebusite city of Jerusalem and made it the temporal and spiritual capital of his people. "King David's many-faceted personality—musician, warrior, statesman, poet/singer and dancer, as well as king and lover—," stated the official program for the festivities, "will provide the inspiration for an entire year of cultural events." Prime Minister Rabin stood on the stage erected for the occasion at the recently opened archeological park in "David's City" and declared: "Jerusalem is the celebration of the glory of the Jewish people from the day it was created in the Image of God. She is its heart and the apple of its eye; and our festivities here today are only meant to once again elevate Jerusalem 'above our chiefest joy,' as was the custom of our fathers and forefathers."

The information sheets distributed to the invited guests stated: "No other people designated Jerusalem as its capital in such an absolute and binding manner—Jerusalem is the concrete historical expression of the Jewish religion and its heritage on the one hand and of the independence and sovereignty of the Jewish people on the other. Jerusalem's identity as a spiritual and national symbol at one and the same time has forged the unique and eternal bond between this city and the Jewish people, a bond that has no parallel in the annals of the nations. Israel's rule over the united city has allowed her to bloom and prosper, and despite the problems between the communities within her, she has not enjoyed such centrality and importance since her days as the capital of the Kingdom of Israel."

The ceremony that launched the events marking "3,000 Years of Jerusalem, City of David" took place in the presence of some 200 invited guests, all of them members of the Jewish establishment from Israel and abroad. For "security reasons" a solid wall of security personnel barred entry to the residents of the Arab neighborhood in which the park is situated. After all, the site of the City of David is located in the heart of Silwan, an Arab neighborhood with a population of 30,000. Ironically, the houses nearest to the site where the opening ceremonies took place have recently been the scene of sporadic violent confrontations between Jews and Arabs, and in 1991–92 a group of Jewish fanatics, assisted by the police, took over several Arab buildings and forcibly ejected their inhabitants.

One Arab resident of Silwan, who had Jewish settlers forced upon him as neighbors, watched the proceedings in bewilderment. He had no idea of the nature of the sudden visit by the prime minister and the mayor. An Israeli journalist who was recording the reactions of the Arab population to the "Jerusalem 3,000" celebrations explained the meaning of the ceremony to him. The Arab, an employee of an East Jerusalem research institute, pulled out a Palestinian history book and read the following passages aloud: "The Philistines, who came from Crete and Asia Minor, merged with the Canaanites, who originated from the Arabian peninsula, and gave the land its name, Falastin. The Jebusites, a Canaanite people, are the ancestors of the

Palestinians. Abraham was neither a Jew nor a Christian, but a 'believer in one God.' The twelve sons of Jacob fled to Egypt, inter-bred with the Egyptians there and became numerous. Moses and his followers wandered in the desert; they were not endowed with any sci-entific or artistic talents and made no cultural achievements whatso-ever. Hence they were influenced by the Canaanites and imitated their religious beliefs. . . .

"Warfare between the Israelites and the Philistines (Palestinians) continued for hundreds of years, and the Bible confirms that the land's inhabitants, who were of Arabian origin, succeeded in zealously main-taining their independence and culture. Jerusalem has been the capital of our Palestinian Arab homeland ever since it was built by our ances-tors, the Jebusites and the Arab Canaanites, in the heart of Falastin. The Arab presence in Jerusalem was never interrupted, in contrast to the Jewish presence, which disappeared. The Arabs tenaciously remained under the Babylonians, the Persians, the Greeks, the Romans, and the Byzantines. There has been Arab rule in Jerusalem and in Palestine ever since the seventh century (except for the Crusader period). The Arab-Muslim tradition was preserved, and flourished under the Muslim Arab dynasties—the Omayyads, the Abassids, the Fatamids, the Seljuks, the Mamluks, the Ottomans . . . until the British conquest of 1917.

"Even your prophets say that you and your king, David, were foreign occupiers," commented the Arab. "This is what the prophet Ezekiel says: 'Thus saith the Lord God to Jerusalem: Thy birth and thy nativ-ity is of the land of Canaan; thy father was an Amorite and thy mother a Hittite'" (Ezek. 16:3).

Had circumstances been reversed and had Jerusalem been under Palestinian sovereignty, the authorities would have been organizing a "Jebusite Festival" to mark Jerusalem's 5,000th anniversary. During this festival, they would have depicted their historical myths in speech and music, exactly as the Israelis did with their celebration of 3,000 years of the City of David. Who is right? The question is superfluous. The chronicles of Jerusalem are a gigantic quarry from which each side has mined stones for the construction of its myths—and for throwing at each other.

The Museum of the City of Jerusalem is located in a fortress called David's Citadel. The citadel, which guards Jaffa Gate and the western section of the Old City walls, is, in its present form, a Mamluk-Ottoman structure, built in the fourteenth to sixteenth centuries. But its foundations, and one tower in particular, date back to earlier periods: Hasmonean, Herodian, and Crusader. The largest of the site's six towers is the Tower of Phasael, which was built by King Herod and was not destroyed at the time of the destruction of Jerusalem and the Second Temple in A.D. 70. The Romans left this huge tower as evidence of the strength of the Jewish city's fortifications, which they had succeeded in overpowering. The architecturally most famous part of the fortress is a mosque crowned by a minaret, used for hundreds of years by the soldiers stationed here. This structure, called the Tower of David, has come to symbolize the city of Jerusalem, its silhouette adorning numerous engravings, paintings, and posters. The museum catalogue emphatically states: "This is the symbol of the longing and yearning for the Holy Land. Life has gone on here continuously for two thousand years." The catalogue does not mention *whose* life.

And indeed, it is this continuity of life in Jerusalem that the Museum of the City of Jerusalem depicts. The earliest date mentioned on the chronological charts that guide the visitor through the museum is 3150 B.C., which is designated as the beginning of the Canaanite period (approximately 3000–1200 B.C.). Perhaps as a way of combatting the Canaanite-Philistine myth, the space devoted to this period—located before the entrance to the first exhibition hall—is small and exposed to sun and rain. Copies of two or three Canaanite and Egyptian artifacts sum up a period of some 2,000 years and together serve as an introduction to what the museum's designers perceive as the real beginning of Jerusalem's history: its conquest by King David.

It is hard to estimate the extent to which the Palestinians themselves believe the Canaanite-Philistine myth, and one hopes that this absurd attempt to give a historical basis to their claim to Jerusalem is simply a political argument that they themselves do not take seriously. After all, some of their Jewish rivals, calling themselves "the Canaanites," have also sought to identify themselves with the indigenous tribes of the Land of Israel/Palestine while dissociating themselves from the "diaspora Judaism" of the intervening period, of which they are ashamed. The myth of the healthy and complex-free "native-born Israeli" who springs from the soil of the homeland involves rejection of the diaspora and has led a number of Israeli intellectuals to erase the memory of 3,000 years of Jewish history and to view themselves as the direct descendants of the Canaanites. Similarly, Maronite Christian Arabs in Lebanon, wishing to deny the Arab connection, have declared themselves to be Phoenicians—descendants of the ancient seafaring people who ruled the Mediterranean from Tyre to Carthage.

But even if the Palestinians take the Canaanite connection with a grain of salt, they have good reason to reflect—as they tour the Museum of the City of Jerusalem—on the fact that history is written by victors, and not the vanquished. On the chronological charts and in the exhibits, the name "Arab" does not appear. Even the accepted designation of the period beginning with the Arab conquest in A.D. 638 and concluding with the Crusader conquest of 1099—the Early Arab Period—was changed not long ago to the Early Muslim Period: it is easier to define the Arabs as Muslims, for there is no "Muslim nation." But there is, of course, a Jewish nation. The Omayyad, Abbasid, Fatamid, Ayoubid, Mamluk, and Ottoman dynasties—all of them Muslim—which ruled Jerusalem for nearly thirteen hundred years (638–1917, except for the Crusader period) appear in the museum chronology by their individual names, thereby turning the city's history into what appears to be a chronology of "foreign" conquerors. Thus one may ignore the Arab identity of the city's inhabitants throughout all that time and the fact that the Arab community played an integral part in the administration of this "foreign rule." There is no need to chronicle the history of the city itself, its institutions, and its public figures; nor is there any need to come to terms with the fact that in the pre-nationalist era, Arabs from Jerusalem held positions throughout the entire Arab world—as government officials in Damascus, Cairo, Istanbul, and beyond, some even serving as governors of Ottoman districts in Iraq and Yemen. Hence, this was not merely a "foreign regime," as it is portrayed in David's Citadel.

In contrast to this historical perspective, when the subject is the Jewish connection to Jerusalem, the museum emphasizes the physical presence of the Jewish community, providing demographic data and describing the nationalist and religious aspirations of the Jewish people in the diaspora toward Jerusalem. This is not surprising. After all, if one treats the history of Jerusalem in terms of regimes, it becomes clear that Jewish rule in Jerusalem spanned only some 600 of the past 3,000 years. In fact, classifying Arab-Muslim rule according to the various conquerors who captured the city from one another is quite convenient; the resulting chronology is miraculously divided into units of time all of which are shorter than the period of Jewish rule in the city.

One of the exhibition halls in the museum is, as previously mentioned, a mosque in which soldiers prayed until the Israeli occupation of the Old City in 1967. The front section of the mosque is now devoted to an exhibit on Islam in Jerusalem. The praying niche and pulpit have been cleaned and whitewashed, but the ancient dedications in Arabic script affixed to the wall have not been given a Hebrew or English translation. The main portion of the mosque is actually devoted to the Crusader period; the 88-year rule of these European knights (1099–1187) gets sympathetic and detailed treatment, including thirteenth-century music playing softly in the background. Not that this prominent reminder of a short episode in the life of the 5,000-year-old city occupies a disproportionate place in the narrative. On the contrary, it emphasizes the universality of the Holy City without impinging on Jewish-Israeli claims, and it reinforces the religious aspect of the city's history. Just as there is no "Muslim nation," there is no "Christian nation" and no fear that the Christians will launch a new crusade to deliver Jerusalem from the hands of the Jews.

The last in the long list of foreign occupiers was Christian—imperial Great Britain. The chronicles of the struggle to liberate Jerusalem from the yoke of the British conqueror are depicted in the final, most dramatic exhibit. A series of slides back-projected onto a large screen illustrates that the struggle and the evolution of the Jewish community, including the bombing of the King David Hotel by the *Irgun* (the underground "National Military Organization") in 1946, the punishment imposed by the British army, and the Jews' eventual victory in their struggle for independence (a large Union Jack is lowered and its place on the flagpole is taken by the flag of Israel). The part played by the Arabs in the history of the British Mandate is depicted as "riots" and as "opposition to the partition of Palestine." Then the Jordanian Arab Legion invaded, and Jerusalem was divided in two for nineteen years.

The lowering of the British flag and raising of the Israeli flag is a concrete example of the standard Israeli point of view, which by now has become a "historical fact": the War for Independence, in whose wake the State of Israel was established, was a struggle against British colonialism and the invading Arab armies. The most critical and cruel stage of the struggle—the bloody communal warfare between Jews and Palestinians—was marginalized and swallowed up in the classic anticolonial, national struggle for independence. The 100-year feud over every residential neighborhood, field, and road, and the killing and expulsion of civilians and looting of their property that accompanied it, were obliterated from the national consciousness. The Jewish victors endeavored to forget that embarrassing chapter: a war against the Palestinian community with whom they had formerly shared the city and the country. The Palestinians, a national community and not a Muslim religious sect—who, vanquished, had disappeared from sight—resurfaced nineteen years later, with the reunification of Jerusalem in 1967. But even then they were not recognized as a national collective, and their struggle against the Israeli occupation is characterized in the catalogue of the Museum of the City of Jerusalem as "municipal and political problems." However, "despite these problems," states the catalogue, "the city is unified, and living in it side by side are Jews, Christians, and Muslims, secular and religious."

This, then, is the narrative recounted at David's Citadel: Jerusalem is the capital of the Jewish people, where they established their kingdom and set up their capital 3,000 years ago. For 2,000 years the city was subjected to the rule of foreign conquerors and the Jewish people were exiled from it. In recent generations they have returned to their capital, expelled the foreign invaders, and reestablished the capital of their sovereign state. Each of the conquerors left a mark, and billions of Muslim and Christian believers have embraced the sanctity of Jerusalem—an attachment they appropriated from the Jewish people. No competing national claim to the city exists, since there is no national collective in Jerusalem aside from that of the Israelis.

A museum is not a political pamphlet, in which one carries on a direct debate with one's interlocutor. In a museum one grapples with the opponent via chronological charts and through the emphasis and deemphasis of exhibits. History is a vast quarry from whose stones a magnificent edifice dedicated to the cult of Israeli Jerusalem has been constructed. In it there is no room for the other—Palestinian-Arab—collective. Its designers, who invested millions of dollars in it, hope that this message will accompany the hundreds of thousands of visitors who go out into the alleyways of the Old City. Those they will meet there are "Muslims and Christians," but not Palestinians, since they have just learned in David's Citadel (whose motto is "here begins Jerusalem") that there was no Palestinian nationality in Jerusalem in the past and there is none in the present. Upon leaving the last exhibition hall, this writer encountered an American tourist couple who were arguing over which of the six towers of the citadel was the real Tower of David. The woman pointed at the mosque with the minaret soaring above it, while the man insisted that it was the massive herodian tower. "But this is the one shown in the catalogue," said the woman. "Maybe you're right," responded the man, "but if so, how is it that David's Tower is shaped like an Arab structure?"

David's Citadel is not Alhambra in Granada, from which the Arabs were long ago expelled, and whose builders can be identified without the identification having political significance. In Jerusalem and its vicinity live one million Palestinians for whom David's Citadel is not a silent monument to a romantic past that has faded, but a living symbol of identity, and its mosque not an exhibition hall, but a holy place. The contradiction between the citadel's being an expression of the Palestinians' attachment to Jerusalem and its being "the symbol of the longing and yearning for the Holy Land" of the Jews makes it truly symbolic of Jerusalem: a conflict-riven city, where each side strives to appropriate for itself both the physical and the chronological space.

History may be written by victors, but the vanquished have not relinquished their version and are diligently cultivating it. Persons wishing a glimpse of the other side's perspective may visit the Museum of Islam on the Temple Mount. There they will find no trace of the Jews. The Palestinians' insistence on promoting their sacred history and geography makes the Israeli victors uneasy. The need to justify their continued dominion over a cohesive Palestinian community, proud of its heritage, has compelled the Israelis to develop symbols and ceremonies aimed at fostering their own legitimacy. They also feel a need to justify the status quo to the outside world—particularly to the liberal Western public.

These needs planted the seeds of the inspired idea of leaping backward 3,000 years in time to anchor Israel's claims to Jerusalem and the legitimacy of its rule over the entire city in a sovereign act by King David at the dawn of history. The "Jerusalem 3,000" celebrations were understood exactly as those who conceived the idea intended, that is, in the immediate political context, and no one took their official rationale or their cultural-historical content seriously. Nonparticipation in the celebrations or pertinent criticism of their content was perceived as a challenge to the legitimacy of Israeli rule and as evidence of an unpatriotic or even anti-Israeli stance. When the ambassador of the United States dared to be absent from the opening ceremonies, the U.S. Jewish community was alerted and protested to the secretary of state. The secretary made assurances that the ambassador's chance absence from the opening did not imply either support for the Arab position or opposition to the status of Jerusalem as Israel's eternal capital. Israeli scientists took issue with the date specified by the organizers as the beginning of King David's reign, arguing that it did not match established scientific chronology, whereas historians protested that the program of events intentionally erased thousands of years of the city's history and glossed over other ties to the Holy City. All of these protestations were dismissed on the grounds that they were not pertinent but were simply being used to camouflage political support for the redivision of "unified Jerusalem."

It is worthy of mention that members of the scientific community in Israel—historians, geographers, and archeologists—have not responded to the unceasing efforts to enlist them in the campaign to provide a basis for nationalist political allegations. The days when research on Jerusalem and the Land of Israel could be used as a means of establishing Jewish ownership claims are gone forever. In the not-too-distant past, the dominant approach of such research was to focus exclusively on periods when there was a massive Jewish presence in Jerusalem and the Land of Israel / Palestine. Archeologists and historians intensively studied the periods of David's kingdom, the Second Temple, and the Mishnah and Talmud. The periods that followed—from the Byzantine era through the time of Ottoman rule—were neglected, since they did not directly touch on the history of the Jewish people.

This disregard for thousands of years in the history of non-Jewish Jerusalem has been replaced by a desire to treat the city's past outside of its ethnic context. Israeli scholars have recently published studies of the history of Jerusalem during the Crusader, Mamluk, and Ottoman periods. They have delved into the archives of the Muslim courts of law in the Old City and elucidated the day-to-day life of the city during periods when the Jewish and Christian communities were under Muslim rule—something that has been given no mention in the official Israeli narrative. Indeed, several of these Israeli scholars have dealt with subjects of particular sensitivity from a political point of view, thereby furnishing the Palestinians with some of their strongest arguments. This liberation from the bonds of politically committed research reflects the scholars' feeling that Israel's claims are accepted as a matter of course and need no reinforcement from selective history. The younger Israeli scholars approach their research with a simple sense of belonging to the city, without dependence on Zionist ideology, feelings of guilt, or the need to vindicate one's own claims.

The problem is that these studies are accumulating in scientific libraries or have been published in professional journals to which the public does not have ready access. Most important, this scholarship has not found its way into school texts, where the ethnocentric Israeli and Palestinian approaches continue to flourish. The stonecutters have proceeded with their work in the quarry of history, but they have no control over the architects of intercommunal strife, who continue building their respective cult sites.

Nevertheless, as we peer into the quarry, the wondrous panorama of Jerusalem's 5,000 years becomes clearer, and the images that give this city its human dimension begin to stand out. Here is Melchizedek, the king of the Canaanite city of Shalem, "and he was a priest of the most high God" who blesses Abraham: "Blessed be Abram of the most high God, possessor of heaven and earth" (Gen. 14:18–20). Here is King David, conqueror of Jebusite Jerusalem— "Nevertheless, David took the stronghold of Zion: the same is the city of David" (2 Sam. 5:6–9)—the king who did not slaughter the Jebusite inhabitants of the city, and who, upon bringing the Ark of the Covenant into the city, unabashedly "danced before the Lord with all his might" (2 Sam. 6:14).

Here is King Solomon, the wisest of men, who built the city and the temple and in so doing established Jerusalem as the political and religious center of the people of Israel. And here is Zedekiah, the last king of David's lineage, who fell into the hands of the soldiers of Nebuchadnezer, King of Babylon, following the conquest of Jerusalem and the burning of the Temple (586 B.C.): "And they slew the sons of Zedekiah before his eyes, and put out the eyes of Zedekiah and bound him with fetters of brass and carried him to Babylon" (2 Kings 25:7).

Following the Jews' return from Babylonian exile and the completion of the construction of the Second Temple (515 B.C.), the most prominent images are those of Nehemiah, a vizier in the court of the King of Persia who built the walls of Jerusalem (444 B.C.), and Ezra the Scribe: "And Nehemiah, which is the Tirshatha, and Ezra the priest and scribe, and the Levites . . . said unto all the people, This day is holy unto the Lord your God; mourn not, nor weep. For the people wept, when they heard the words of the Law. Then he said unto them, Go your way, eat the fat, and drink the sweet and send portions unto them for whom nothing is prepared: For this day is holy unto our Lord: neither be ye sorry; for the joy of the Lord is your strength" (Neh. 8:9–11). A hundred years passed from the days of Nehemiah until the advent of Alexander of Maccedon (332 B.C.), and approximately 200 years of corrupt and repressive Hellenistic rule led to the Hasmonean revolt, where Judah the Maccabi stands out: "He was like a lion in his exploits, like a lion's whelp . . . he pursued and tracked down the renegades, he consigned those who troubled his people to the flames" (1 Macc. 3:4–5). In the year 165 B.C., Judah the Maccabi restored the Temple "to the sound of zithers, harps and cymbals, at the same time of year and on the same day on which the pagans had originally profaned it. And all the people fell prostrate in adoration, praising to the skies him who had made them so successful" (1 Macc. 4:54–5).

From 37 B.C.–A.D. 4, following approximately 100 years of Hasmonean rule, Herod the Edomite reigned over Jerusalem, and the city and the Temple reached the peak of their greatness and splendor. Jesus of Nazareth looked down on this glorious city from the heights of the Mount of Olives "and wept over it, saying, If thou hadst known, even thou, at least in this thy day, the things which belong unto thy peace! but now they are hid from thine eyes" (Luke 19:41–42). And forty years later (A.D. 70), the great Jewish revolt against the Romans culminated in total defeat and exile: "Then one of the soldiers, without waiting for orders, without a qualm for the terrible consequences of this action . . . Snatched up a blazing piece of wood and climbing on another soldier's back hurled the rand through a golden aperture. . . . As the flames shot into the air the Jews that watched the calamity sent up a cry. . . . The Temple Mount, enveloped in flames from top to bottom, appeared to be boiling up from its very roots: yet the sea of flames was nothing to the ocean of blood" (Josephus, *The Jewish War*, Book 6, Chap. 4).

The eradication of Jewish Jerusalem was accomplished by constructing a Roman city on its ruins (A.D. 130) and by changing its name to Aelia Capitolina. Its transformation into a Christian city was the doing of the Emperor Constantine (A.D. 324) and his mother, Queen Helene: "The pious emperor judged it incumbent on him to render the blessed locality of our savior's resurrection [on the Mount of Olives] an object of attraction and veneration to all . . . [then] he adorned the sacred cave [of Christ's burial place] itself as the chief part of the whole work and hallowed monument . . . with rare columns and profusely enriched with most beautiful decoration of every kind" (Eusebius).

Constantine's mother, Helene, found the holy cross upon which Jesus had been crucified and the sacred tomb, after digging in "a mound of garbage that was piled upon them." In the course of the next 300 years, dozens of churches and monasteries were built in Jerusalem, including the gigantic "New Church" (Nea), whose builder, the Emperor Justinian, said upon its completion: "I am greater than you, King Solomon." The image of this magnificent Christian city was immortalized in the famous mosaic floor of a church in the city of Madaba in Moab (now in the Kingdom of Jordan). The armies of the Persian Empire destroyed the churches in 614, but they ruled Jerusalem for only fifteen years, and shortly afterward a new era in the annals of the city commenced with its conquest by Caliph Omar in 638.

The Arab conquest was accomplished without bloodshed. It bore the stamp of an Arab commander blessed with generosity, integrity, and simplicity. The terms of surrender he dictated were generous: security was granted to the city's inhabitants, their children, their churches, and their right to worship. But some humiliating conditions were imposed upon them as well: they were forbidden to ring the church bells, to wear crosses, or to conduct religious ceremonies in public; non-Muslims were forbidden to bear arms or ride horses; a head tax was imposed, and they were even obliged to shave the front of their heads.

So began a period of more than 400 years of Arab rule, during which the Temple Mount mosques were built (see Chapter 3). The makeup of the population changed and Jerusalem became an Arab city, even if Christians were numerous. The Jews, permitted to return and live there after hundreds of years of Christian rule during which they had been banned from the city, were grateful to the Arab regime. The Jerusalem-born Arab historian Al-Muqadassi describes his city at the close of the tenth century: "And as to her being the finest city, why, has any seen elsewhere buildings finer or cleaner, or a mosque that is more beautiful? . . . Still, Jerusalem has some disadvantages. . . . In this city the oppressed have no succor; the weak are molested and the rich envied; also schools are unattended [and] everywhere the Christians and the Jews have the upper hand" (quoted in Guy Le Strange, *Palestine Under the Moslems* [Beirut: Khayats, 1965]).

The buildings of this lovely city fell into the hands of the Crusaders in 1099, almost without being damaged, but their Muslim and Jewish inhabitants perished in an orgy of killing the likes of which have seldom been seen. A Crusader chronicler describes the scene: "It was impossible to look upon the vast numbers of slain without horror; everywhere lay fragments of human bodies, and the very ground was covered with the blood of the slain . . . still more dreadful it was to gaze upon the victors themselves, dripping with blood from head to foot, an ominous sight which brought terror to all who met them" (William of Tyre, *A*

History of Deeds Done Beyond the Sea. Trans. E.A. Babcock and A.C. Krey. [New York: Columbia University Press, 1943], 372).

Eighty-eight years later, Crusader Jerusalem was besieged by the Muslim army commanded by Sultan Salah al-Din (Saladin). The besieged Jerusalemites trembled for fear that the Muslims would make them pay for the slaughter of their people. But the sultan was made of different stuff. He was humane, generous, sensitive, merciful toward the weak, honest, skillful in statesmanship, and courageous in war. In short, the image of Saladin the infidel matched the ideal of the Christian knight. Saladin set generous terms of surrender, and no Christian was killed. The Christians left the city after paying a ransom, the mosques that had been turned into churches were ritually purified, and several churches were made into mosques. The Church of the Holy Sepulchre was closed for a short time, after which it was reopened and Christian worship restored. The image of the generous enemy, the unbeliever who demonstrated the Christian spirit more than the Christians themselves, kindled the imagination of the Europeans. They merged the romance of Saladin with that of another ideal knight of the Middle Ages, Richard the Lion-Hearted. These two fearless and irreproachable knights fought one another, conducted negotiations, and respected each other. When Richard left the shores of the Holy Land, he sent Saladin a message that he was returning home only in order to raise money to enable him to complete the liberation of Jerusalem. Saladin responded: "Truly, if God wills that Jerusalem pass into other hands, it cannot fall into any more noble than those of the great *Malik Rik* (King Richard)."

The Holy City remained in Muslim hands for 730 years (1187–1917). During those centuries Christian pilgrims visited the city, splendid Mamluk structures were built, and a large Jewish community gathered there. From time to time Christian rulers called for the "deliverance" of Jerusalem, and Muslim monarchs fought each other for control. "However," states an English historian writing in the 1870s, "during the interval of five hundred years Jerusalem has been without a history. Nothing has happened but an occasional act of brutality on the part of her masters toward the Christians." History returned to Jerusalem during the nineteenth century, when the European powers began to show an interest in the city and to squabble over chunks ripped from the ailing body of the Ottoman Empire.

But the annals of the Jewish community in Jerusalem during those 500 years show that life was not devoid of incident. It was hard, full of persecution on the part of the authorities and provocation by the Arab inhabitants of the city. "The peoples scorn the Jews so much that they do not allow us to walk on the streets, but rather a Jew must descend from the path so that a Gentile may pass, and if the Israelite does not descend by himself, he is lowered against his will," recounted one rabbi. A traveler reported that "the Jews there exist in a state of the cruelest and most shameful poverty and subjugation. They are less sensitive to their misfortune than to the well-being they expect after their death, by reason of which they live there in hopes of dying there and being buried with their ancestors." There are many testimonies to the poverty, the terrible living conditions, the filth, and the neglect that prevailed in the Jewish quarter, but this quarter was not exceptional. As late as the nineteenth century, European travelers were describing Jerusalem in the bleakest terms: "Ruins everywhere, and everywhere the odor of graves," wrote the French author Gustav Flaubert. "It seems as if the Lord's curse hovers over the city. The Holy City of three religions is rotting away from boredom, dejection, and neglect."

The language of these testimonies describing the shocking condition of Jerusalem—repeated in nearly all the accounts penned by European travelers—does indeed reflect the actual situation. However, these descriptions are not so innocent and free from bias as they might seem. They were written with the intent of providing justification and an excuse for colonial aspirations, and they evinced a Eurocentric arrogance regarding the "white man's burden" or its French equivalent, *mission civilisatrice*. The backwardness of the Orientals—so the argument went—the dirt and neglect, the prejudices and religious fanaticism, the cruel and corrupt despotism of the Ottomans, and the misery of the Jews, all cried out for salvation by the West. Only the European powers and their emissaries were capable of bringing Progress to the Orient. The era of colonialism in the Middle East did not officially commence until after the First World War and lasted a very short time (1917–1947), but its seeds were sown in Jerusalem's soil during approximately the same period that European colonial regimes were being established in Africa and the Far East. Strategic considerations precluded the dismantling of the Ottoman Empire at that time; therefore competition between the aspiring colonialist nations assumed a cultural, religious, and economic guise. But the pretense of bringing progress to the backward city of Jerusalem fooled no one, and even the "primitive natives" understood its significance and exploited it to their own ends.

Were it not for the habit of the Israelis and Palestinians of always returning to the quarry of history to dig up arguments to aid them in their present-day quarrels, the historical description of Jerusalem relevant to our needs could have begun with the mid-nineteenth century. It was then that the internal and external political forces, interests, ideologies, and processes that provided the background for the Jewish-Arab struggle, which burst into the open around the time of the First World War and immediately afterwards, first began slowly to take shape. And indeed, the mid-nineteenth century will serve as our point of departure for most of the subjects discussed in this book.

For many generations intra-European competition in this "backward and neglected" city had been left to the fanatical and small-minded clergy. But in the fourth decade of the last century, the agents of European progress arrived, seeking to bring change—not because of their concern for the good of the city and its inhabitants, but because of fear that the city would fall into the hands of others. The English were first, as usual. They suspiciously eyed the French and the Russians, whose involvement in Levantine matters was longstanding. The Russians considered themselves heirs of the Byzantines; the French, successors of the Crusaders. Both demanded for themselves the noble status of "defenders of Christianity and the holy places"—each, of course, in the name of a different Christianity. The pretensions of the French and the Russians were not accompanied by concrete efforts to improve the state of the oppressed Christians, who strained under the Turkish yoke. Only when Great Britain arrived on the scene and gave notice—in the name of a third (Protestant) Christianity—that it too had something to say and that it too demanded "influence," were the "defenders" aroused to action. The French came to the rescue of the Catholics, and the Russians championed the Greek Orthodox. The British, finding only two Protestants in all of Jerusalem, became the saviors of the Jews.

All of the Europeans took pains to do good deeds in the holy city: tending the sick, introducing technical and scientific innovations, improving the sewer system and purifying the water, eradicating ignorance, unearthing the past, and revealing "the truth" (that of Jesus of Nazareth) to the masses of primitive natives. The emissaries of each nation also had additional motives (that some might regard as the more important ones); to outdo their rivals, to win over more natives, and to create solid political and physical "facts" that would improve their country's standing in the competition to inherit pieces of the crumbling Ottoman empire. When one built a church, the rivals built four; when a hospital was established, three more followed in its wake; when a bishop was appointed, two patriarchs were named without delay; when a Frenchman published an earthshaking scientific discovery, German and English scientists hastened to refute it. When the Russians sought to attack the Turks and plunder their land, they could find no better excuse than an alleged violation of Greek Orthodox rights; and when the English wished to spy out the land, their best pretext was that they were investigating the wanderings of the Children of Israel in the desert.

The compulsive need to "display the flag" was usually expressed by a "friendly visit" of gunboats to Jaffa, Jerusalem's port city. But in Jerusalem the rivalry over the flag became comical when it turned into a struggle over postage-stamp licking. In 1859, a post office was opened in Jerusalem in front of which the symbol of the Hapsburg Empire fluttered and on whose stamps appeared the image of His Apostolic Majesty the King-Emperor of Austria. For many years the Austrians enjoyed practically a monopoly on mail service (except for an unsuccessful attempt by the local imperator to provide Ottoman mail service). Finally, the German Empire could no longer bear the humiliation of having Jerusalem residents lick only stamps upon which the likeness of Emperor Franz Josef appeared. In 1900 a German Imperial Post Office was opened. The Germans (always more efficient than their Austrian cousins) found a sophisticated way to display a flag on every street corner: they distributed blue mailboxes throughout the city. No more than six months passed, and the French opened their own post office, which also distributed mailboxes—in art nouveau style, of course. In 1901 the Imperial Russian Post Office was opened and, last but not least, the Italian Mail (in 1907), when even Italy had awakened to the need to exhibit its presence in the East.

The first French consul in Jerusalem, Comte Gabriel Marie Jean Benoit de Lantivy de Kerveno, who served in 1843–44, described the competition among the European powers (disguised as religious-humanitarian activity) as follows: "The Anglicans (Episcopalians) prosper and are making great efforts, which have not borne fruit as yet, to create an English nation here via the conversion of the populace. The Anglicans are striving to attract the Jews of Jerusalem, as they already have the Druze in Lebanon, so as to cut this population off from the influence of French patronage. To this end, they are making efforts the likes of which have never before been beheld." The consul enumerated some of the innovations introduced by the Anglicans: a physician, an architect, and a pharmacy, as well as a well-equipped hospital. "I consider it urgent," concluded de Kerveno's letter to his minister, "to establish two Catholic institutions in Jerusalem—that will be obviously French as well—so as to balance the opposing influence of the Anglicans and the Greco-Russians."

The foreign consuls were demigods. One of them commented: "After God, the consuls were the most exalted personalities in Palestine. Not even the Ottoman pasha was so venerated by the populace." They were the long arm of the European powers. A series of agreements, called "capitulations," permitted the consul to establish a sort of island of European sovereignty—not territorial, but personal—in Jerusalem. From the Ottoman authorities they appropriated jurisdiction and control over their respective "protected populations," and the consul himself was authorized to determine which individuals fell under this "protection" and were thereby shielded from the arbitrariness of the authorities and the violence of the "natives." The consul also dispensed justice to those under his protection, in accordance with the laws of his land, and was authorized to imprison or fine them, employing for this purpose armed men called *kavasses*. Protected persons, both European citizens and local people (who had obtained certificates of protection on various pretexts), were extremely grateful. Only the consul's protection enabled them to exist in this barbaric land and to work toward the realization of their religious aspirations or their commercial ambitions.

There were almost no limits to the range of the consuls' activities or to their ability to implement the power vested in them. Paradoxically, the principal constraints were a consequence of the weakness of the local regime: coping with the corruption, the inefficiency, and the rivalries among various factions of the population exhausted the consuls. Furthermore, the authorities made effective use of the weapons of the weak, employing cunning and flattery to stir up dissension among the consuls. The otherwise helpless Turks played the consuls against each other. When they gave in and granted one consul a permit from the Sultan (*firman*) for the construction of a building, or some other concession, they would hurriedly dispense a similar concession to a rival consul, thereby intensifying the competition between them. When France and Britain came to collect on their debt for having assisted the Turks in the war against Russia (the Crimean War of 1853–56), the Turkish regime hastened (in 1858) to bestow its army parade ground on the Russians, of all people, for the purpose of setting up a gigantic complex of buildings which is called the Russian Compound to this day.

The consuls, "champions of progress," limited their attentions to "enlightened" persons. Thus, during the 1870s, all of the consulates in Jerusalem together "cared for" only 670 German, British, Russian, and Austrian subjects, in addition to some 3,000 local "protégés," out of a total population of 25,000. The fate of the others did not interest the consuls, and their "progress" was of importance only if it furthered the latter's imperial interests or religious aspirations. The relatively wide scope of the "personal sovereignty" enjoyed by the foreign powers did not change significantly until the period of Ottoman rule was drawing to a close. With the British occupation and the establishment of the Mandatory regime, the "capitulations" were repealed, and the foreign consuls lost the perquisites of their status, with the exception of a few ceremonial courtesies.

Jerusalem's development during the second half of the nineteenth century was extremely rapid. In the space of two generations, the Holy City passed from medieval darkness into the modern age. The "primitive natives" began showing signs of a sense of nationhood, a factor that seriously threatened the old world order. Massive Jewish immigration to Palestine as a whole and to Jerusalem in particular—and the establishment of the Zionist movement—provoked strong reactions from the Arab population, and a Palestinian national movement began to take shape.

"The problem of Jerusalem"—demanding a political, religious, and communal solution secured in international agreements—arose at the close of the First World War, when, following centuries of Ottoman sovereignty, the city was occupied by Great Britain. This was not the first time in modern history that Jerusalem had been the object of international contention. A hundred years before, European states had clashed with one another over the holy places; however, those international disputes were not related to the question of sovereignty over

Jerusalem, but arose from religious disputes that served as a pretext for increasing the spheres of influence of the international powers outside the city (see Chapter 3). Communal strife, too, was dormant until the British occupation. The various communities residing in Jerusalem differed in religious identity only. The Jewish community, which constituted the majority of the city's population by the mid-nineteenth century, uncomplainingly accepted the favored status accorded the Muslim Arabs and contented itself with religious autonomy. Muslim ascendancy was conspicuous in all areas of life in Jerusalem.

The disintegration of the Ottoman Empire exacerbated the problems. Immediately preceding and following the British occupation, the European powers sought to solve the problem of sovereignty by proposing the imposition of international rule over Jerusalem. The Sykes-Picot agreement of 1916 specified that, following the division of the Ottoman Empire, the region between Dan and Beersheba (biblical Palestine) would be placed under "international administration," but this treaty was never implemented. With the conclusion of the war and the dismemberment of the Ottoman Empire, Great Britain received a League of Nations Mandate granting it rule over Palestine, including Jerusalem. This was the solution to the sovereignty problem. The European powers and other interested parties attempted to resolve the issue of the holy places as well. Long and tortuous negotiations were conducted over an international agreement regarding the holy places, which, if signed, would have imposed certain restrictions on British sovereignty in Jerusalem. The negotiations collapsed, however, and in late 1924 it was decided that the British administration would also be responsible for the holy places, without the involvement of outside elements. This was the solution to the religious problem. The problem of Jerusalem ceased, for the time being, to be an object of international concern. The city reverted to being simply the capital of a political entity under British sovereign rule.

It was the ongoing intercommunal conflict that returned the problem of Jerusalem to the international arena. The Jewish and Arab

(Muslim and Christian) communities embarked upon a prolonged, tangled, and bloody struggle for national hegemony in Palestine. Throughout the years of the British Mandate, Jerusalem was the principal point of contention and main arena in this struggle. Conflicting interests came to light in all areas of the city's life: municipal administration, economics, the holy places, national symbols, transportation, commerce, construction, and land ownership. The principal political struggle focused on municipal government. From the time of the municipality's inception during the Turkish period, a Muslim Arab had always served as mayor, and the Arabs demanded the continuation of this practice. However, Jews constituted a majority of the city's population, and they demanded the democratic election of the mayor and members of the city council. The British searched for a compromise solution, but in the end they decided in favor of continuing the status quo (see Chapter 5).

No one was satisfied with this arrangement. The Jews developed their own elaborate system of municipal and communal services, but the existence of separate communal organizations only increased the polarization and tension. The conflict was reflected in the economic and commercial spheres as well—essentially in every aspect of the city's life.

Intercommunal strife in Palestine peaked in the mid-thirties. With the outbreak of the Arab Revolt in 1936, all hope for reconciliation and coexistence evaporated. The British government drew the logical conclusion and for the first time proposed partitioning the country into Jewish and Arab states, in keeping with the recommendations of the Peel Commission (1936). According to this plan, Jerusalem was to remain united and to come under a permanent British Mandate. Elections would be conducted based on ethnically determined electoral districts and voters' lists. In 1938 another commission (the Woodhead Commission) was appointed to implement the partition plan.

Plans to implement partition were suspended in the atmosphere of increasing tension leading up to the Second World War. In May 1939, a White Paper was issued in which the British declared their intention to establish a unified Palestinian state at the end of ten years. In this state a two-thirds Arab majority would be guaranteed by means of restrictions on Jewish immigration, and Jerusalem would have no special status apart from the guaranteed freedom of access to its holy places. Understandably, the Jews rejected the White Paper of 1939; but so did the Arabs.

Meanwhile, the Second World War broke out, and as a result the problem of Jerusalem was temporarily marginalized, even though intercommunal tensions persisted. During the last days of the war and especially in 1946–47, Jerusalem was the scene of violent clashes between Jewish underground organizations and British authorities, which reached a climax with the July 1946 bombing of the British governmental offices in the King David Hotel.

In 1947, the Palestine problem again returned to the international stage. As in 1917, the questions requiring resolution concerned sovereignty, the holy places, and municipal administration. On November 29, 1947, the United Nations General Assembly approved a proposal for the partition of Palestine into two states, Jewish and Arab. The Jerusalem district would become a *corpus separatum*, under UN Trusteeship. A representative of the United Nations was to be designated as responsible for the holy places, whereas municipal administration would be divided between the Jews and Arabs. However, the internationalization of Jerusalem was never accomplished. In the wake of the UN decision, Jews and Arabs embarked upon a war that rapidly expanded into an armed conflict between the Arab countries and the nascent State of Israel.

In the weeks following the proclamation of the state on May 14, 1948, the Israeli government had no time for political decisions that did not relate directly to the most important problem of the hour: the conduct of the war. No steps were taken to define the legal status of those portions of Jerusalem that fell to the Israeli Defense Forces (IDF). The government refrained from political actions liable to provoke the various countries with interests in Jerusalem, even at the price of lack of clarity regarding the form of civilian government in the city.

At that time David Ben-Gurion defined the question of who would govern Jerusalem as "a question of military ability." This was not a decree based on principles, but an interim decision of a practical nature. At that time Israel had not yet abandoned the effort to conquer the entire city. Only in July 1948, when the second cease-fire came into effect, did the Jewish community's leaders begin a process of adjustment to the bitter reality that the Old City would remain outside Israeli jurisdiction. The sole official step taken by the government at that time in Jerusalem was the application of Israeli law to those portions of the city under Israeli control, which was not perceived as an attempt to annex the area to the State of Israel, but as a way to create a "controlled territory," subject to military administration. This step by the government was acceptable to the international community, whose representatives in Jerusalem began referring to the Israeli military governor as "the military governor of Israeli-occupied Jerusalem."

Throughout the summer of 1948 the Israeli government continued to vacillate on the question of Jerusalem. There were three options to choose from: internationalization of the entire city, as demanded by the partition resolution of 1947; partition of the city between Israel and Transjordan, along the military lines established in the aftermath of the war; and occupation of the remainder of the city.

In late August 1948, the Israeli cabinet convened to deliberate the question and decided—by a majority of one (five to four)—that given the choice between the partition and the internationalization of the city, the latter option was preferable, electing to relinquish its sovereignty over Jerusalem entirely rather than divide the city. This decision aroused the ire of the Jewish residents of Jerusalem. Their spokesperson, the military governor Dov Joseph, stated, "It is hard for me to understand the brand of political thinking that says that instead of the Arabs having something it is better that neither they nor we have anything."

David Ben-Gurion laid the military option before the cabinet. He proposed launching a campaign beginning with "storming Latrun and continuing from there north to Ramallah and to Jericho and the Jordan, so as to liberate the Hebron district and the whole area between Latrun and Ramallah and all the way to Jericho and the Dead Sea." He was careful not to mention the Old City explicitly. Foreign Minister Moshe Sharett expressed the opposite opinion: "I am certain that the lesser of the evils is part of Jerusalem for the Arabs—if absolutely essential—rather than international rule over all of Jerusalem."

The final debate, held on September 26, 1948, concluded with two historic votes. Ben-Gurion's proposal regarding a renewed military campaign was rejected by a seven to five majority; and the cabinet decided, with a seven to four majority and two abstentions, that "should the partition [of Jerusalem] be necessary, the [Israeli] delegation to the United Nations would agree."

These decisions defined Israel's policy regarding Jerusalem: first, it must accept the partition of the city as a fact and strive for stabilization of the political-military status quo, while maintaining dialogue with the Transjordanians and opposition to the internationalization of the city; second, the military status quo must not be altered by force via pre-emptive military action, even with a good chance of success.

Faithful to these decisions, Ben-Gurion initiated the renewal of secret contacts with Transjordan, which went on intensively throughout November and December of 1948. Early in 1949, Israeli army officers proposed a plan to capture Judea and Samaria in a lightning attack lasting three days; however, the prime minister rejected it. Even so, Israel still refrained from publicly announcing its official stance on the future of Jerusalem. In accordance with a motto coined by Ben-Gurion, "Declaration—no; deeds—yes," Israel embarked upon a series of vigorous steps to consolidate its rule and its legal status in the city and to make it the capital of the state in practice. In February 1949, military administration of Jerusalem was abolished, and a government decision stated the intent "to implement [in Jerusalem] all the governing arrangements customary elsewhere in the State of Israel." In December 1949, the Knesset began holding its sessions in Jerusalem, and on the sixteenth of that month Ben-Gurion moved his office to the city, designating the beginning of January 1950 as the date when the remaining governmental offices, with the exception of the Foreign Ministry, the Ministry of Defense, and the National Police Headquarters, must make the move. The final step in Israel's effort to establish political faits accomplis in Jerusalem was taken on July 12, 1953, when the spokesperson for the Foreign Ministry announced that "in accordance with the government's decision and following the completion of arrangements for the accommodation of the ministry and its employees, the Foreign Ministry will today move to Jerusalem." The foreign diplomatic missions in Israel reacted lukewarmly to this latest step by the government. Some boycotted the ministry's Jerusalem offices, but only briefly, and ever since 1954, all foreign diplomats have presented their credentials to the president of Israel at his Jerusalem residence and have paid a visit to the Foreign Ministry.

By the time of the 1967 war, there were twenty-three diplomatic missions in Jerusalem. Most missions, however, including all of the major embassies, did not relocate from Tel Aviv. In any case, the prolonged process of creating political "facts" and turning Jerusalem into the capital of the state continued for some six years, concluding in 1954.

The Arab Legion—Transjordan's British-commanded army— entered the battle for Jerusalem on May 18, 1948, thereby preventing the complete collapse of the Arab-Palestinian military campaign in the city and determining the position of the front lines, which, in the form of armistice lines, have remained more or less stationary since then. After a relatively short period of military rule of East Jerusalem, King Abdullah convened the Jericho Conference, at which 2,000 Palestinian public figures expressed their desire for "the unification of Palestine and Transjordan as a step toward full Arab unity." The Jericho Conference proclaimed "His Majesty Abdullah as King of all Palestine." On December 7, 1948, the Transjordanian government declared its intention to implement "the unification of the two sister countries . . . legally and internationally, when the time is ripe." On that day the name Transjordan was abolished and the kingdom renamed "the Hashemite Kingdom of Jordan." Abdullah was forced to postpone the annexation of the West Bank because of vehement opposition from the other Arab countries, but not for long. All the inhabitants of Palestine residing in the West Bank became citizens of the Hashemite Kingdom. The post of Governor General of the Jordanian-occupied territory was abolished and its civilian administration brought under the jurisdiction of the minister of the interior in Amman. In April 1950 parliamentary elections were held with the participation of all the citizens of the kingdom, from both banks of the Jordan River. The unified parliament, made up of twenty representatives of the East Bank and twenty representatives of the West Bank, was called upon to ratify the formal unification of the two banks. The following decision was passed with a large majority and no votes in opposition, several Palestinian delegates having absented themselves before the vote: "Full unification between the two sides of the Jordan Valley, the eastern and the western, and their merger into one state, the Hashemite Kingdom of Jordan." Thus, in mid-1950 East Jerusalem, and with it the West Bank, became an integral part of the Hashemite Kingdom of Jordan.

As we have seen, by late 1948 Israel and Jordan were ripe for negotiations regarding the future of Jerusalem. The Israelis, as previously mentioned, had ratified a decision to accept in principle the partition of the city, and were seeking allies in their struggle to prevent its internationalization. King Abdullah had institutionalized his rule in the West Bank, and at the Jericho Conference assured himself some public support for annexing it to his kingdom. There was room, therefore, to assume that political dialogue between the partners in ruling Jerusalem would bear fruit. These were not the first political negotiations between Jews and the Bedouin king. Throughout the winter and spring of 1948 talks had taken place between representatives of the Jewish Agency and King Abdullah, and there was no difficulty reviving them. Negotiations were resumed in November 1948 and continued without interruption until early 1951. They revolved around military issues, such as the terms of the armistice agreement, the future of the West Bank, a nonaggression pact, and a peace agreement. Concerning Jerusalem, the two sides agreed to regard the ceasefire lines determined in November 1948 as agreed-upon boundaries. The Jordanian negotiators did indeed, from time to time, demand the return of Arab neighborhoods in the western part of the city, but these claims were rejected by the Israelis and King Abdullah did not press the matter. On February 22, 1949, the king stated to the Israeli delegation: "I have no demands with regard to new, that is, West Jerusalem, but I will not agree to hand over the Old City to the Jews or accept its internationalization." The Israelis did not challenge the Old City's remaining in Arab hands; this would have meant an end to the negotiations. What they did want was a guarantee of free access to the holy places, the use of the ancient Jewish cemetery on the Mount of Olives and of the Hebrew University campus on Mount Scopus, and the restoration of the flow of water in the pipeline from Rosh Ha'ayin to Jerusalem via Latrun, then in the hands of the Arab Legion.

The rapid progress being made in the negotiations prompted the Israelis and Jordanians to view these matters as minor details that could be resolved easily and that need not delay the signing of the armistice agreement. In any case they figured that this agreement was just a step on the way to a comprehensive settlement. The two sides therefore agreed that resolution of the remaining issues would be worked out by a special committee appointed in accordance with Article 8 of the Israeli-Jordanian Armistice Agreement. However, this committee's deliberations went badly from the very beginning. It became clear that the sides had conflicting interests. Israel was relatively satisfied with the territorial division that had been settled upon, being interested, as mentioned, chiefly in free access to the holy places and Mount Scopus.

Jordan, by contrast, was not interested in freedom of access but in territorial changes. The pressing issue for the Israelis was their being cut off from the Western Wall and the Israeli sector of Mount Scopus. For the Jordanians it was the tens of thousands of Palestinian refugees who had left the Arab neighborhoods in the "new" city. The Israelis refused to link freedom of access to the return of the refugees, and the Jordanians claimed that the "restoration of normal life," upon which the demand for freedom of access was based, meant the return of the refugees to their homes. The committee's deliberations continued until the end of 1950, but nothing practical came of them. Jerusalem remained divided in half between Israel and Jordan along the cease-fire lines of November 1948, and from the point of view of both states, the question of sovereignty over the city remained open. The Armistice Agreement states categorically that "no provision of this Agreement shall in any way prejudice the rights, claims, and positions of either side hereto in the ultimate peaceful settlement of the Palestine question" (Art. 3). On the basis of this article of the agreement, the Arab states maintained—throughout the years that the armistice remained in force—that the entire agreement was temporary and did not abolish the state of belligerency between Israel and Jordan, that the boundaries designated in the agreement were merely military lines, and that Arabs' signing the document in no way implied their recognition of permanent borders.

The Israelis' argument was the reverse. Israel's version was that the Armistice Agreement had indeed created a permanent situation. Government positions stated in the Knesset make it clear that Israel also did not regard the annexation of the West Bank by Jordan as illegal. As to Jerusalem—there Israel and Jordan accepted each other's de facto rule. Indeed, throughout the years that the armistice held (1948–1967), there were continuous incidents, both minor and major. However, on the whole it may be said that the two sides strove to the best of their abilities to refrain from provoking each other, both being guided by the desire to maintain the status quo as far as possible. During the nineteen years that the city was divided, the two sides essentially sought to cover up the fact that the final outcome of the military campaign for Jerusalem

1. The Tower of David and Jaffa Gate

had not been decided, and by drafting the series of agreements and setting up the proper administrative bodies, this was accomplished. As long as neither side violated the status quo by deliberately attempting to capture territory, the armistice in Jerusalem could be preserved.

On the Israeli side of the city, a sense of forced acquiescence to its division prevailed. The sadness and longing caused by being cut off from the sacred places of the nation were from time to time expressed in works of literature or in emotional outbursts, but these never developed into any political initiative calling for the conquest of the Old City. On the Arab side of Jerusalem, there were severe political tensions between the local people and the Jordanian regime. Jerusalem, more than any other city in the West Bank, was a gathering place for those factions who regarded the Jordanian regime as an invader that had destroyed their hopes for independence. Through violent demonstrations and terrorist acts they attempted to disrupt the plans of those who adopted the idea of integration with Jordan. The regime fought these factions, which were centered around the Mufti Hajj Amin al-Husseini and the leftist parties. The Arab Legion jailed them or banished them from the city. The Jordanians cultivated and fostered the rivals of the Husseinis. On the assumption that diplomatic support for the strengthening of Jerusalem as the political center of the West Bank would promote the Palestinian separatist cause, the Jordanians persistently and vigorously worked to establish Amman's status as the sole political and economic center of the kingdom. They purposely held back Jerusalem's development, deprived the city of any political power base, abolished its limited administrative independence, and turned it into a backward provincial town. The Palestinians followed these actions angrily, but were powerless to oust the regime. They persevered in their protests against Jerusalem's backward and neglected state, but bowed to the superior force of the Jordanians. Thousands of Jerusalemites emigrated to settle in Amman. The Palestinians continued to clash with the Jordanian authorities over one issue only; the latter's attitude in relation to Israel and Jerusalem. The Arab residents of the city did not accept its division as a fait accompli. Many of them supported the activities of Palestinian infiltrators to Israel and grumbled over the Jordanian army's harsh repression of attempts to provoke Israel. For some twenty years there was continuous tension between the people, whose attitude toward Israel was relatively extreme, and the government, which knew that any ill-considered act on its part was liable to provoke the Israelis to murderous retaliatory attacks. Despite the massive exodus of 1948-era refugees from the city to all parts of the Arab world, thousands remained there whose homes were in West Jerusalem. Many of these people, who had not managed to take their belongings with them when they fled, still zealously guarded their house keys.

The partition of the city separated the warring communities. The struggle for control that had characterized Jerusalem during the

Mandatory period ceased. The two sections of the city became homogeneous districts, separated from each other by a fortified border, bristling with barbed wire and roadblocks. Separate municipal governing bodies were established in West and East Jerusalem respectively. The first municipal elections were held in West Jerusalem in 1950, and in East Jerusalem in 1951.

The problem of the holy places was not solved, and as long as the sovereignty question remained unanswered, it was impossible to find a lasting solution. Jordan, in whose custody most of the holy places remained, took legal and practical steps to protect them. In January 1951, a "custodian of the holy places" was appointed and the Jordanians assiduously preserved the status quo there. Locations sacred to the Jews—particularly the Western Wall and the cemetery on the Mount of Olives—remained closed to worshipers for nineteen years.

In June 1967, the status quo that had prevailed in Jerusalem for nineteen years was violently upset. The Jordanian attempt to capture the former British High Commissioner's mansion in no-man's-land—which was the first attempt by either side to take territory by force since 1948—launched an inevitable chain of events that necessarily decided the city's fate. Israel, which had not initiated the war with Jordan—and had even tried to prevent it—was left in control of the whole city. The Israeli government's original perception of the Six-Day War as a defensive war with no territorial objectives changed after its occupation of the West Bank. And the first practical expression of this change, of course, pertained to the Old City of Jerusalem. Less than one week after the end of the war, the cabinet had already approved a decision to annex it to Israel.

The Israeli occupation reopened the question of sovereignty in all its intensity. The obliteration of the border restored Jerusalem's physical integrity; however, it revived both the national conflict and the struggle on the local front over the economy, development, resources, and land. The reunification of the city did not bring an agreed-upon settlement on the question of the holy places any closer.

The occupation and the reunification of Jerusalem altered not the parties to the conflict but the character of the struggle. During the British Mandate, the Jews and Arabs had fought each other while both were subject to the domination of a third party. The major part of the struggle had not been carried on between these two communities themselves, but via the efforts of both to achieve their objectives through pressure and influence on the colonial regime. With the ouster of the British, the struggle had assumed the character of a military confrontation that had concluded in a temporary compromise. The Israeli occupation created a new situation. The ongoing conflict was now between one community, which ruled over the entire city, and another, which had been vanquished and had become a subject minority.

The international competition over sovereignty also assumed a different character. In 1949 two national states, Israel and Jordan, had reached a (temporary) agreement on the division of the city and had cooperated in thwarting the attempt by Christian states (albeit with the participation of other elements, including Arab ones) to impose the rule of an international religious patron on the city. The agreement between the partner-rivals had made it possible for them to stand together against the Christian religious interests; to challenge and defeat them; and then to prove that they were capable of finding their own solution without compromising their national sovereignties. In 1967 an entirely new state of affairs came into being. One of the two ruling states had upset the delicate balance in the city, and because of this strategic error, Jordan had lost control of its part of Jerusalem. Yesterday's partner was today's ruler of the entire city; the renewed national conflict had culminated in the victory of one side. But now Israel faced two contenders in the campaign for Jerusalem: international Christian interests (as in 1949), and Arab and Muslim interests.

Israel's success in blocking the internationalization of Jerusalem had been due not only to its cooperation with Jordan, but also to the world powers' view of the Jerusalem issue as marginal in 1949. The political conditions that came into being following the Six-Day War were substantively different from those that had prevailed during the period when the city was divided, and international pressure on Israel assumed new dimensions.

The Jews' return to the actual sites of the historical events that had forged their nationhood was a unique experience, the intensity of which had seldom been paralleled, even in the history of so ancient a people. As a sovereign state, Israel was obliged to give concrete expression to the profound connection between the people and the capital city. To this end, the government enacted of a series of legislative actions and administrative measures that were later called "the reunification of Jerusalem." It was inevitable that the reunification legislation—smelted in the furnace of such a profound spiritual experience—would be regarded as eternal and irreversible from the moment of its enactment. Even the boundaries of the unified city, drawn in accordance with military and demographic considerations, took on profound political and symbolic significance: they too, like the reunification legislation, became an unchallengeable part of the national myth. Israel's policy regarding the political future of Jerusalem was formulated in a variety of ways, but the overwhelming majority of Israelis agreed that the reunified city, with the boundaries determined in 1967, would "eternally" remain under exclusive Israeli sovereignty, and that no compromise would be allowed granting sovereign status in the city to any other state. Yet for many years the Israeli government accepted a policy formulation that committed it to conduct negotiations "with no preconditions" with any Arab state that consented to sit down at the negotiating table. When asked how their uncompromising stance on Jerusalem could be reconciled with this commitment, the Israelis explained that the official Israeli policy formulation did not contradict it. For example, in a letter to UN Secretary General U Thant in 1967, Foreign Minister Abba Eban wrote that, "The term *annexation* is out of place." In 1978, the foreign minister Moshe Dayan stated, in an address to the UN General Assembly, that "one of the subjects that will undoubtedly be discussed [in peace negotiations] is problems regarding Jerusalem." In Israel's view, there was no contradiction, said Dayan, between "absence of preconditions" and "demands that each side might bring up."

The official Israeli stance, which enjoyed wide-ranging support within the Jewish population of Israel as well as in the diaspora, was one of emphasizing unwillingness to make any compromises regarding sovereignty over reunified Jerusalem. This fact disquieted Israeli policymakers. With their thorough knowledge of the Arabs' no less determined stance, they were particularly aware of the necessity of introducing fresh ideas with regard to the future of Jerusalem and of the danger that, if this did not happen, the problem could become an obstacle blocking any chance of a settlement. However, since they did not dare deviate from the national consensus, they concentrated their efforts on making proposals that did not clash with the principle of total Israeli sovereignty (see Chapter 7).

The Israeli proposals were directed at finding ways to satisfy the religious and communal needs of Jerusalem's non-Jewish residents and to solve the problem of the holy places. For example, Israel suggested granting extraterritoriality to the Christian holy places, self-administration to the Muslim holy places, and autonomy of religious jurisdiction to all of the city's religious communities. Ideas such as the decentralization of Jerusalem's municipal government and the establishment of an Arab sub-municipality in the context of an overall Israeli municipality were proposed. None of them ever came to anything since it was clear, from sounding out the Jordanians and Palestinians on the subject, that these ideas could not provide a basis for negotiations. In any case, no meaningful negotiations concerning Jerusalem were taking place, so priority was not given to political planning on that issue. Instead, Israel's position was expressed in practical terms by the establishment of demographic and physical "facts" in East Jerusalem. A massive building program (see Chapter 5) totally changed the face of the annexed areas. The Israelis had faith that in this way, physical facts would create political ones. They supposed that as time went by, the international community would grow used to the new situation and would moderate its opposition to the unilateral measures Israel was taking.

The Israeli occupation dealt an immeasurably powerful blow to the Palestinians, paralyzing them totally. When political activity finally began to revive, one policy line united all Palestinian streams—that of ending the occupation. No agreed upon political program outlining the manner of achieving this objective was in evidence. The ouster of the Israelis was, in effect, an ideal that they did not know how to realize. The possibilities they explored were armed insurrection, active nonviolent resistance, feigned acquiescence (while exploiting the enforced "rules of the game" to their own ends), and complete dependency on Jordan and the Arab states. The possibility of negotiating an agreement with the Israelis was not considered. As far as the Palestinians were concerned, the "abolition of the results of aggression" was not a matter for negotiation, and certainly not one on which there could be compromise. Moreover, there was no agreement about what the character of Palestinian relations with Israel should be after the termination of the occupation. Opinions were divided as to the political future of the West Bank and Jerusalem.

As a result, no clear Palestinian position regarding the solution of the problem of the occupied territories was formulated. The only common denominator to be found was refusal to recognize Israel as a legitimate negotiating partner. In the aftermath of the Yom Kippur War of October 1973, there began a process of political consolidation, reflected in the universal acceptance of the PLO as the sole representative of the Palestinian national movement. However, because this organization was a coalition, the disagreements continued. A moderate minority within the PLO supported the establishment of Palestinian rule in any territory of Palestine that became liberated, as an interim phase on the way to "the liberation of all of Palestine," and acknowledged that this objective could only be attained politically. In contrast, a majority opposed any political course of action and did not agree to the political objective of establishing a mini-state that would live in peace, even temporarily, with Israel.

Jordan's stance passed through a number of permutations. In the period following the 1967 war, King Hussein uncompromisingly demanded the restoration of his total control over East Jerusalem. Late in 1971, he began hinting at a willingness to be satisfied with sovereignty over just part of it: in conversations with the Israelis, he proposed leaving the Jewish Quarter and the Western Wall in Israel's hands. He supported the principle of an "open city," meaning the physical reunification of Jerusalem. Despite these signs of flexibility regarding a territorial settlement, the Jordanian king stood by his demand for the restoration of his country's sovereign status in at least part of Jerusalem. He regarded himself as ordained by fate to preserve the Arab character of Jerusalem, and to hold it in trust for all Muslims. Hussein could not take any stance that would make him responsible for "the loss of the Holy City." In the plan for a Jordanian-Palestinian federation that he published in 1971, Hussein designated Jerusalem as the capital of the Palestinian province "of the federated United Arab Kingdom." His position became more rigid after the Yom Kippur War, but in March 1976 he declared: "In the context of a peace agreement, if Arab sovereignty is restored to (the Eastern) part of the city, I see no reason that the city should be divided. Jerusalem must be the city of all believers."

Ever since 1948, the United States has found itself in a strange position. It has been the principal supporter and promoter of the legal fiction called the "internationalization of Jerusalem," despite actively opposing it and cautioning others against its adoption. In 1949, when the UN General Assembly was debating the ratification of a resolution calling for the installation of an international regime in Jerusalem, the American representative warned that approval of the plan would involve the United Nations in countless difficulties in an attempt to attain objectives that were not all pertinent to the international community. The Americans maintained that the resolution did not take into account the interests of the city's inhabitants and that it endangered international interests in Jerusalem. The General Assembly ratified the internationalization resolution despite U.S. opposition. That same year, the United States supported a Swedish proposal for the functional internationalization of the holy places, in place of territorial internationalization. On that occasion also, the U.S. position was rejected. In spite of taking this stand, the United States adhered to the legalistic position that it was bound by the General Assembly resolutions regarding the internationalization of Jerusalem. Officially, it recognized Israeli and Jordanian rule in Jerusalem as de facto only.

In the first weeks of Israeli occupation (in 1967), the United States took political stands favorable to Israel. It headed the bloc that thwarted a Soviet-Arab proposal wherein the General Assembly would have declared Israel an "aggressor" and ordered it to unconditionally withdraw from Jerusalem. The United States thereby prevented the Israeli occupation's being defined as illegal in international law. It acknowledged Israel's right of "belligerent occupation," a form of occupation whose legality is recognized in international law as extending until the time a peace treaty is signed. When Israel took measures to annex East Jerusalem, the United States was critical. The official American position was formulated by Arthur Goldberg, U.S. Ambassador to the United Nations, as follows: "The United States does not accept or recognize these measures [Israeli annexation] as altering the status of Jerusalem. My government does not recognize that the administrative measures taken by Israel on 28 June 1967—the passing of the Reunification Law—can be regarded as the last word on the matter . . . [but can only be interpreted as] interim and provisional, and not as prejudging the final and permanent status of Jerusalem."

That is, Israeli claims notwithstanding, this was how the United States related to the Reunification Law. This critical stance was convenient for Israel because it expressed only moderate censure and left an opening for discussion of the "measures" themselves. Ambassador Charles Yost reiterated this position on July 1, 1969: "The United States considers that the part of Jerusalem that came under the control of Israel in the June 1967 war, like other areas occupied by Israel, is occupied territory and hence subject to the provision of international law governing the rights and obligations of an occupying power...We have consistently refused to recognize those measures as having anything but a provisional character."

These declarations, as we shall see further on, were reiterated on various occasions, and represented the official U.S. policy on Jerusalem. Their verbal gymnastics, however, enabled the United States to take a moderate position in regard to Israel's massive construction activity in East Jerusalem.

The visit of President Sadat to Jerusalem in the fall of 1977 ushered in a new era in the history of the conflict over Jerusalem. The fact that the Egyptian president visited the city and spoke before the Knesset was interpreted by the Israelis as recognition of Jerusalem's status as Israel's capital. However, it quickly became clear that the problem had not been miraculously solved. The question of Jerusalem was raised at every bilateral encounter between Israel and Egypt, and at Camp David it even threatened to scuttle the entire conference: the Egyptian president brought up the issue and offered several draft proposals, but the Israelis refused to discuss any alteration to the status quo and objected to any reference being made to the problem of Jerusalem in the text of the documents of the accords. The Americans tried, under pressure from Sadat, to find some sort of symbolic solution—such as flying Muslim flags on the Temple Mount—but their suggestions were vehemently rejected by the Israelis. When it became clear that there was no chance of arriving at any agreement, the conference participants agreed to mention the Jerusalem problem only in letters that would be exchanged among the delegation heads—Carter, Begin, and Sadat—and appended to the body of the Camp David Accords. President Sadat, as one interested in a change in the Jerusalem situation, initiated the correspondence. In his letter to President Carter, Sadat made the following points:

1. Arab Jerusalem is an integral part of the West Bank. Legal and historical rights in the city must be respected and restored.

2. Arab Jerusalem should be under Arab sovereignty.

6. The holy places of each faith may be placed under the administration and control of their representatives.

7. Essential functions in the city should be undivided and a joint municipal council composed of an equal number of Arab and Israeli members can supervise the carrying out of these functions. In this way the city shall be undivided.

These formulations reflected a noticeable effort on the part of the Egyptians to adopt a moderate stance, similar to the official American position, as well as a clear attempt to present themselves as not opposing the physical unity of the city. Even so, the Egyptian position was completely contradictory to that held by the Israelis, who regarded political division and physical unity as diametric opposites. Prime Minister Begin wrote to President Carter: "On 28 June, Israel's parliament [the Knesset] promulgated and adopted a law. . . . On the basis of this law, the government of Israel decreed in July 1967 [*sic*] that Jerusalem is one city, indivisible, the capital of Israel." President Carter replied to the Egyptian president's letter, saying that "the position of the United States regarding Jerusalem remains as stated by Ambassador Goldberg to the United Nations General Assembly on 14 July 1967, and subsequently by Ambassador Yost, to the UN Security Council on 1 July 1969."

The position taken by President Sadat at Camp David did not differ greatly from that of King Hussein, nor was it more moderate with regard to Arab demands. However, the fact that Sadat agreed to sweep the Jerusalem problem aside and sign a document that made no reference to it upset the Saudis and was one of the main factors contributing to the tension between the two countries. The fact that the issue of Jerusalem was not part of the peace process was also one of the factors given by Jordan as a reason for its nonparticipation. The Palestinians took a negative position vis-à-vis the peace process as a whole, as a matter of principle. And unlike the Egyptians, Jordan and Saudi Arabia were unwilling to agree to continued Israeli sovereignty even over West Jerusalem.

Differences of opinion regarding the application of the Camp David Accords to Jerusalem arose immediately with the start of negotiations concerning Palestinian self-rule. At every meeting the Egyptians demanded that the matter of Jerusalem be discussed and the Israelis rejected the demand. Each side based its stand on the Camp David Accords and accused the other of deviating from them. The argument mainly revolved around the Egyptian demand that the residents of East Jerusalem be granted the right to vote in elections to choose the Palestinian self-governing authority. In the early stages of the negotiations, Foreign Minister Moshe Dayan was not opposed to this demand; however, after a short while the Israeli government officially stated that it would not agree to the demand, since doing so would set a precedent for Jerusalem's being considered part of the "occupied territories" where autonomy was to be implemented.

This continual reference to the problem of Jerusalem was contrary to the scenario to which the Camp David participants had agreed, wherein Jerusalem was to have been last on the political agenda. The Israelis, Egyptians, and Americans all recognized the centrality of the Jerusalem problem, but since they also knew that this was the most complex and delicate of all the problems in the Middle East conflict, they sought to isolate it and agreed not to seek a resolution to it until other, smaller obstacles had been removed from the road to a comprehensive settlement. There was much logic to this position, except that the Egyptians and Israelis did not succeed in operating in accordance with it, and the Jerusalem problem was quickly moved to the center of the deliberations.

A number of factors combined to bring this about. Those who opposed Camp David—the "rejectionist front" in the Arab states and extremist elements in Israel and Egypt—stubbornly insisted on raising the question of Jerusalem in hopes that discussing it would sabotage the autonomy talks and perhaps the entire process of normalization of diplomatic relations between Israel and Egypt. Within the Egyptian administration itself, opinion was becoming increasingly strong that their not mentioning the issue of Jerusalem would be construed as meaning they were neglecting it. The Americans, who were striving to expand the scope of the peace negotiations and to end Egypt's isolation, saw a need to help create the conditions necessary for the integration of Jordan and Saudi Arabia into the peace process. In Israel there was a new school of thought—at variance with the conventional wisdom that Israel must work to the postpone the resolution of the Jerusalem problem—whose adherents demanded its being placed at the top of the agenda. However, Israeli statesmen had always considered leaving Jerusalem for last to be an extremely important tactical objective, since postponement of the debate would enable Israel to continue establishing faits accomplis in the city, thereby reinforcing its status.

The debate over Jerusalem took on the character of recurrent conflagrations, flaring up with increasing frequency and intensity. Positions became polarized and additional players were drawn into the fray. The Egyptians intensified the dispute by accentuating positions that they had always held but that they had blurred and downplayed in the past. The Israeli government reacted by establishing physical "facts" (through land confiscations and construction of government offices in East Jerusalem) and by making strong statements that were construed as closing the door on further negotiations. The Israeli reactions, unlike the Egyptian positions, made real alterations in the situation in the city, and Israel was thus blamed for the intensification of the dispute. Every Israeli reaction led to a counter reaction, and an unending cycle of escalating extremism resulted. A salient example of this process was the Knesset's ratification of the Law of Jerusalem—Capital of Israel. This law was introduced as a private member's bill in July 1980, by Knesset members opposed to the peace agreement, with the announced objective of scuttling it. The Likud cabinet, which agreed with the wording of the proposed law (merely a reiteration of the prime minister's formulations from Camp David), dared not oppose it. The opposition likewise did not dare stand against it, for fear of being accused of "destroying the national unity over Jerusalem." Following the ratification of the law, Egypt withdrew from the autonomy talks, and Sadat publicly initiated an exchange of angry letters with the Israeli prime minister. Even countries friendly toward Israel were convinced that the law had altered the status of Jerusalem and therefore reacted by removing the few embassies remaining there.

This reaction to the Jerusalem Law provoked an Israeli counterreaction, which again took the form of establishment of a physical presence in the city. The endless chain of reactions and counterreactions resulted in increasingly entrenched positions on all sides. Chances of arriving at a solution to the problem seemed more remote than ever.

The Lebanon War (1982) and, in its aftermath, Israel's massive settlement activities and the construction of gigantic Jewish neighborhoods surrounding Jerusalem, led to the intensification of Palestinian protests, and Jerusalem became the focus of demonstrations and acts of terrorism. The sporadic rebellion, which was accompanied by efforts to improve the standard of living in Arab East Jerusalem (see Chapter 6), obscured the accumulation of rage by the Arab populace of Jerusalem from many observers until it erupted all at once toward the end of 1987. The Intifada totally altered day-to-day reality in Jerusalem. Months of commercial strikes, demonstrations, murders, stone throwing, and car torching caused Israelis to cease visiting East Jerusalem; the intercommunal rift deepened and became an abyss. The impact of the Intifada internationally forced all parties to the conflict to realize the necessity of embarking on diplomatic initiatives, and these directly affected Jerusalem.

In July 1988, King Hussein announced that he was cutting all legal and administrative ties with the West Bank. The king understood that there was no longer any chance of returning to the status quo ante of the unity of the two banks that his grandfather, King Abdullah, had created in 1948. Even so, Hussein maintained a direct connection with the Muslim holy places in Jerusalem and continued to finance the activities of the Muslim institutions in the city. In November 1988, the Palestine National Council declared the establishment of "the state of Palestine, in the land of Palestine, with its capital at Jerusalem."

In May 1989, the Israeli government published a "peace plan," the gist of which was the holding of elections for representatives who would carry on negotiations with Israel regarding an interim settlement and self-rule. This initiative foundered, one major reason being Israel's refusal to permit the Arab residents of East Jerusalem to vote in the elections on the grounds that the city was part of the State of Israel and not of the West Bank. The issue became a point of contention inside Israel, when the Likud-led government (and, following the election of a Labor-led coalition in 1992, the right-wing opposition) opposed the Jerusalem Arabs' voting, whereas the Labor government agreed to it under specific conditions.

In October 1990, the intercommunal tensions—which had increased in the face of the political paralysis, the continuing Intifada, and the Iraqi invasion of Kuwait—erupted again. The Temple Mount massacre, in which seventeen Palestinians were killed in clashes with Israeli security forces (police and border guards) in and around the compound of the Al-Aqsa Mosque, was the most serious episode in the twenty-three years of Israeli occupation. It, in turn, generated a chain of serious acts of violence that continued until the convening of the peace conference in Madrid (October 1991).

In the discussions preceding the Madrid conference, the question of Jerusalem occupied a central place. Israel demanded that the city not be mentioned in the official invitations to the conference and that the Palestinian participants (within the Jordanian-Palestinian delegation) not be residents of East Jerusalem. The Palestinians, on the other hand, demanded that the United States issue them a letter of assurance in which it would reiterate its known (though downplayed) position regarding nonrecognition of the annexation of Jerusalem, whose future would be determined by negotiation. The Americans solved the problem by not mentioning Jerusalem in the letters of assurance it sent to the Israelis, but by giving the Palestinians what they had requested in theirs. Thus, the Israelis and Palestinians both went to Madrid thinking that their (contradictory) preconditions had been met, and this anomaly was not discovered during the conference.

However, immediately following the conclusion of the ceremonial event and with the commencement of the bilateral talks in Washington, the dispute over Jerusalem erupted openly. The Palestinians stuck by their claim that Jerusalem was an inseparable part of the occupied territories and that therefore all of the agreements in the interim settlement that applied to the West Bank must apply to Jerusalem as well, and that Jerusalem must become the capital of the Palestinian state in the context of the permanent settlement. Israel vehemently opposed any discussion of East Jerusalem, even though the ban on East Jerusalemite Faisal al-Husseini's participation in the deliberations of the Israeli-Palestinian committee was lifted in the wake of Labor's ascent to power (in mid-1992). The Americans recommended postponing discussion of the question of Jerusalem until after the negotiations for the permanent settlement, but the Palestinians refused, since "Israel is establishing physical and other sorts of 'facts' that could potentially predetermine the situation and leave nothing to discuss in the future." When the talks reached a stalemate (and there are those who claim that this was a deliberate tactic on the part of PLO Chairman Yassir 'Arafat), it was suddenly revealed that the Madrid process was merely a diversionary tactic, and that the real deliberations had been conducted in Oslo in complete secrecy.

In the Israeli-Palestinian Declaration of Principles signed in September 1993, the Palestinians agreed to what they had rejected at the bilateral talks in Washington, namely the removal of discussion of Jerusalem from the context of the interim agreement: "Jurisdiction of the [Palestinian] Council [self-governing authority] will cover the West

Bank and Gaza Strip territory except for issues that will be negotiated in the permanent status negotiations: Jerusalem, settlements, etc."

Right-wing circles in Israel regarded Israel's willingness to discuss Jerusalem at all as undermining its status as "Israel's unified capital," but as we have seen previously, the Likud government headed by Menachem Begin had also been prepared to discuss the issue of Jerusalem in the context of peace negotiations. The Declaration of Principles also stated that "Palestinians of Jerusalem who live there will have [the] right to participate in the election process." Both sides exhibited apparent flexibility on issues regarding Jerusalem. The Israelis agreed to a liberal interpretation of the passive and active voting rights of the Palestinians (i.e., the right to vote and to be elected)—an issue that had been a source of disagreement for years—leaving the way open for interpretations defining Jerusalem as a part of the West Bank. The Palestinians relented on their principal demand for immediate discussion of the Jerusalem issue and agreed to postpone it despite the fact that they well knew the Israelis were energetically at work establishing irreversible "facts" in East Jerusalem. However, this mutual flexibility was not actually an indication that their polarized positions had become less so. The Declaration of Principles and the agreements that were signed in its wake allowed Israel to specify that the Palestinian Authority would be entitled to operate only in the territories turned over to its control, and that it was forbidden to maintain any official institutions in Jerusalem. The Palestinians, for their part, agreed to postpone the discussion of Jerusalem only after Foreign Minister Shimon Peres promised the PLO chairman (in a letter addressed to the Norwegian foreign minister) that the Palestinian institutions in East Jerusalem were very important and would be preserved. All of these institutions, "including economic, social, educational, and cultural institutions as well as Christian and Muslim holy places, fulfill a vital role for the Palestinian population. Needless to say, we shall not interfere with their operation. On the contrary, the fulfillment of this important role merits encouragement." These institutions, and particularly Orient House, which had become the hub of Palestinian political and diplomatic endeavors, stepped up their activities, and this became an embarrassment to the Israeli government. The Palestinian Authority's activities in East Jerusalem became a weapon in the hands of the right—especially Jerusalem's mayor, Ehud Olmert, Teddy Kollek's successor (see Chapter 4)—who denounced the government for pursuing a policy promoting the redivision of the city and its abandonment to the Palestinians.

Under pressure from the right, the government was compelled, in late 1994, to pass a special law authorizing the police to close any institution connected with the Palestinian Authority, and requiring any activity of the Authority "within the precincts of the State of Israel" (i.e., East Jerusalem) to have the approval of the Israeli authorities. This attempt by the Israeli government to treat the Palestinian Authority like a foreign governing body forbidden to operate outside its area of jurisdiction was indeed based on the Palestinian Authority's commitment not to do so, but was, of course, pathetically futile. No law can sever the Palestinian people's attachment to Jerusalem and make it into a "foreign country." The very fact of Israel's recognition of the Palestinian national collective, embodied in the Declaration of Principles, and the willingness to conduct negotiations regarding the realization of its national rights created an entirely new state of affairs in Jerusalem. It essentially imparted legitimacy to this national collective in Jerusalem as well, and recognized its attachment to the city. The approximately 200,000 Palestinians (who have not taken Israeli citizenship) living in East Jerusalem feel that they are entitled to be a part of their own national body, to organize their communal life and to unite around their national slogans and the governing institutions they agree upon.

The internal contradiction in the Declaration of Principles between the "principles" component—mutual recognition between Israel and the PLO—and the practical component—the setting up of a Palestinian Authority with limited authority—was temporarily dealt with by postponing discussion about the full extent of Palestinian self-determination. But both sides well knew that no problem had really been solved, and both therefore set out to establish additional "facts" to improve their situation, come the hour of decision.

The Israelis persisted in their policy of establishing a physical presence and accelerated the pace of construction of Jewish neighborhoods in the city and its surrounding areas. They also attempted to hamper the Palestinians' activities by shutting down their institutions in East Jerusalem. However, they were unable to actively prevent the Palestinians from establishing their own presence: the establishment of research institutes and cultural and educational centers, and the transformation of their political center, Orient House, into a virtual foreign ministry, where the prime ministers and foreign ministers of many countries came to pay official visits. The Israelis, of course, enjoyed a clear advantage, having all the force of a sovereign state at their disposal, but they repeatedly were made to realize their limitations: no form of coercion that they could apply was capable of suppressing the Palestinians' collective attachment to Jerusalem and its concrete manifestations. The struggle for Jerusalem has not been decided, and the need to mobilize the rival communities to continue it "till victory" has generated ceremonies like the "Jerusalem 3,000" on the Israeli side and the commemoration of "5,000 years since the Jebusites" by the Arabs. Nearly 100 years after the problem of Jerusalem arose, it still awaits a solution.

Is it possible to unravel the enigma of Jerusalem? In order to seriously deal with this question, one must leave the quarry of history and walk through the shadows and twisting alleyways of the earthly Jerusalem.

CHAPTER TWO

THE MUTE HILLS

In the winter of 1988, the Israeli Ministry of the Interior, as empowered by the Municipalities Law, appointed a commission of inquiry to consider a request by the Jerusalem Municipal Council to expand the city's municipal boundaries. Several months later the commission's purview was extended to include determination of the municipality's "optimal boundaries."

The municipal council was seeking approval to annex thirty square kilometers of land to the west of the city, thereby increasing the area under its jurisdiction by 30 percent. The first argument put forward by the council in support of the annexation was that in recent years the demographic balance between Jews and Arabs in Jerusalem had been upset, and the growth of the Arab population was threatening to disrupt the ratio that had been determined as optimal—72 percent Jewish to 28 percent Arab. The council chose to annex land in the west, inhabited by Jews, in order to increase the city's Jewish majority. This would also enhance Jerusalem's status internationally as a Jewish city. Of course, wrote the council in a memorandum to the commission, it would be possible to expand Jerusalem's boundaries eastward, into the West Bank, but such a move would arouse controversy in the international arena.

The suburban and rural communities whose land Jerusalem wished to annex opposed the annexation. They argued, among other things, that in political terms, Jerusalem's westward expansion would lead to neglect of the eastern and northern sections of the city (the territory annexed in 1967 and the sections of metropolitan Jerusalem inside the West Bank). That is, westward expansion might be interpreted as surrendering to the pressures of the Intifada and was liable to give the impression that Israel was relinquishing those parts of the city.

After four-and-one-half years of deliberations, the commission decided to add twenty-three square kilometers to Jerusalem's jurisdictional area. The most important principle motivating the commission members was "the state's obligation to strengthen and shore up the status of Jerusalem as Israel's capital through increasing its [Jewish] population and expanding its economic base. The large-scale immigration from the Soviet Union affords a unique historical opportunity to realize these objectives." By mid-1993, the farthest point from the Old City walls—within the boundaries of the Holy City—was more than ten kilometers distant as the crow flies. The Old City itself (covering less than one square kilometer) was now less than one percent of the city's total area.

The commission was ostensibly concerned with setting the municipal boundaries within which the local authority would be responsible for carrying out the tasks allotted to it by law: disposal of garbage, construction of roads, provision of water, and granting of building permits. But it was clear, from the arguments for annexation and from the wording of the decision, that the practical aspect of its work, as important as this might be, was subordinate to "higher" interests. The optimal boundaries of Jerusalem were not to be determined according to the criteria of economy of scale or efficiency of service delivery to its citizens, but in conformity to nationalist parameters. The bare hills and populated suburbs were being conscripted to the internal and external political struggle, and from the moment they were declared part of the city, they were imbued with its sanctity.

Evidence of the connection between the act of designating Jerusalem's boundaries and the nationalist-religious sentiments they evoke can be found in an ancient talmudic text, which relates how the

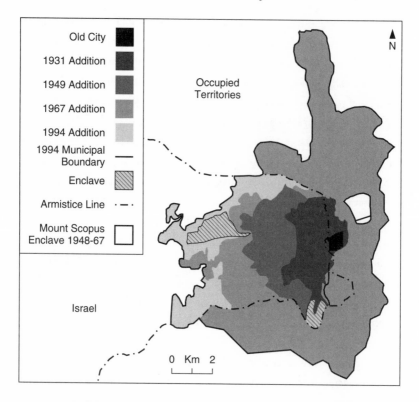

Old City
1931 Addition
1949 Addition
1967 Addition
1994 Addition
1994 Municipal Boundary
Enclave
Armistice Line
Mount Scopus Enclave 1948-67

Occupied Territories

Israel

N

0 Km 2

MAP 1. Municipal boundaries, 1931–94

sages of Israel declared that the holiness of Jerusalem applied to a certain area outside the city walls "in order to arouse the warriors of Israel to be willing to give their lives for its sake." Two thousand years have passed, but the rationale has not changed. The fact that in ancient times the city's boundaries were determined by religious authorities according to Jewish religious law (halacha), whereas today they are drawn by secular authorities, does not constitute a substantive change. Modern-day halacha follows in the wake of administrative decisions and extends the boundaries of the city's sanctity accordingly. All of the territory within its municipal boundaries is regarded as "the Holy City" by the religious establishment. And this is no trivial matter, since from the moment a particular area is designated as part of the Holy City, it comes under Jerusalem's religious laws, whose sole objective is to strengthen the spiritual ties between the Jews and their sacred city, imbuing them with the sense that, because they live in Jerusalem, they are contributing to the salvation of their souls and the redemption of their people; and, of course, to "arouse them to give their lives for Jerusalem."

The perception that Jerusalem's sanctity pervades the entire city is uniquely Jewish. As Professor Zwi Werblowsky of Hebrew University explains, "For the Jewish people Jerusalem is not a city containing holy places or commemorating holy events. The city as such is holy." A similar attitude is prevalent among Muslims—but regarding Mecca, not Jerusalem. Even those Muslim religious scholars who consider al-Aqsa Mosque ("the precincts whereof we have blessed") a focus of holiness radiating throughout the city, do not perceive the concept "Holy City" in the sweeping, comprehensive way that Jews do. "It would be an exaggeration to call every building, every neighborhood, and every street corner around the Old City, and stretching for many kilometers beyond it 'holy,'" according to one Arab scholar, but his religious Jewish counterpart would disagree.

The Christians, too, have grappled with the question of Jerusalem's boundaries, but in an entirely different context. The boundary of the Old City walls is of crucial importance in determining the authenticity of the Church of the Holy Sepulchre. The grave's location inside the city is confusing to Christians, since Jesus was a Jew, and Jews are forbidden to bury their dead within the city walls. An acrimonious dispute broke out between those who venerated the traditional site and those who sought to fix its location outside the walls of the Old City, at a place known as the Garden Tomb. The final outcome of this dispute depends on the precise location of the city walls in Jesus' time, but the archeological findings are ambiguous. Although a wall line was found that, according to some scholars, places the Holy Sepulchre outside the city, other researchers claim that what were identified as city walls are actually nothing but the walls of a Roman temple, and that in Christ's lifetime, the city walls followed the same line as today.

This controversy, like all controversies in Jerusalem, is not free from sectarian influences: Protestants venerate the Garden Tomb, while Catholics remain faithful to the Holy Sepulchre. Whatever the location of the authentic grave, both sites, as well as other Christian holy places, have given European Christian powers a pretext for extending Jerusalem's administrative boundaries. The British Peel Commission of 1936 gave the Jerusalem enclave boundaries that stretched all the way to the Mediterranean (see Chapter 7). The UN Partition Plan of 1947 designated municipal-political boundaries that encompassed an area 200 square kilometers in size, extending as far south as Bethlehem. These borders never got beyond the mapping stage, but the pretext for drawing them that long and the considerations determining their shape were both political and demographic. And so has it been always. The process of making the latest boundary determination, in 1993, was no different from that of seventy years before. Those who drew the line were not defining a simple geographic space, they were delineating a holy enclosure. Thus, the history of the boundaries of Jerusalem has been a history of the conflicts over it.

For hundreds of years Jerusalem's boundaries coincided with the walls of the Old City. These walls hermetically sealed the city off from its surroundings. Until the 1870s, the gates of the Old City were closed at sunset and opened at sunrise, and no one entered or left Jerusalem without a prior arrangement with the Ottoman pasha. Only as the end of the century approached were the gates left open all night.

When the city began to expand beyond the walls, the Ottoman authorities were compelled to define its limits. According to the earliest clear map of Jerusalem, on the eve of the First World War its municipal boundaries enclosed an area of approximately seven square kilometers (including the Old City). The built-up area fanned out along the principal traffic routes to the north, west, and south of the Old City. It is interesting to note that although the "new" city (i.e., the area outside the walls) was sparsely inhabited and abounded with open spaces, its municipal boundaries had already reached the limits of city's "natural" site: in the north, the slopes of Mount Scopus and French Hill; in the east, the Valley of Jehoshaphat and the Kidron Valley; in the south, the edge of the Baq'aa plain; and in the west, the crest of the slope leading to Nahal Soreq. These boundaries (with the addition of certain areas to the southwest) remained in force until 1948.

The British authorities introduced modern municipal government to Jerusalem during the Mandatory period. In particular, they developed an advanced physical planning system (see Chapter 5). Initially, the city's boundaries took in about seventeen square kilometers, but by the end of the Mandate they had expanded to include forty-four square kilometers. The British were the first to discover the connection between the drawing of boundaries and the political conflict over Jerusalem: the placement of border lines determines the demographic balance between Jews and Arabs. The Jews had an interest in keeping the city's area to a minimum, because the population of almost all of the adjacent communities was totally Arab. For this reason they were willing to forgo incorporating the few Jewish suburbs, whose residents were in any case not enthusiastic about being part of Jerusalem and paying municipal taxes. In this they were like the Arab villagers, who also preferred to preserve their rural status.

In order to surmount conflicting interests as well as to attend to urban and planning concerns, the British designated three types of boundaries for Jerusalem: municipal boundaries; urban boundaries, which included additional built-up areas; and town-planning boundaries, which encompassed all of the areas that were sensitive from a physical planning point of view, and which extended far beyond the municipal boundaries. Only those who resided within the city limits were eligible to vote in the Jerusalem municipal elections. The British placed forty-six highly visible markers along the boundaries, which they both sketched on a map and described verbally. The verbal description was based on a detailed record of land holdings, and bears witness to the ethnic mix of Jerusalem: "thence south following the eastern boundary of this property and that of Fouad Nashashibi to the corner of the wall of the property of Issaf Nashashibi . . . thence to the property of the Jewish Sephardic community . . . to the eastern boundary where it meets the property of Mr. F. Vester (American colony) etc., etc."

But the British were not content with simply defining the city's borders. The last Jerusalem municipal elections to take place under Mandatory rule, in 1934, were conducted according to a ward system, and these wards were ethnically defined. For election purposes, the British designated twelve wards, each one having a majority of Jews, Christians, or Muslims. Six of the wards were designated as Jewish, two as Christian, and four as Muslim. The efficiency of those who laid out the boundaries of the wards was reflected in the fact that most of the Jewish areas did not include a single Muslim, and vice versa. Despite the de facto ethnic segregation that prevailed in the Jerusalem neighborhoods of the day, it was not at all easy to arrive at such a result. And indeed, in the northern ward, there were 124 Jews and 41 Christians in addition to 563 Muslims, despite the gerrymandering efforts of British officials. These Mandatory boundaries remained unchanged until 1948. To illustrate how small the area included within these boundaries was, suffice it to say that the Knesset, the Israel Museum, and the government offices at Kiryat Ben-Gurion, which are now well inside the city, were outside the city limits in Mandatory times.

The next redrawing of the boundaries was a military, not an administrative matter. During the months from December 1947 through June 1948, there was heavy fighting in Jerusalem and its immediate vicinity. The city was divided in two by the front lines, which shifted hither and thither until stabilizing in late July, to remain unchanged for the next nineteen years (1948–1967).

The statutory basis on which the partition of Jerusalem rested was the cease-fire agreement signed on November 30, 1948 between Moshe Dayan, "commander of all the Israeli forces in the Jerusalem region," and Abdullah al-Tal, "representing the Arab Legion and all the other Arab forces in the Jerusalem area." This agreement states, among other things, that "there shall be a complete and sincere cease-fire in the

Jerusalem area." The cease-fire was defined as "sincere" at the suggestion of Moshe Dayan, who wished to emphasize thereby the wish of
both sides to cease hostilities without being compelled to do so by outside forces. The principal component of the agreement was a map
signed by both sides, which fixed the location of the lines that marked
the boundaries of Israeli and Jordanian-held territory, respectively, and
the no-man's-land in between.

For nineteen years this map remained the only binding document for
determination of the demarcation lines in the city. It was an unprecedented
piece of work. Had it merely been a cartographer's nightmare and a geogra-
pher's catastrophe, that would have been bad enough; however, a great deal
of blood was shed as a result of its vagueness and ambiguity. The lines were
sketched on a Mandatory 1:20,000 scale map. Moshe Dayan drew the Israeli
front line with a green grease pencil, while Abdullah al-Tal marked his front
line with a red one. The grease pencils made lines three to four millimeters
wide. Sketched on a map whose scale was 1:20,000, such lines in reality
represented strips of land sixty to eighty meters in width. Who owned
the "width of the line?" Had it been a matter of an open desert area, the problem would have been insignificant. But this was a densely built-up city, whose
streets were mostly nine meters wide—or thirty meters, including the houses
on both sides. In addition, when they drew the demarcation lines, no one
had taken the trouble to have a flat surface beneath the map. As a result, the
grease pencils skipped over some places. And the lines were also disjointed,
zigzag, or sketchy due to uncertainty or error in their initial drawings.

This cartographic monstrosity haunted both sides throughout the
years that the armistice was in force. In defense of the map makers, it
should be said that neither of them dreamed that the document they were
signing would stand alone for so many years. In the text of the agreement,
they wrote: "The undersigned envisage that additional talks will be held
in the near future, for the purpose of expanding the scope of this agreement." Indeed, within six months the General Armistice Agreement
between Israel and the Kingdom of Jordan was signed on the Greek
island of Rhodes. However, this agreement affirmed that "the armistice

lines were identical with the lines set out in the agreement of November 30, 1948." In other words, the Moshe Dayan–Abdullah al-Tal map remained the authoritative document. True, maps were affixed to the Rhodes agreement. But the six copies of the Rhodes map differed both from the Dayan–al-Tal map and from one another. The sole copy of the Dayan–al-Tal map was taken to the UN offices in New York, where additional colored copies were made and presented to the two sides.

The lack of clarity concerning demarcation lines diminished in April 1949, when an agreement between Israel and Jordan was signed, dividing the no-man's-land to the north and south of Jerusalem between them. This agreement created a single line of demarcation, which divided the no-man's-land more or less equally; however, it did not apply to Jerusalem. King Abdullah of Jordan gave in to Arab League pressure and did not permit the unoccupied area located within the city's municipal boundaries to be divided. The Arabs regarded such a division as the relinquishing of Arab territory.

Thus, it was precisely in this most complex area—the built-up part of Jerusalem—that the cartographic tangle was not resolved. In the heart of the divided city, there remained extensive stretches of contested land to which neither side was permitted access. The ruins were left as visible reminders of the 1948 war. These areas became a severe sanitary problem; only rarely would Israeli and Jordanian authorities cooperate in the removal of mosquitoes or contamination caused by sewage or stray dogs.

The Israelis and Jordanians did not become aware of the confusion caused by the Dayan–al-Tal map until 1950, since until then the demarcation lines had not been marked by fences, but by isolated military positions. But early in 1950, an Israeli soldier was killed south of the Mandelbaum Gate (the only crossing point between the two parts of the city) while walking down a street that the Israelis considered to be theirs. When the incident was discussed by the Mixed Armistice Commission, it suddenly became clear that the Jordanians, the Israelis, and the United Nations each had a different interpretation of the map accompanying the "sincere cease-fire" agreement. The differences were

2. Divided Jerusalem (1948–1967). "No-man's-land" in front of Jaffa Gate

not about trivial matters, but concerned entire streets. For example, one street in the Misrara section, houses and all, appeared within the width of the Israeli grease pencil line, but the Jordanians held that the border ran down the middle of the street. In another case, when a photograph of the building called Steinitz House, near the Mandelbaum Gate, was magnified, it turned out that its eastern side was within the Jordanian area, its western side in the Israeli zone, and its southern terrace in the no-man's-land. The problem was complicated by the fact that there was a Jordanian fortified position inside the house.

The Israeli Survey Department attempted to project the 1948 map onto a very large-scale Israeli municipal map. The outcome would have been laughable had it not concerned matters of the utmost seriousness. Some 125 houses were caught in the "width of the line" all along its length; at least 50 within the Jordanian line and 75 within the Israeli one. The adversaries could not agree on an authoritative interpretation of the November 1948 map, and the resultant severe friction led to several incidents of shooting in which lives were lost.

EL MISRARA

MAP 2. Areas within the "width of the line"

Both Israel and Jordan had fortified buildings in the no-man's-land, while some areas regarded as no-man's-land were, in fact, under the control of one or the other of the states. In February 1955, an attempt was made to define the ownership of at least those areas within the "width of the line." A vote was taken, and the Israelis and the UN-appointed chairman of the commission agreed, with the Jordanians abstaining, that "the Armistice Commission has, throughout the years, been accustomed to regard as binding the outside edge of each line." In other words, the territory within the width of the grease pencil line was under the sovereignty of the side whose territory was bounded by that line, reducing the no-man's-land to a minimum. The Jordanians did not want to vote in support of a resolution extending Israeli sovereignty, but were unable to vote against it, as it happened that the entire area of the Old City walls fell within the width of the Jordanian pencil line, that is, between Jordanian territory and the no-man's-land. Had the decision been to make the inner edge of the line binding, they would have had to abandon their positions on top of the wall.

For fourteen years following the war, the demarcation lines within the city boundaries were not fenced, nor even marked. Only the areas outside the built-up sections were fenced—those to the south, immediately after the war, in 1949, and to the north, in 1956. In 1962, with increasing infiltration and many cases of the border being crossed by civilians unaware of its location, it was decided to fence the border line. The intention was not to create an impenetrable barrier but only to mark the border. The initiative came from the Israelis, who hoped thereby to achieve a division of the no-man's-land. The Jordanians were opposed in principle to any such division, and hence to the marking of the border. A compromise was found whereby the fence was defined as a "fence to prevent infiltration," which did not imply agreement regarding the border line. At the same time that work was begun on the fence, arguments as to its position arose. In some places two fences were erected—one complying with the Israeli interpretation of the map, the other with the Jordanian. In the Hinnom Valley, where there was no demarcation line on the Dayan–al-Tal map—due apparently to the grease pencil's having skipped—three successive fences were put up and taken down because the Israelis and Jordanians could not reach agreement as to positioning.

It is surprising that the inextricable tangle caused by the cease-fire maps did not result in daily shooting incidents. Of course there were incidents—both minor and major—continually throughout the armistice period, but it can be said that both sides strove to avoid exacerbating the tension, and opened fire only in exceptional cases. Both Israelis and Jordanians were motivated by the desire to maintain the status quo as far as possible. In many instances, infringements and violations of the agreement were tacitly tolerated, or at most, gave rise to formal complaints to the Mixed Armistice Commission. The status quo proved stronger than the formally signed agreement.

Within the width of the grease pencil line, in the no-man's-land, in the towers of the Old City wall, on the roofs of monasteries and churches, in communications trenches and concrete pillboxes, Israel Defense Force units and Arab Legion forces faced each other for nineteen years. The improvised positions left over from the days of the 1948 war were reinforced and improvements were made; concrete

3.   Israeli and Jordanian soldiers on the "width of the line"
(1950s)

communications trenches were built, some of them subterranean. On both sides, the border line became a wall of fortifications. The soldiers, as is often the custom, gave picturesque names to their positions. In Israeli military parlance, for instance, we find Jordanian positions with nicknames like "the red-tiled house," "the arch house," "the monkey house," "the climbers' house," "the rags," "the tins," "sacking," "yellow shutters," and "palm branch." Israeli positions were given names like "vegetable garden," "the mission," "the cellar," "the classroom," and "the solitary house." Along the armistice line within the city, there were thirty-six Jordanian and nineteen Israeli fortified positions in all.

Israel regarded the grease pencil line as being a border in every sense of the word, and recognized the Jordanian line on the opposite side of the no-man's-land as the boundary of the sovereign territory of the Hashemite Kingdom. Following the occupation and annexation of East Jerusalem in 1967, the Israeli Foreign Ministry was called upon to pass judgment on the question of the status of the no-man's-land as regards sovereignty. This was no small matter, since these areas totaled some three thousand dunams (750 acres), some of which were located in the center of the city, where the price of land was extremely high. A statement by the Foreign Ministry declaring that the no-man's-land belonged to Israel would have made possible the immediate confiscation of property located there from its Arab owners under the Absentee Property Law, the law under which all of the property of Palestinian refugees who left the State of Israel had been seized. The Ministry refused to publish the requested announcement, and the government was compelled to take other means of action. Israel's legal recognition of the 1948 lines as the agreed-upon boundaries of sovereignty between itself and Jordan did not prevent the Israeli government from making the politically motivated claim, from 1967 onward, that it had never recognized Jordanian rule in Jerusalem and that the cease-fire line was of an exclusively military character.

The municipal council of Israeli Jerusalem that was set up in 1948 conducted an independent foreign policy of its own. It did not recognize the cease-fire line, and in January 1949, demanded the expansion of the city's municipal boundaries to include areas that were held by the Jordanians, such as the Mount of Olives, French Hill, and Shu'afat village. A commission of inquiry, appointed by the minister of the interior, recommended the annexation of this territory. "Part of this territory is, indeed, held by the Jordanians," commented the commission, "but we cannot relinquish Hadassah Hospital and the university," nor the German Augusta Victoria Hospice compound, "which is our due as a part of the reparations for loss of life and damages inflicted upon the Jews in Central Europe [at the hands of the Germans]." In the end, the minister of the interior approved the westward expansion of the city's boundaries only, to include Jewish neighborhoods and abandoned Arab villages that had been previously excluded from the city's jurisdictional area. The annexation of sections of East Jerusalem would have to wait nineteen years.

In contrast to the huge expansion of the municipal area of Israeli Jerusalem—whose area reached thirty-eight square kilometers by 1967—the area of the Arab city had grown hardly at all. The

jurisdictional area of the Arab municipality was just six square kilometers, including the Old City, and of this, the built-up area never
exceeded three square kilometers. In 1952, the village of Silwan, in the
Kidron Valley, was annexed to Arab Jerusalem. The shortage of land for
building within the borders of the city impelled many to find places to
build outside its confines, especially along the road to Ramallah. These
areas were located in small rural jurisdictions where modern planning
practices were not employed. The municipal council of Arab Jerusalem
was not interested in having them included in its jurisdiction, since
their addition was liable to alter the balance of municipal political forces
and place the rule of the governing coalition at risk. Problems of town
planning, however, compelled the Jordanian authorities to declare, as
had the British before them, town-planning boundaries that extended
beyond the city's municipal boundaries.

The most dramatic and far-reaching redrawing of boundaries
occurred in 1967, in the aftermath of the Six-Day War. Following the
Israeli government's decision to annex East Jerusalem, it became necessary to determine the precise boundaries of the area slated to be incorporated into the state. The basic policy assumption was that all of the
annexed territory would be added to the jurisdictional area of the
Jerusalem municipality, because the objective of the annexation was
officially "unification of the divided city." The political imperative
which dictated that the geopolitical and municipal boundaries of
Jerusalem must be identical, of course, made any urban considerations
subject to overriding political or security requirements. It also meant
that decisions regarding the placement of these boundaries fell to the
highest political echelon: the Israeli cabinet.

Prime Minister Levi Eshkol appointed a committee of experts to
deal with this issue, and its members presented the cabinet with no
fewer than five proposals. The most sweeping of these was that of the
army's representative, according to which some 200 square kilometers
would be annexed to Jerusalem, a broad band that would cut off the
north of the West Bank from its southern half. Another, less ambitious

proposal entailed the adoption of a Jordanian plan, prepared in 1964, to extend Jerusalem's town-planning (but not municipal) boundaries to include some seventy-five square kilometers from the border of Ramallah in the north to that of Bethlehem in the south. Other proposals recommended the inclusion of the Kalandiya Airport to the north and the villages of Azariyeh and Abu Dis to the east. The army's proposal endeavored to respond to military needs, "so that Jerusalem would henceforth not be subject to the whims of artillery batteries able to bombard the city mercilessly—being within sight of its buildings."

The civilian members of the committee were concerned about the demographic ratio between Jews and Arabs that would be produced by excessive expansion of the city's boundaries, and advised the cabinet "not to include too many Arab residents in the annexed area, and to include open areas, for the development of Jewish neighborhoods." All of the committee members were convinced that the boundaries they were drawing would also constitute the borders of the State of Israel, and that it was therefore necessary to relate to the territory beyond them—the West Bank—as an area that would be under different sovereignty. Representatives of the Jerusalem municipal council, though they participated in the deliberations, dared not bring up urban concerns such as town planning or provision of municipal services. How significant could these be in comparison to the overwhelming importance of vital national interests?

The man who, more than anyone else, influenced the demarcation of the boundaries was Defense Minister Moshe Dayan. He did not support the army's maximalist approach. "You are going too far," he said to one Israeli officer. "Why do you come with such a big appetite?" And to the cabinet, Dayan stated, "I know the Jews' appetite. It is possible to take the entire West Bank, but we are talking about the annexation of East Jerusalem. [Even so] it is possible to be generous. . . . I am not in favor of annexing ten additional villages with 20,000 inhabitants and cutting off the northern from the southern West Bank." A compromise was finally agreed upon whereby the boundaries were drawn according to overtly tactical considerations, ensuring Israeli control of the hills and passing through wadis that were convenient to defend. The residential sections of villages were excluded from the annexed territory, and to the north of the city, the line was shifted to a position fifty meters east of the main Jerusalem-Ramallah road, in order to bypass urban neighborhoods and refugee camps (situated just to its east) that had constituted an integral part of the built-up section of the expanded city.

The sum total of annexed land was seventy-one square kilometers and, as previously mentioned, only six of these had actually been part of the Arab municipality of Jerusalem. The rest was land belonging to twenty-eight villages, only a few of which were annexed in their entirety. In most cases only a part was annexed, leaving the populated area of the village outside, but stripping it of its agricultural land and/or potential building sites. The annexed territory also included some land from the neighboring municipalities of el-Bireh, Ramallah, and Bethlehem. In terms of local government, the area comprised one municipal council and seven rural or village councils.

The cabinet, during its session of July 26, 1967, voted to approve the boundaries that the committee of experts had unanimously agreed upon, euphemistically referring to their action as a "declaration regarding the expansion of the jurisdictional area of the Jerusalem municipality." It was accompanied by a verbal description of imaginary lines connecting reference points and altitude points that appear only on printed maps. The following is a sample of this description: "From map reference point 1678613520 northward along Wadi 'Isa to map reference point 1673613678, and thence in a straight line northeast until it meets the road at map reference point 1675413700, and thence eastward along the road until map reference point 1678813706, and thence in a straight line to altitude point 777.3 located at map reference point 1685413710. . . ." The people who drew these imaginary lines were military men who had learned well the lesson of Moshe Dayan's 1948 grease-pencil line. Perhaps Dayan himself cautioned them against making the same mistake he had nineteen years previously: the line from one point to the next is as thin as a hair. In any case, the 1967 border—

drawn in haste and without serious consideration or attention to urban exigencies, and on the basis of short-sighted historical and political presumptions—has come to have vital political and emotional import.

Town planners with the Jerusalem municipality thought that errors had been made in drawing the border, and recommended changes, seeking the inclusion of even larger areas within the jurisdictional area of the municipality. Their 1968 master plan recommended "redefining the boundaries by shifting the line between four and six kilometers eastward and adding territory to the west." However, because of the political difficulties caused by any discussion of changes to the boundaries of the territory annexed to the city, the eastern boundary remained as it had been in June 1967. Annexation of territory west of the city did not cause political problems, and therefore the Jerusalem municipality did succeed in expanding its boundaries westward in 1993.

To the east of the city, other means were found for adding territory to the State of Israel without defining it as annexation. The settlement of Ma'ale Adumim, which began as a workers' dormitory camp beside an industrial park, had by 1995 developed into a city with a population in excess of 20,000. The municipal jurisdictional area of its local council—which became a municipal council when Ma'ale Adumim officially became the first Jewish city in the West Bank in 1991—has since grown to encompass thirty-eight square kilometers. In 1994, the jurisdictional area of this Jerusalem suburb—theoretically located in the West Bank and ostensibly subject to military government—was further expanded until its western boundaries merged with the eastern boundaries of Jerusalem, thereby creating a continuous stretch of "Jewish" land extending from the approaches to Jericho in the east to the western slopes of the Judean Hills. All of this huge area acquired sacred status from Jerusalem in accordance with the halachic (Jewish legal) principle that it and the city were "contiguous and visible."

The Jewish holiday of Purim is celebrated on the fourteenth of the month of Adar, except in cities surrounded by "a wall from the time of Joshua Bin Nun," where the holiday falls on the fifteenth. Since Jerusalem is in the latter category, a question arose as to the geographical definition of the city, and whether its suburbs could be regarded as being surrounded by a wall from Joshua's time. Here the twofold test of visibility and proximity was applied: if the houses constituted a single built-up area all the way to Jerusalem, then they were part of Jerusalem. However, some areas were "contiguous but not visible," and some were "visible but not contiguous." According to tradition, houses that were not part of a continuously built-up area, but from which the city was visible, were regarded as belonging to the Holy City. And vice versa: houses from which Jerusalem could not be seen but which were part of a continuously built-up area were likewise sanctified. This adaptable definition of connection to Jerusalem matched the similarly adaptable definition employed by bureaucrats and politicians who permitted themselves to designate bare hills, trees, and Arab houses—far from the traditional boundaries of the city—as belonging to Jerusalem, "the eternal capital of the Jewish people."

Map making, determination of boundaries, and naming are all acts of taking possession. Human beings are not the creators of any of the features of the natural world, but they can give them names and designate their locations on maps. By so doing they believe that they have created the world anew. People can react to an attempt to change their identities, but inanimate objects cannot protest when their identity is altered. They are mute. The hills of Judea cannot rebel against being turned into building lots. Had they a voice, they would surely forgo the honor of being thought of as holy ground, if that status means forfeiting their tranquility and becoming pawns in a political game. In Jerusalem, of all places, whose historical site is so precisely defined, and so eternal, commissions of inquiry grant themselves—and military officers—license to inflate its jurisdictional boundaries, thereby turning its very geographical definition into a farce.

It would seem that before we can answer the question, Whose is Jerusalem? we will first have to agree on the answer to the question, What is Jerusalem?

CHAPTER THREE

HALLOWED GROUND

At number 24 Misgav Ladach Street in the renovated Jewish Quarter of the Old City, in an apartment that has been con-verted to a museum, there stands a mold for casting a seven-branched candelabrum. The mold, with its forty-two goblets and the flower-and-bud pattern crowning its candlesticks, stands empty, await-ing the pouring of the gold that will transform it into the candelabrum of the Third Temple. Donations totaling 1.75 million dollars are required for the completion of this important ceremonial object. And this is not the only temple implement on exhibit at the Temple Institute, whose windows look out on the mosques on the Temple Mount. Many others have already been fashioned from pure gold, in anticipation of the great moment when they will be installed in the sanctuary to be built on the Mount once the Muslim houses of prayer currently occupying its summit have been removed. Indiana Jones needn't have done battle with the raiders of the lost ark—an exact model of the Ark of the Covenant, bedecked with cherubs with outstretched wings, stands at the center of the exhibition, flanked by the High Priest's ritual garments, musical instruments for the Levites, and golden censers.

Rabbi Yisrael Ariel, head of the Temple Institute—whose experts and artisans painstakingly produced these ritual objects—has no doubt that the great day is at hand: the Third Temple will very soon be rebuilt. Unlike the rabbis of Israel's religious establishment, Rabbi Ariel asserts that the rebuilding of the Temple is within human capabilities and is not a miraculous feat that can only be accomplished with the coming of the messiah. Several groups share his belief, and among them operate no fewer than ten institutes, seminaries, and other institutions devoted to practical preparations for the reconstruction of the Temple and elucidation of the pertinent points of Jewish law. Though composed of fanatical extremist elements, these groups enjoy the moral support of respected religious personalities and receive financial aid from government ministries and other official bodies. Rabbi Yisrael Ariel and other Third Temple activists are, however, confronted by two major stumbling blocks. First is the prohibition imposed by the Chief Rabbinate against Jews' entering the Temple Mount, not to mention their making changes there. And second is the fact that worship on the Temple Mount is today limited to Muslims, whose rights to the site are recognized by the Israeli authorities.

Two inscriptions were placed on the gates leading to the Temple Mount during different historical periods. One, carved in stone in ancient Greek (currently on display in a museum) and bearing a warning directed at any "gentile" who might dare to enter the Temple precincts, guarded the approaches to Herod's Temple: "No gentile shall enter within the partition and barrier surrounding the Temple. Whosoever is caught shall be solely responsible to himself for his subsequent death." The second inscription, painted on a metal signboard, and set in place 2,000 years after the first, carries a pronouncement by the Chief Rabbinate: "Entrance to the area of the Temple Mount is forbidden to everyone by Jewish law owing to the sacredness of the place."

These two inscriptions epitomize the stormy history of this holy place, the most sacred of all to the Jewish people; the only place on this earth where, according to the Jewish faith, the human being stands fully in the presence of God, and from which—despite the Temple's destruc-

4. The Temple Mount

tion 2,000 years ago—the Shechinah (God's presence) has not departed. The sanctity of the place is so great that halacha (Jewish religious law) decrees that human beings are too impure to set foot there and must await the coming of the Messiah, who will purify them. The Temple, when it was standing, symbolized the sovereignty of the people of Israel, and the destruction of the one signified the loss of the other. With Israel's exile from the land, "the gentiles" gained possession of the Mount and erected their places of worship on its summit; henceforth it was forbidden for Jews to pray there to their God. The Chief Rabbinate maintains that the sanctity of the Temple Mount did not depart with the destruction of the Temple, and that the various degrees of holiness of its different areas continue to prevail. That position is upheld by ancient halachic rulings, foremost among which is that of Rambam (Maimonides): "Although the Temple is today in ruins because of our transgressions, a person is obligated to regard it with awe, even as he would have when it was standing."

There were areas within the precincts of the Temple Mount that it was permissible to enter after performing certain acts of purification, such as immersion, that can be carried out even today. However, one area could be entered only after purification with the ashes of a red heifer. Such ashes are no longer obtainable, since the strain of cattle that was used has died out, and the chances of being able to breed a red heifer that would meet all the special halachic requirements are exceedingly slim. In the absence of a red heifer's ashes it is not possible to purify a person who has been contaminated by contact with the dead or by contact with another person who is "unclean"—in other words, any Jew. Hence the conclusion that only the Messiah can solve the problem, since only he is capable of finding a suitable red heifer, whose ashes, mixed with holy water, can purify the Children of Israel. The area requiring purification with a red heifer's ashes is actually not extensive, but since the location of the central sanctuary—the holy of holies—cannot be precisely determined, it is also impossible to gauge the exact whereabouts of other areas on the Mount.

This confusion regarding the reference point from which the location of different sections of the Temple can be determined means that Jews are absolutely forbidden to climb the Temple Mount, and desecration of this holy place is considered a serious transgression, punishable by death at the hand of God. The Chief Rabbinate's unequivocal ruling in this matter is supported by the signatures of more than 300 rabbis from all streams of Judaism, in Israel and abroad. Summarized, it reads: "We hereby repeat the warning that we have made in the past, that no man or woman shall dare to enter any part of the area of the Temple Mount, regardless of which gate they gain entry by."

Rabbi Yisrael Ariel and other rabbis before him chose a different approach: they did not take issue with the enduring sacredness of the Temple grounds, but rather they claimed that it was indeed possible to determine the site of the holy of holies and from there to ascertain the location of the various other sections of the Temple. According to their calculations, there are large areas at the southern and northern ends of the Mount that are entirely outside the Temple precincts, and where, not only is it permissible to pray, but a synagogue should be erected immediately.

All this is quite apart from the practical preparations for the erection of the Third Temple, which, from these rabbis' perspective, would constitute fulfillment of a major religious obligation, perhaps even a commandment. Year after year, ever since 1967, on every holiday during which Jews used to ascend the Temple Mount when the Temple was still standing, groups of religious fanatics and nationalist activists have attempted to push their way onto the Mount and to hold public prayers there. The police, however, have not permitted this, and have forcibly ejected them from the area. The police response is based on a cabinet decision in accordance with which "explicit orders have been given not to allow Jews to hold prayers in the Temple Mount compound so as not to bring about confrontations and disturbances of public order." Nearly every year these groups petition the High Court of Justice in an attempt to have the orders repealed. However, the court has consistently rejected their pleas and reaffirmed the decision of the government.

Immediately following the occupation of the Temple Mount in 1967, Moshe Dayan officially endorsed the status quo, and it has endured to this day. The entire area, including the mosques, other buildings, and all the gateways to the Mount save one, remained in the hands of the Muslim religious authorities (the *Waqf*). Jews were permitted to visit, but not to pray. Dayan's decision was astounding in its daring. The Jews returned after thousands of years of exile and conquered their holy place and symbol of their national independence, and despite this enormous load of emotional baggage, an Israeli leader made a rational decision in order to prevent a religious war whose consequences were beyond conjecture.

Fanatical groups have sought to alter the status quo on the Temple Mount, for the most part through legal protest-movement tactics such as demonstrations and ceremonies, for the benefit of television cameras. Some have engaged in confrontations with the police, while others have gone even further in their violence, conspiring to blow up the Temple Mount mosques. This was not an isolated incident, but was attempted repeatedly, only to be thwarted by the authorities. The conspirators, however, did not give up. Five times they tried to blow up the mosques and each time they miraculously failed in the attempt, were caught and brought to justice. But the potential for destruction remained great, because among the architects of these schemes were not only disturbed persons, but also people of sound mind with solid ideological grounding, access to explosives, and an admiring public. They relentlessly made attempt after attempt. Their motivation was not only religious-ideological, but nationalistic-political as well, and the attempts to blow up the mosques coincided with critical points in the peace process— from the Disengagement Agreements of 1974, which preceded the pullout from the Sinai Peninsula, to the Oslo Accords in 1993. The members of the extremist opposition to a peace involving territorial concessions hoped that blowing up the mosques would "torpedo" the peace process. The frequency of their provocative attempts to force their way onto the Temple Mount and to pray there increased each time signs of moderation appeared and efforts to put an end to the Israeli-Palestinian conflict intensified.

The symbiotic connection between the religious and the nationalistic components of Israeli-Jewish and Arab-Palestinian identity turned the struggle over the Temple Mount into a time bomb, ticking away in the heart of Jerusalem with a destructive potential of truly apocalyptic proportions. The red heifer's ashes have served as a mechanism for delaying its detonation. They are a reminder that the Israeli government has succeeded in preserving the status quo only because the religious establishment has persisted in maintaining its position that the ritual impurity of the Jews prevents them from taking possession of the Temple Mount. However, this mechanism is not reliable, since the dissension cleaving Israeli society in regard to the peace process with the Palestinians has led to the intensification of attempts to commit unlawful, provocative acts.

The Palestinians react vigorously and forcefully to any attempt to alter the status quo on the Temple Mount, and the inevitable result of this confrontation is bloodshed. The violence reached its zenith in October of 1990, when seventeen Muslims were killed and over a hundred were wounded by Israeli police and border guard fire. Those killed in the incident were declared *shuhada* (martyrs) who had fallen in the holy battle for the Noble Haram (the compound of the Al-Aqsa Mosque). The hundreds of young men who took part in the bloody clashes with the Israeli police were suffused with a sense of participation in a battle whose outcome would determine whether Palestine would be delivered or lost.

The Jewish zealots of the Temple Mount asserted that the status quo amounted to "handing over the Mountain of the Lord to its desecraters" and abandoning the Jewish people's holiest place and symbol of their national sovereignty. The Palestinians, in contrast, viewed the status quo as a humiliation that carried with it the danger of the loss of their exclusive control of the Temple Mount, and even if they became accustomed to the practical arrangements that were made, they never ceased to regard them as having been imposed by the hated occupier. The Palestinians assumed that the objective of Zionism, as hinted by its name, was to take over the Temple Mount and rebuild the Temple there. Therefore they believed that the schemes of the Jewish fanatics represented Israel's true ambitions, and they mistrusted the intentions of the authorities and the words of reassurance offered by Israeli moderates.

The provocative actions of the Jewish fanatics fueled Muslim fanaticism and vice versa, in a vicious circle of violence and hatred. The zeal of the Muslims was no less intense than that of the Jews. Although many Jews were unable to come to terms with the symmetry in the degree of religious and national significance ascribed to the Mount by the two conflicting sides, it would be impossible not to acknowledge the supreme importance of the Noble Haram in the religious and national identity of the Palestinian people. Jews emphasized the difference between Muslims' connection to the site and their own; for Jews it is the actual, undisputed location of the ancient Temple. However, Muslim belief relies on legend, on tradition, and on the aura of sanctity imparted to the place by Jewish sources. Islam became associated with Jerusalem's holiness via Muhammad's night journey to the city: "Glorified [be] He who carried His servant by night from the Holy Mosque to the Farthest Mosque, the precincts whereof we have blessed" (*Qur'an*, sura 17:1).

The Farthest Mosque, or al-Aqsa, came to be identified with the southern end of the Temple Mount, and the night journey was linked to Muhammad's ascent to heaven astride a winged beast. These traditions gained concrete expression when Caliph Omar conquered Jerusalem (A.D. 638). The Temple Mount was cleansed of the piles of rubbish and the ruins that had accumulated during the Byzantine period, and a mosque was built there and given the name Al-Aqsa, thereby anchoring tradition in physical reality. The Temple Mount area as a whole—which includes some thirty-five acres, with mosques (Al-Aqsa and the Dome of the Rock) and dozens of small shrines and other religious structures, and is surrounded by walls containing nine gates (as well as five that are sealed)—became "the Noble Haram," "the precincts whereof we have blessed"; in its entirety an indivisible, sanctified site.

Jerusalem's ascent in level of sanctity was accompanied by theological disputes, but these had already died out before the Crusader conquest of 1099. And when Sultan Salah al-Din (Saladin) rid the Mount of the Christian symbols placed there during Crusader rule and purified the mosques with rosewater, the Temple Mount was established in the Muslim faith as a holy place associated with Mecca and Medina, even if not on the same level of holiness as they. For the Muslims of Jerusalem and the country surrounding it, the fact that their city was perceived by Muslims in general as their third holiest site was not the sum total of its significance. In the context of their spiritual life, the emotional connection to the nearby Temple Mount was even more powerful than that to distant Mecca. One cannot escape the irony of the fact that history has decreed that the places held sacred by the Jews are the same ones that are sacred to the Arabs of Palestine. Conflict over these sites became inevitable when the two communities welded nationalistic designs to religious symbols, to an extent that blurred the distinctions between them.

For hundreds of years no conflict erupted between Jews and Muslims over possession of the Temple Mount and the rest of Jerusalem's holy sites. Arab writers like to regard the tension-free atmosphere that prevailed in Jerusalem until early in the twentieth century as testimony to the fact that "all of the troubles were the product of Zionist incitement." But the truth is that there were no religious tensions only as long as the Jews continued to acquiesce to absolute Muslim control over Jerusalem and its holy sites. Entry to the Temple Mount was absolutely forbidden to non-Muslims, and even at the western wall of the Mount, the "Western Wall" or "Wailing Wall," Jewish worshipers were subject to the whims of the Muslims. The inferior status of Jews and Christians was maintained while the Muslims ruled Jerusalem. They imposed laws and customs based on the classic Muslim attitude that the Jews and Christians, as "people of the Book," were to be tolerated, but only if they were willing to put up with discriminatory treatment. The British conquest changed the situation totally, and the religious-nationalist conflict burst forth, its components remaining unchanged to this day.

The focal point of the conflict during the British Mandate was not the Temple Mount compound itself, but the Western Wall below. Being forbidden to enter the Mount did not especially upset the Jews, since the religious prohibition served, then more than now, as an obstacle to head-on confrontation. Both sides regarded the Western Wall and the summit of the Mount above it as a single unit—located on different levels topographically, but constituting an integral whole.

In 1920, Rabbi Avraham Yitzhak Hacohen Kook, revered Chief Rabbi of the Ashkenazim, defined the relationship between the Temple

5. The Western Wall Plaza

Mount and the Wall: "The Temple Mount is Israel's eternal holy place, and even should it be under the hand of others for long days and periods of time, it will finally come to our hands. . . . That we do not enter within from [beyond] the Wall is not because of the slightness of our rights and the slightness of our connections to this holy place, but rather because of the greatness of our connection to it. . . . The Western Wall, especially, was left to us as a remnant and a sign and as proof of our salvation and of the assurance of our return to the sacred standing-place [before God]." A Palestinian leader, the Mufti Hajj Amin al-Husseini, took Rabbi Kook's yearning to return to the Mount with the advent of the messiah and turned it into a concrete political plot. He stated in 1925 that "the weeping of the Jews beside the Wall and their kisses [of its stones] do not arise from their love for the Wall itself, but from their concealed aspirations to take control of the *Haram a-Sharif* (Temple Mount), as everyone knows." Hajj Amin, who led the Palestinian national movement in violent and futile struggles against the

Zionist movement and the British authorities, used the Temple Mount as a rallying point for the masses. He exploited the holy places for their powerful symbolism, which spoke to the hearts of millions of believers far more strongly than abstract nationalist slogans.

Had the Palestinians been able to see what was on the horizon, they might have contented themselves with exclusive control of the Temple Mount, which the British Mandatory regime agreed to. Article 13 of the Mandatory Charter states that "nothing in this mandate shall be construed as conferring upon the Mandatory authority permission to interfere with the structure or the management of purely Muslim sacred shrines, the immunity of which is guaranteed." The authorities absolutely did not interfere in the management of the Muslim holy places, even though the religious institutions headed by Hajj Amin used donated funds, which had been collected for the upkeep of the mosques, to finance subversive activities and even to obtain weapons for use against British soldiers. The Temple Mount itself was turned into a hiding place for weapons and explosives and a haven for murderers fleeing the police. Only when the Palestinians declared a general revolt against the British (in 1937), did the authorities decide to dismantle the "state within a state" that had grown up around the Muslim religious institutions. The British tried to arrest and exile the Palestinians' religious-nationalist leader, but Mufti Hajj Amin escaped to the safe haven of the Temple Mount. He stayed for three months (mid-July to mid-October, 1937), and from there directed the Arab Revolt. The authorities dared not attempt to penetrate the Haram. Only in mid-October did the Mufti flee, under cover of darkness—sliding down a rope slung over the Temple Mount walls—and find asylum in Beirut. The Arab Revolt was crushed, and the catastrophic effects of this failure left the Palestinian community powerless when the time came that it was really put to the test: the 1948 war. Had they been wise enough to follow a realistic policy, they would not have begun a hopeless battle. Had they understood that behind "the Jews' weeping beside the Wall" was hidden a might born of desperation, they would not have provoked them, thereby creating a store of hatred and vengeful feelings that would, in the fullness of time, burst forth and threaten their holy places.

The Muslims turned the Jews' prayers at the Western Wall into a focus for incitement and political struggle. They tried their utmost to interfere with Jews' access to the Wall, and to disturb them at prayer, even deliberately pelting worshipers with trash. They attempted to use the Mandatory government's commitment to preserve the status quo to compel the authorities to forbid the Jews to conduct public prayers, allowing them only "the right of a simple visit to the Wall." Because the Muslims owned the Wall itself (which is a section of the Temple Mount walls) and the pavement in front of it, they complained to the authorities about things the Jews did that could be construed as attempts to assert possession of the site, such as placing benches, chairs, and the screen dividing the men's and women's sections near the Wall, and repairing the stone pavement of the plaza. The government took its time responding, so the Muslims began initiating provocations. The Muezzin would begin the call to prayer at precisely the time Jewish prayers were going on. Muslims set up a prayer corner near the wall and held Dervish services there with drumming. An opening was made in a wall at the edge of the prayer area, through which Muslims led cattle during Jewish worship. They smoked cigarettes on the Sabbath, and would deliberately pour out the waste water from the adjacent Arab neighborhood by the Wall. Of course the Jews reacted strongly to this, and on the night of the Ninth of Av, 1929, when Jews traditionally lament the destruction of the First and Second Temples, they held a gigantic demonstration during which the Zionist flag was displayed and *Hatikva* (the Zionist anthem) was sung. The Arab response was not long in coming, and an inflamed mob first attacked Jewish neighborhoods in Jerusalem and then dozens of other Jewish communities. In the course of these disturbances the Jewish community in Hebron was wiped out and a number of isolated settlements were burnt to the ground.

The Mandatory government acceded to most of the Muslims' demands, but left to the League of Nations the dubious honor of making a final ruling on "the question of the rights and claims of the Jews and Arabs regarding the Western Wall." The Jews demanded only that they be allowed to continue their prayers "under fair and dignified terms and without impinging on the religious rights of others." But the decisions of the international body and the Mandatory authorities who implemented them were very restrictive. The Jews were permitted free access to the Wall at all times, but they were allowed to bring with them only religious articles and portable objects whose number and dimensions were precisely specified. On the eve of every holiday, the British District Commissioner would verify their compliance. It was forbidden to bring chairs or benches, to blow the shofar, or to sing. Until the conclusion of the British Mandate, the Jews had to put up with humiliating conditions during worship: they were allowed to read from the *Torah* only on official holidays; on the Sabbath they had to leave the Wall and read the *Torah* in synagogues in the Jewish Quarter; and elderly and sick people were forced stand on their feet throughout the prayers on High Holy Days, when the services go on all day. It was forbidden to blow the shofar even at the most sacred moment in the Jewish liturgy, the *Ne'ila* prayer at the close of the Yom Kippur fast.

During all those years, the *yishuv* (Jewish community in Mandatory Palestine) followed a policy of self-restraint and conciliation, but not all its members acquiesced to the humiliating conditions at the Wall, and some clashed with the authorities. The British, however, did not deviate from their policy; the vociferous protests of the Muslims and the fear of religious riots ensured that. It is easy to imagine the force of the Jews' angry feelings and the lust for revenge that accumulated over the years, and the period (1947–1967) of being denied access to the Wall only increased their longing to return to this remnant of the Temple. That torrent of feelings was loosed on the eighth of June, 1967, when the first Israeli soldiers reached the paved area in front of the Wall.

Immediately following the paratroopers—the conquerors of the Temple Mount—came personnel from the Military Rabbinate. With them they brought a *Torah* scroll, a shofar, and a bench. Upon their arrival, they held the scroll aloft, blew on the shofar, and sat on the bench. Each of these acts was symbolic, because all had been forbidden to the Jews. Echoes of the past resounded in every Israeli act and statement. Just forty-eight hours after the conquest of the Wall, the entire densely built-up area adjoining it was demolished. The narrow Western Wall pavement was transformed into a gigantic plaza, and more than 100 Arab families were evicted from their homes, which were torn down to make way for the hundreds of thousands of Jews seeking to reach the Wall. The former space in front of the Wall could not have accommodated the 400,000 people who swarmed to the site; the maximum number able to pray there during the period of the Mandate was 12,000 per day. Practical considerations were the determining factor in the demolition of the buildings of the Arab quarter, but undoubtedly an irrational force was also at work. This was the settling of historic accounts with those who had provoked the Jewish people, placed obstacles in their path, humiliated them at their most sacred place, and denied them access to it for twenty long years.

Echoes of bygone days could also be discerned in the declarations of Israel's leaders regarding the government's treatment of the holy places in Jerusalem. In contrast to the city's other twentieth-century conquerors (see page 99), the Israelis refrained from committing themselves to preserving the existing arrangements, since this would mean perpetuating the humiliating situation at the Western Wall. Indeed, one of the Palestinians' major grievances against the occupation was that the Jews had disrupted the status quo at the Wall, "which is an exclusively Muslim [piece of] property, since it is contained within the area of the Holy Enclosure and also because the Muslims possess the property rights to the pavement [*al Rasif*] which lies before the Wall." In a complaint lodged with the Security Council in August of 1967, the Palestinians stated that "the Jews have the right of access to the Western Wall to conduct prayers and supplications subject to rules. . . . These rules have settled the Jewish-Arab dispute concerning this Holy Place, and under no circumstances should this dispute be allowed to arise again."

The Palestinians not only sought to reinstate the humiliating conditions of the Mandatory years, they also rebuked the Jews for displaying ingratitude toward the Muslims, who "had acted as the Jews' protectors and had provided them with a refuge from the aggression from which they suffered throughout the non-Muslim world." They maintained that "the site of the temple has not been established categorically in any religious text, and is a controversial issue amongst historians and archeologists." Other Muslim spokespersons asserted that no remains had been found on the Temple Mount that proved the Jewish claim that the Temple had been located there, and even declared that the Temple had stood on another hill altogether—Mount Zion.

Just as the Muslims had turned the Temple Mount into a focal point for nationalist activities, the Jews have transformed the Wall into a national site. The sacred wall, in whose crevices worshipers place slips of paper bearing entreaties to the Almighty for a life of tranquillity and for peace in the world, is also the place where soldiers' swearing-in ceremonies are held and where their weapons are consecrated.

The coexistence of these two neighboring places of worship is not peaceful, nor is the conflict over them merely religious. There is an obvious contrast between the elevated enclosure, crowned with magnificent structures, above, and the bare pavement, with a stark wall at its end, below. As author A. B. Yehoshua describes the situation: "The problem [of the Western Wall] stems from both its architectural meagerness and the fact of its being a remnant of a marginal part of an ancient structure that was destroyed two thousand years ago, as well as from its absurd juxtaposition with the Temple Mount, of which it once was a part and to which it has now become something supposedly contradictory—in the national sense, above all." To Yehoshua, the Western Wall embodies "religious exclusivity" and is "symbolic of destruction," and the overwhelming impression it makes is of "Jews standing uncertainly, pessimistically, stranded there before the harsh, bare stone Wall."

Yet there are those who hold that the spiritual yearning for universal human salvation—which is not focused on some ritual object or magnificent building, but precisely on harsh, bare stone—best expresses the authentic essence of Judaism. As Rabbi Avraham Yitzhak Hacohen Kook stated: "And all the air above the Wall and up to the heavens is regarded by us as exalted and holy and it is our right not ever to depart from this place. It is there for us forever, and it is not our business from what period its stones [originated]. For us the main thing is the place and the holy air that extends from it to the high heavens." However, this religious and spiritual way of perceiving the Wall does not satisfy those who view it as the embodiment of "the innermost heart of the historical national experience"—the return to the *moledet* (homeland) and the renewal of Jewish sovereignty. They seek a concrete expression for this experience—one that "could be the equal, architecturally and in content, of the mosques on the Temple Mount and the Church of the Holy Sepulchre"—as the first among equals. And since those who are of this opinion refrain from drawing the simplistic and barbarous conclusion that the mosques must be demolished, another, "temporary," solution is required: the renovation of the Western Wall plaza.

Since the time that all the buildings in the area fronting on the Western Wall were torn down in June of 1967, transforming it overnight into a dusty lot, many groups have sought to provide it with a form befitting its importance and symbolism. But design requires agreement concerning the significance of the site. The indissoluble connection between religion and nation was acceptable to everyone, but left many questions unanswered. Should the area be designated an orthodox synagogue, where custom dictates the separation of men and women? Was the entire plaza a holy place, where those in attendance must cover their heads, or was it necessary to define separate areas for worshipers and visitors? How far did the holiness of the Western Wall extend? Was only the small portion of the Wall where Jews have prayed for a thousand years holy, or was the entire Temple Mount Wall? What expression should be given to the secular perception of the Wall as a national-historical site? What should be done with the archeological artifacts discovered there?

All of these problems required both pragmatic and administrative solutions, and in the absence of agreement it was impossible to arrive at an overall plan. Thus, temporary, fluid arrangements were adopted that reflected the changing political power relationships. Plans for the comprehensive design of the Western Wall area were suspended amid vociferous debate. Because of the political power of the religious sector and its ability to mobilize a sizable public in the struggle for its particular perceptions, the area closest to the Wall functioned as an orthodox synagogue, while the more distant section (and the area outside the traditional prayer section) was treated as a secular site. None of the plans for giving the plaza as a whole a permanent form, including some impressive architectural conceptions, were approved or implemented.

However, there was a more profound reason that the Western Wall plaza remained without distinctive form or character: the concern that making significant structural improvements would turn the Wall area into a substitute for the Temple Mount. Rabbi Kook's perspective, that the Wall symbolized "the assurance of our return to the sacred standing-place [before God]," or a promise of return to the Temple Mount, clashed with the view that it was necessary to build a religious and spiritual sanctuary beside the Wall that would function as a "kind of temporary-permanent substitute for the Temple." The perspective of those rejecting any substitute triumphed, and perhaps the suggestion of constructing one was no more than the frivolous brainchild of secular liberals. There *is* no substitute for the Temple Mount. The inherent tension caused by the juxtaposition of the Temple Mount and the Western Wall has not dissipated. The fact that, in this of all places, sovereign and victorious Israel is unable to express its religious and national affinities, and thus actually seems to acquiesce to this allegedly humiliating situation—that of gentiles looking down on Jewish worshipers—has led fanatical elements to unceasingly concoct schemes to blow up the mosques. These fanatics have found unlikely allies: Christian fundamentalists.

Many individuals and groups have made monetary contributions to Rabbi Yisrael Ariel's Temple Institute and similar institutions. Most of these donations come from marginal Jewish circles, but some donors of substantial sums are members of evangelical-fundamentalist Christian groups in Europe, Japan, Korea, and especially the United States. These groups not only support Jewish fanatics who aspire to destroy the mosques on the Temple Mount and replace them with the Third Temple; they also take an active part in practical preparations to alter the status quo on the Mount. What brings together devout Christians—who make pilgrimages to Jerusalem by the thousands and work themselves into trances of religious ecstasy—and pious Jews, who view these Christians as "goyim" whose sole intention is to convert them? This strange alliance of fanatics is based upon their shared belief that the End of Days is at hand and that there is no more reliable means of hastening the advent of the Messiah—that of the Jews (for the first time) and that of the Christians (for the second)—than the building of the Third Temple.

Evangelical fundamentalists from various denominations believe literally in the Old Testament and in the prophesies found therein. They believe that the "ingathering of the exiles" (the Jewish people), the reinstatement of King David's lineage, the rebuilding of the Temple, and the revival of the Temple cult are prerequisites for the return of Jesus of Nazareth. The Second Coming does not bode well for the Temple, however. It will again be destroyed, during the Battle of Armageddon, at the end of which Jesus will triumph and the Millennium—the era of justice and peace on earth—will commence. The Jewish fanatics are not worried about the apocalyptic battle that will supposedly take place after the Temple is rebuilt; they prefer to have allies in this world, even ones who will become their enemies in the world to come, and to depend on their Messiah, son of David, to deal with Jesus, son of Mary.

Many fundamentalists do not visit the Church of the Holy Sepulchre at all, regarding it as a center of Eastern Orthodox and Catholic idolatry.

6. The Holy Sepulchre

They absorb the sanctity of Jerusalem while surveying the city's sublime panorama from the summit of the Mount of Olives, not in the depressing darkness of the church. There is an element of paradox in the fact that it is precisely those who relate to the Old Testament literally, as accounts of actual historical events, who scorn the places revered by the mainstream churches that emphasize the spiritual and allegorical meaning of the Holy Scriptures. Yet this paradox is just another expression of the complexity of Christianity's attitude toward Jerusalem and its holy places.

On the one hand, Christians hold sacred the sites of the great mysteries—the passion, resurrection, and ascension; all actual locations in the earthly Jerusalem—regardless of whether they have been accurately identified. On the other hand, they emphasize the spiritual, ethereal significance of those events that are not identified with specific locations, but whose holiness dwells in the heart of the believer and in the community of Christians. Since they regard the Old Testament as an allegorical preface to the chronicles of "spiritual Israel" (the universal Christian community), earthly Jerusalem loses its importance as the concrete, physical stage upon which history unfolds, and is replaced by the heavenly Jerusalem. The celestial Zion is manifest wherever a person is in communion with God, whether in the bosom of the Catholic Church or while singing gospel hymns.

This concept, an attempt to distill the religious experience and free it from dependence upon the physical site, did not diminish the powerful and understandable longing of many people to be close to the objects of religious adoration; to see them and to touch them. The tradition of pilgrimages and the cult of the holy places responded to basic needs of believing Christians, and the church fathers neither desired nor were able to impose their cold, rationalistic, theological perspective. Therefore they asserted that "although God's presence is close to us everywhere, even so, the human spirit, dependent as it is on the influence of the world of the senses, soars to states of spiritual exaltation in certain places more than in others."

Jerusalem is not the only holy place and pilgrimage site, but it has had a special role because of its connection with the life of the Christ. In its earthly dimension, the holy city held a dominant position in the chronicles of the Christian world, as the focal point for the yearnings of millions, and as the means whereby spiritual interests were transformed into political claims. The holy places became sectarian battlefields, and visiting them turned into a cult of worshiping the relics of saints, as well as a method of accumulating "points" to the credit of souls suffering the torments of purgatory. According to the author of one classic guidebook (Father Barnabas Meisterman), "Plenary and partial indulgences have been attached to the Holy Places . . . all of which may be applied to the souls in Purgatory . . . [I]n order to gain these indulgences even several times a day, it is sufficient to be in a state of grace . . . at the privileged place" (*Guide to the Holy Land* [London: Burns, Oates & Co., 1923], xxvi).

I invite any Jews inclined to mock this cult to participate in one of the celebrations held at the graves of Jewish holy men and to visit the stands selling holy water and other objects blessed by the touch of some saintly rabbi. Perhaps the Jews do not keep complicated accounts with the Holy One Blessed Be He for the expiation of sins, but the cult of the holy men's graves and the purchase of talismans for long life or the birth of a son are much further from traditional Jewish precepts than the worship of saints' relics is from the Christianity of Saint Augustine. Early in the 1970s, Jerusalem municipal workers bored small holes in a section of the western wall of the Temple Mount, far from the traditional "Western Wall," in order to place wooden beams there to support some buildings from the Mamluk period that were sagging. Large groups of ultra-orthodox Jews gathered there, at "the Little Wall," tore down the supports, diligently gathered up all of the fragments of stone they could find, and placed them in large urns. The urns were borne through the streets in a pagan funeral procession accompanied by mournful cries, and buried at the Western Wall.

The conflict over Jerusalem's holy places is currently perceived in the context of the Israeli-Palestinian struggle, and no wonder: the explosive Temple Mount issue bears within it the potential to ignite a worldwide conflagration, and it is, therefore, a conflict of international importance. However, that struggle is not only what has earned the holy places in Jerusalem notoriety as an international political problem, but also internal Christian quarrels over Christian holy places. Ironically, more Christians have been injured in violent confrontations among themselves over control of their sacred sites than have Jews and Muslims in conflicts over the sites in dispute between them. From Crusader times to this very day, a mighty struggle has been going on continuously among the Christian denominations. This is a reflection not only of sectarian zeal and theological dissension, but also of the tortuous political battles of the Christian world powers, wherein religious conflicts were exploited to further imperialist goals and to gain strategically advantageous positions.

The entire complicated and sometimes bloody history of the Christian sites and the struggle over their control cannot be outlined here. This discussion will go only as far back as the period when the arrangements prevailing today were concluded. First of all, though, it may be helpful to enumerate the Christian communities that maintain a presence in Jerusalem, whose sheer number sheds light on the potential for confrontation and tension.

The churches in communion, either directly or indirectly, with the Holy See in Rome are: Roman Catholic, Greek Catholic (Melchite), Armenian Catholic, Syrian Catholic, Maronite, Chaldean Catholic, and Coptic Catholic. The Greek Orthodox denominations are: Greek Orthodox, Russian Orthodox ("White" and "Red"), and Rumanian Orthodox. Other religious communities include: Armenian (Georgian), Coptic Orthodox, Ethiopian, Syrian Orthodox, Evangelical Episcopal (Anglican), Lutheran, Southern Baptist, Seventh Day Adventist, Presbyterian (Scottish), Pentecostal, Nazarene, Mennonite, Mormon, and Makoya (Japanese).

For the purposes of pursuing our interest in the holy places, we can ignore all but two or perhaps three of the above denominations: the Roman Catholics (referred to in Jerusalem as the Latins), the Greek Orthodox, and the Armenian Orthodox. The conflict between the two major churches dates from the Middle Ages, when the Eastern and Western churches separated once and for all (the Great Schism of 1057). It revolved around the ownership of and the right to worship at principle holy places: the Church of the Holy Sepulchre, the Church of the Ascension on the Mount of Olives, the Tomb of the Virgin in the Valley of Jehoshaphat, and the Church of the Nativity in Bethlehem. Confrontations that threatened to turn into bloody incidents obliged whoever was ruling the city to intervene, to contain them, to take sides, and sometimes to restore order by force.

The political conflict quickly became an important issue in international politics, and after the Ottoman conquest of 1517, the problem of the holy places was mentioned in a long series of international agreements between the Ottomans and the European powers of the day, who acted as patrons for their co-religionists and their interests in Jerusalem.

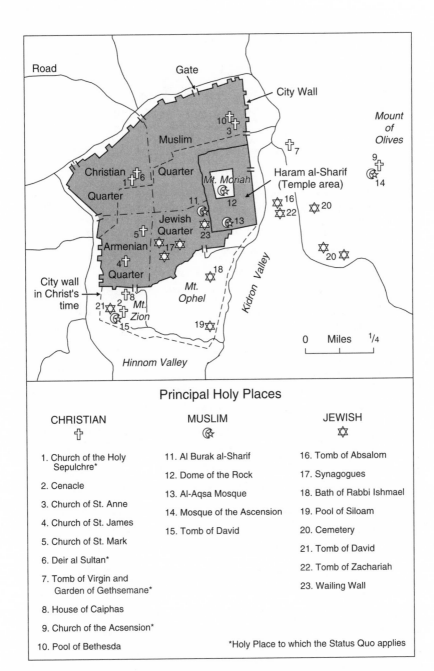

Principal Holy Places

CHRISTIAN ✝	MUSLIM ☾	JEWISH ✡
1. Church of the Holy Sepulchre*	11. Al Burak al-Sharif	16. Tomb of Absalom
2. Cenacle	12. Dome of the Rock	17. Synagogues
3. Church of St. Anne	13. Al-Aqsa Mosque	18. Bath of Rabbi Ishmael
4. Church of St. James	14. Mosque of the Ascension	19. Pool of Siloam
5. Church of St. Mark	15. Tomb of David	20. Cemetery
6. Deir al Sultan*		21. Tomb of David
7. Tomb of Virgin and Garden of Gethsemane*		22. Tomb of Zachariah
8. House of Caiphas		23. Wailing Wall
9. Church of the Acsension*		
10. Pool of Bethesda		*Holy Place to which the Status Quo applies

MAP 3.   Holy Places (1947 map)

Throughout the 400 years of Turkish rule, the power of the Greek Orthodox church in the holy places was steadily reinforced at the expense of the Latins and the smaller Christian denominations.

The sultan, who regarded the Orthodox as his subjects, supported their claims over those of the Latins, who were of the same religion as his enemies, the European powers. Military victories by European nations, particularly France (over the Ottomans), brought the Latins a number of rights, though these were later revoked. Meanwhile, the Orthodox gained a powerful international supporter in the form of Czarist Russia. During the eighteenth and nineteenth centuries, the problem of the holy places became an international issue of primary importance.

L.G.A. Cust, a senior official in the British Mandatory administration who investigated the problem and published a classic work on the subject, describes the conflict thus: "The history of the Holy Places is one long story of bitter animosities and contentions, in which outside influences take part to an increasing degree, until the scenes of our Lord's life on earth becomes a political shuttlecock, and eventually the cause of international conflict. If the Holy Places and the rights pertaining thereto are an 'expression of man's feelings about Him whose story hallowed these sites,' they are also an index of the corruptions and intrigues of despots and chancelleries during eight hundred years. The logical results have been the distrust and suspicion, and the attitude of intractability in all matters, even those of only the most trivial importance, concerning the Holy Places" (*The Status Quo in the Holy Places* [Gov't. of Palestine, 1929], 4).

It is no wonder that those attempting to resolve the conflict sought out a magic formula and found one in the form of reinstatement of the status quo ante—the situation that existed before. Rights to ownership and use of the holy places and parts thereof would be determined according to what had been established at a certain point in the past, and no change would be permitted. Had the status quo been clearly defined and accepted by all, matters would have been relatively simple. However, for political and historical reasons, several rulings had been made and then arbitrarily revoked. Thus the codification of the Status Quo created one of the most fluid and imprecise codes in the world.

In 1757, at the time of the Seven Years' War in Europe, the Greek Patriarch of Jerusalem succeeded in obtaining a *firman* (edict) from the Ottoman sultan designating the Orthodox as the primary church at the holy places. For many years the Latins sought the repeal of this edict, receiving unstinting aid in their efforts from the European powers. In 1850, the French ambassador demanded, in the name of his country and the kingdoms of Austria, Spain, Sardinia, and Belgium, that Istanbul restore control over parts of the Church of the Holy Sepulchre and other sites to the Latins. Russia vigorously opposed this demand, and the ensuing diplomatic dispute was one of the causes of the Crimean War (1853). In February 1852, the sultan issued an edict rejecting the Latins' demands as formulated in 1850 and stating that the status quo would be maintained in all of the places specified. This decree constituted the official codification of the Status Quo. Subsequently, in various international treaties, such as the Treaty of Paris (1856) and the Treaty of Berlin (1878), it was explicitly agreed to preserve the Status Quo in the holy places of Palestine, with any changes to be made only with the agreement of all parties.

After the First World War the situation changed drastically. Turkey was defeated, a European power became ruler of the Holy Land, and Russia, now part of the Soviet Union, no longer intervened in matters pertaining to the holy places. Changes were also taking place in Christian Europe. Whereas previously the French had been recognized as the protectors of the Catholics in the Ottoman Empire, now Italy had become their principal diplomatic support. It was the Vatican's goal to abolish the Status Quo codified in 1852, and to that end it demanded that a commission be set up to examine the various claims and arrive at a new arrangement. The Vatican had reason to hope that this attempt would succeed, since the Bolshevik revolution in Russia had left the Orthodox Patriarchate of Jerusalem without a powerful European patron. Greece, it is true, had begun to represent the patriarchate in international forums, but was clearly no match for Italy and France.

The League of Nations Charter of the British Mandate for Palestine included many provisions concerning the holy places. These included the following: "All responsibility in connection with Holy Places and religious buildings or sites in Palestine, including that of preserving existing rights and of securing free access to the Holy places, religious buildings and sites and the free exercise of worship, while ensuring the requirements of public order and decorum, is assumed by the Mandatory."

The Vatican's demand for the appointment of a commission of inquiry was also mentioned in the charter. "A special commission shall be appointed by the Mandatory to study, define and determine the rights and claims in connection with the Holy Places and the rights and claims relating to the different religious communities in Palestine. The method of nomination, the composition and the functions of this Commission shall be submitted to the Council of the League [of Nations] for its approval, and the Commission shall not be appointed or enter upon its functions without the approval of the Council."

The Mandatory Charter, then, obligated the British government to act to preserve "existing rights" and to set up a commission to examine requests for changes in the Status Quo. There was no doubt that this problem affected only the Christian holy places, since it was explicitly stated that the British were forbidden to interfere with the Muslim holy places. As to the Jews, they were not represented in the League of Nations, their status under Ottoman rule was inferior to that of the Christian and Muslim communities, and their holy places were not included in any codification of the Status Quo. Nevertheless, the Charter referred to holy places in general, and this had serious consequences as regards the Jewish holy places (as we have seen).

The composition of the commission was the subject of extensive debate in the Council of the League of Nations. The Vatican did not hide the fact that it was not seeking a just and impartial investigation, but rather the augmentation of its rights in the holy places. It therefore demanded that the commission include a Catholic majority and not be permitted to rule on rights already possessed by the Catholics. Britain endeavored to find all manner of compromises in an attempt to ensure that the makeup of the commission would not sabotage the effort to solve once and for all, in a just and unbiased manner, all the conflicts between the Christian denominations. In the course of the debate, the British proposed dividing the commission into three subcommittees, to deal with Christian, Muslim, and Jewish holy places, respectively. They suggested that the Christian committee be made up of three Catholics, three Orthodox, one Ethiopian, and a neutral chairperson. The Catholics were adamantly opposed. When it became clear that there was no chance of reaching agreement on the composition of the commission of inquiry, Britain took on the entire burden of responsibility for the holy places. According to Article 13 of the Mandatory Charter, the British had committed themselves to protecting "existing rights," and they interpreted this as meaning those rights that were recognized by the Ottoman government as of the eve of the First World War. Thus, the *firman* of 1852 remained in force.

Conflicts and claims relating to the holy places were removed from the jurisdiction of the courts and handed over to the executive branch exclusively. The latter attempted to fulfill its role in accordance with precedents based on the Status Quo, where these were clear. Given the differing interpretations of that Status Quo by members of different denominations, the Mandatory government tried to mediate, reject, or take on itself—as a neutral party—roles that were in dispute, such as responsibility for building maintenance and repair.

The following are examples of matters that the British government was compelled to deal with. The stairs leading to the Chapel of St. Mary's Agony in the Church of the Holy Sepulchre are Latin property. The question was, whose right was it to sweep the lowest step, situated only slightly above the level of the church forecourt, or parvis, which was common property. In 1901, a bloody dispute broke out between the

Greeks and the Latins over this issue. Today the arrangement is that the Latins sweep the step at sunrise, while the Orthodox sweep it when it is their turn to clean the parvis. The columns supporting the dome of the rotunda belong to various denominations, whose ownership is signified by the icons set in them. Beginning from the east side, columns 15–18 are the Armenians', 12–14 belong to the Orthodox, and the Copts are entitled to use columns 10 and 11, although they are owned by the Armenians, as are columns 8 and 9. Columns 5–8 belong to the Orthodox, 1–4 to the Latins. In 1924, there was a clash over the right to clean the dust from the door leading to the Copts' room between columns 10 and 11. The Armenians claim full possession of the area and of the room, and argued, therefore, that they had the right to clean the dust from the doors, while the Copts demanded this right for themselves. In the end, the government recognized the Armenians' claim. It should be pointed out that sweeping and other cleaning is considered an indication of ownership, since why would one sweep what is not one's own?

As it became apparent that the British Mandate was drawing to a close, the Vatican made a renewed effort to gain what it had been unable to achieve thirty years before. However, this time it did not employ the stratagem of demanding a judicial inquiry into the rights of the other denominations, but rather involved itself in the plan for the internationalization of Jerusalem. Internationalization in itself did not necessarily guarantee Catholic interests, as it did not deal with the matter of conflicts among Christian denominations. However, here again the Vatican depended on its political influence, which was immeasurably greater than that of the other denominations, and it hoped that a United Nations Trusteeship over Jerusalem would serve its interests. The other Christian communities, especially the Greek Orthodox, reacted to the internationalization proposal with suspicion; the Vatican's intentions were clear to them, as was the danger to their status. Thus, for example, the Greek Orthodox patriarch demanded that the maintenance of the Status Quo be guaranteed in the constitution of the international city and that the governor of the city be a person "whose lack of bias is beyond doubt."·

Following the war of 1948–49, the internationalization plan foundered in the face of vigorous opposition from both Israel and Jordan, and the sites in Jerusalem sacred to Christianity, most of which were located in the Old City (now occupied by Jordan), were once again predominantly in Muslim hands. The Jordanian government endeavored to prove its ability to handle the difficult job of protecting the holy places responsibly. For this purpose King Abdullah created a new post, "the Guardian of the *Haram a-Sharif* and the Supreme Custodian of the Holy Places." In his eagerness to reassure everybody, the king not only charged the Guardian with maintenance of the Status Quo, but directed him to see to it "that all the *firmans* of the sultans and the traditional rights held by the patriarchs be examined and recorded impartially in a special official registry, in case any person might need to refer to them."

The Jordanian government successfully maintained law and order in trouble spots like the Church of the Holy Sepulchre and the Church of the Nativity in Bethlehem. Incidents were not frequent, both because of the strict enforcement of the Status Quo, and because on holidays such as Easter, the Jordanians posted 150–200 policemen in the Church to preserve order. The only major conflict during Jordanian rule was the traditional one between the Ethiopians and Copts. At first the government ruled in favor of the Ethiopians, but subsequently relented under Egyptian pressure, and changed its verdict to favor the Copts.

There were developments regarding the repair and restoration of the Church of the Holy Sepulchre. Ongoing disputes among various denominations regarding responsibility for its upkeep had sometimes required the intervention of the Mandatory Public Works Department, or in certain instances the municipal government, to carry out urgent repairs. In 1951, the Christian denominations initiated plans for cooperation on renovation work, but negotiations dragged on for eleven years. Only in 1962 did the Latins, Greek Orthodox, and Armenians establish a joint technical office, which began work on reinforcement and renovation. These activities were carried out at a leisurely pace, both because of the delicate nature of the work and the site's inaccessibility by vehicle, and the mutual suspicions of the participants. The advent of the Israeli occupation found the work well under way.

The occupation of the Christian holy places by Israel was an event whose symbolic and practical significance to Christians is hard to exaggerate. Following in the footsteps of the Byzantines, the Omayyads, the Fatimids, the Crusaders, the Mamluks, the Ottomans, the British, and the Jordanians, Israel was responsible for the safety and integrity of the sites most sacred to hundreds of millions of Christians of all denominations. Here were the Jews—the chosen people who had forfeited their primacy for not heeding the gospel—returning to conquer the Holy City and to rule over the sites of the passion, resurrection, and ascension. What was the significance of this event for Christians, who were "Israel in spirit," the heirs of historic Israel in heaven and on earth? What would happen now that the holy places had come under the sovereignty of a state that identified itself with one religion and had never hidden the fact that, regarding Jerusalem, its political objectives were identical with its religious objectives? And how would the Israeli occupation influence the Status Quo? Would the new occupiers learn to exploit sectarian rivalry for their own purposes?

The Israeli authorities well understood the nature of the responsibility they were assuming with regard to the holy places, but their initial actions suggested that they were not yet fully conversant with the matter. Following the occupation of the city, Prime Minister Levi Eshkol announced to the heads of all the religions that Israel would base its policy regarding the holy places on their self-management by the leaders of the various religious communities. In his declaration he explained that "the arrangements at the Western Wall will be determined by the Chief Rabbis of Israel; the arrangements at the Muslim holy places will be determined by a council of Muslim clergymen; and the arrangements at the Christian holy places will be determined by a council of Christian clergymen."

The promise of self-management was intended to assuage fear in religious Jewish circles about intervention by secular elements. It was also meant to lessen apprehension in the Muslim community about Israel interfering with the management of Muslim religious institutions, as it had done in Israel proper, and as it indeed attempted to do in East Jerusalem also (see the following discussion). But the self-management formula was not suited to the Christian holy places. It was, after all, because of Christian inability to resolve problems concerning internal management of the holy places that the status quo had become an institution. Israel sought to reassure the Christian denominations, but it did not do this in the traditional manner, and failed to use the magic words *status quo*.

It is interesting to compare the Israeli government's declaration of July 1967 with those of the two other countries that established their regimes in Jerusalem during the twentieth century. General Allenby, upon officially entering Jerusalem on December 11, 1917, issued a proclamation to the city's population. Concerning the holy places, he proclaimed that all of the sites sacred to the three religions would be maintained and protected "in accordance with existing customs." On January 5, 1951, King Abdullah of Jordan issued a manifesto in which he stated, among other things, that "law and order will be preserved in accordance with the Status Quo, and the rights of all religious communities, mosques, and churches will be guaranteed."

The Israeli post-conquest proclamation speaks of "faithful preservation of the principles laid down in Israel's Declaration of Independence." Israel's policies were based, then, upon this statement from the Declaration: "The State of Israel shall guarantee freedom of religion, of conscience, of language, education, and culture; [and] shall protect the holy places of all religions."

It was not by chance that the Israeli proclamation did not repeat the accepted formulation of maintaining "existing customs," or the "Status

Quo." Had it done so, Israel would have been obligated also to maintain the Status Quo in the Jewish holy places, in whose name the British had obstructed Jewish practices at the Western Wall and had imposed humiliating and discriminatory regulations, as we have already seen.

Israel promulgated the Law for the Protection of the Holy Places, which stated that the sites "shall be protected from desecration and any other harm, and from any thing liable to infringe upon the freedom of access by members of the religions to the places sacred to them or offend their sensibilities." However, this law did not solve what was precisely the most complicated problem: What was to be done in a place sacred to two religions? The law allows every member of a religion "access" to this place for the purpose of prayer, but what if this prayer "offends the sensibilities" of another?

Everyday life in the Christian holy places ran its own course, and to the surprise of those who had diligently read the old descriptions of intercommunal violence at these sites, the atmosphere was relaxed and relatively free of sectarian conflict. Cooperation among the larger denominations grew, and the renovation work on the Church of the Holy Sepulchre was completed. Only two small denominations, the Copts and the Ethiopians, kept the experts on the Status Quo occupied, as they continued to fight over the Chapel of the Four Bodiless Creatures.

A kind of fluid and complex state of affairs prevailed in the inter-religious conflict in Jerusalem. The Israelis conducted a protracted dialogue with the Vatican on the issue of Jerusalem and its holy places. The Holy See initially based its stance on the old demand for the internationalization of Jerusalem; however, over the years it moderated its position and brought forward proposals more acceptable to Israel. One such proposal was an agreement that would have guaranteed the security of the holy places and the universal sacred character of Jerusalem. The Vatican held fast to its point of view that the problem of Jerusalem involved not only the management of the holy places, but also an array of issues associated with the Christian presence in Jerusalem, including administration of educational institutions; monasteries and convents; and orphanages. The historic Fundamental Agreement of 1993, wherein the Vatican recognized Israel, and an exchange of ambassadors took place, provided a fitting context in which to continue the complex dialogue between the "historical" Israel and the "spiritual" Israel. One of the articles of the agreement asserted that "[the signatories affirm] continuing commitment to maintain and respect the Status Quo in the Christian Holy Places to which it applies." Day-to-day relations between the authorities and the Eastern denominations (especially the Orthodox and the Armenians) were also generally good, although attempts to intervene in the appointment of prelates of the Church gave rise to short-lived tensions.

Israel's relations with the Muslim religious authorities, which were initially stormy and conflict-ridden, soon settled into a routine based on mutual nonrecognition coupled with unofficial contacts. Following the 1948 war, which caused the total disintegration of the Muslim religious and judicial systems in Israel, the administration of the Arab-Muslim community had been in the hands of Jewish government officials. In the first months of the occupation, Israel attempted to impose this policy—devoid of autonomous Muslim authority in religious, administrative, or judicial matters—on the elaborate and highly-influential Muslim establishment in Jerusalem. The Muslims of East Jerusalem neither desired nor were able to accept this Israeli *diktat*, on either political or religious grounds. When an Israeli official requested a copy of a sermon to be delivered during Friday prayers, and even deleted some Qur'anic verses from it, there was an explosion. On July 24, 1967, the Muslim establishment published a sharp retort, asserting that "the principles of Muslim law obligate Muslims, under the prevailing conditions [of non-Muslim rule], to assume responsibility for their religious affairs and it is forbidden for non-Muslims to be responsible for Muslim religious affairs. . . ." The signatories to the document constituted themselves as "the Muslim Council in the West Bank including Jerusalem until the Termination of the Occupation."

The Israelis reacted characteristically: they exiled some of the signatories, but ceased to interfere in the religious affairs of the Muslim community. With time, a fragile, unofficial modus vivendi evolved. Israel did not recognize the Muslim Council's authority or its decisions, but did not disrupt its activities. On its side, the Muslim Council did not recognize Israeli authorities or laws, but refrained from acting as an anti-regime political body. However, this mutual nonrecognition was not absolute. The Muslim Council was functioning as a religious and judicial authority, and so it required some contact with the Israelis. The Israelis needed the cooperation of the Council on certain vital issues as well, the first and foremost being the maintenance of public order on the Temple Mount.

The contacts between the two bodies continued, albeit with the pretense of being ad hoc and nonbinding. Both sides from time to time chose issues that they could dispute publicly, in order to prove the contradictory principles each supported: the Muslims, that they did not recognize Israeli authority, and the Israelis, that their authority was in force. An important moderating factor was the fact that the Muslim institutions—especially the Temple Mount Management and the *Waqf* (religious endowment)—operated under the financial oversight of the Jordanian government, which covered their deficits. The entire situation irritated fanatical Jewish groups, because the presence of an independent Muslim authority, with its own guards and overseers, on the Temple Mount was perceived as a continuation of the subjugation of the Mount to foreign rule. "The Temple Mount is not in our hands!" they cried, reversing the famous announcement by Mota Gur, commander of the army unit that conquered the Temple Mount in 1967, that "the Temple Mount is in our hands."

"In our hands" or "not in our hands" shout the Jewish extremists (there is no "a little bit in our hands and a little bit in theirs") and the Arabs echo their cries; not because the two sides are not peace-seekers searching for compromise, but because they believe that they are not entitled to relinquish the holy place. It is not theirs to give, for it belongs to God, whose commandments determine the physical shape of the place of worship, as well as the substance, form, and timing of the prayers and ceremonies. None of these can be compromised. The authorities designated by God's commandments to mediate between Him and humankind possess absolute power and exclusive rights to the holy place. It follows, then, that any site that is sacred to more than one religion or more than one denomination will be a source of ceaseless conflict, requiring the intervention of a secular authority who is capable of enforcing law, order, and decorum. The actions of this secular authority may be based on impartiality, but in the polarized atmosphere of a disputed holy place, every action will be construed as favoring one of the sides, since if it does not rule in favor of one side, it is necessarily ruling against it.

In Jerusalem today, this authority is in the hands of a state that identifies itself with one religion and does not conceal its intention to exploit its dominant position and its control of the holy places for the advancement of its political interests. However, Israel's power advantage does not permit it to act totally without restraint. The holy places in Jerusalem are dear to the hearts of over two billion people, and any overt attempt to substantively alter the fragile status quo is liable to severely damage Israel's interests and image. It is also liable to lead to bloodshed, and has done so in the past. Dominion over members of another religion is, of course, also perceived in its political context, and therefore it is impossible to differentiate between the holy places and their control as a religious matter, on the one hand, and their significance as an expression of national identity, on the other.

This religious-nationalist tangle results in the problem of the holy places being perceived in the context of the issue of governing authority, as defined by the term *sovereignty*. The combined conflict over religious dominion and sovereign rule—both of which are by nature absolute and exclusive—creates an insoluble problem. Therefore, those seeking to solve the problem attempt to sever the connection between the two components. Whoever aspires to sovereignty, or actually has political control, can offer religious autonomy, acknowledging the centrality of the religious dispute and proposing a compromise solution that seems flexible and conciliatory, without relinquishing that control. On the other hand, those to whom power is denied, and who are striving to obtain it, reject the separation of religious dominion from political sovereignty, and demand a solution to the problem of sovereignty first. Disinterested parties who are not involved in the national conflict tend to propose religious sovereignty as a solution, that is, they would give secular authority to religious or supra-national elements. The 1947 plan for the internationalization of Jerusalem was based on the desire "to satisfy the interests of the three monotheistic religions of the civilized world, to which Jerusalem is sacred." This radical attempt to turn all of Jerusalem into a "holy place" did not succeed, because it was absurd from the very beginning: the city's inhabitants are not members of a monastic order prepared to forfeit their national claims; as far as they are concerned theocratic rule is no different from autocratic rule, even with the promise of municipal autonomy.

The internationalization plan did not die, however, and was recently revived with a constricted domain; it no longer encompasses the entire city and a broad expanse surrounding it, but only the walled Old City that includes most of the sites sacred to the three religions. In 1994, King Hussein remarked: "The Islamic, Christian, and even the Jewish holy places should not be placed under the sovereignty of this or that country. . . . The holy places should unite all those who believe in God, and all of them should have the same rights. . . . Interfaith dialogue will turn Jerusalem, this small city and small land, into what God wanted it to be, a destination for [pilgrims] of all faiths."

Indeed, this approach compels one to give thought to the violent "interfaith dialogue" that has been going on these past two thousand years among all the legions that have come to Jerusalem seeking salvation. It was voiced by a ruler who has relinquished his claim to sovereignty over Jerusalem, but the Israelis and the Palestinians have not done likewise. The Israelis hold fast to the idea of a "unified Jerusalem, eternal capital of sovereign Israel," in which context they are willing to grant autonomy in the administration of the holy paces. In 1994, they even recognized "the present special role of the Hashemite Kingdom in the Muslim holy places in Jerusalem"—that is, the institutionalization of the status quo.

The Palestinians have rejected any separate arrangement for the holy places. As far as they are concerned, it is not possible to divorce the problem of the holy places from the issue of political control. The Muslim world has supported their stance, and has rejected King Hussein's suggestion to fabricate such a separation. A congress of Islamic states in December of 1994 issued the following statement: "The congress emphasizes that holy Jerusalem is an inseparable part of the Palestinian land and stresses the necessity of restoring it to Palestinian sovereignty as the capital of Palestine." Any other position implies willingness to recognize Israeli sovereignty in exchange for the surrender of the Muslim holy places to a pan-Islamic religious authority.

The solution to the problem of the holy places is intertwined with the problem of a permanent political solution for all of Jerusalem, and failing that, the situation will continue to be fragile and volatile. A bomb is waiting to go off in the heart of Jerusalem, its fuse burning with the fire of the religious fanaticism of Jew, Muslim, and Christian.

CHAPTER FOUR

THE LORD MAYOR

By June of 1995, tension was high between Ehud Olmert, the mayor of Jerusalem, and Faisal Husseini, the Palestinian Authority appointee responsible for Jerusalem affairs. The Israeli mayor vigorously objected to the recent diversification of the political activities whose focal point was Orient House, an abandoned East Jerusalem hotel—formerly a Husseini family mansion—that had become the hub of Palestinian resistance to the Israeli occupation. These activities consisted primarily of political conferences and meetings with diplomats, but also increasingly encompassed involvement with municipal issues. Mayor Olmert was angered by all of the political activities, but what especially upset him was Faisal Husseini's chutzpah at daring to occupy himself with matters that were "under the sovereign authority of the Jerusalem City Council," such as education, school renovations, and the development of infrastructure (water, electricity, etc.) in East Jerusalem. Olmert was furious when he found out that the Palestinians were planning to establish a Palestinian municipal authority in Jerusalem and even had gone so far as to call a meeting of those members of the Arab municipal council of Jerusalem (elected in 1963) who were still living. The Arab council was disbanded after the unification of Jerusalem in 1967. This blatant expression of the

Palestinians' delegitimation of the Israeli municipal authority and its head provoked a harsh response. Not confined to efforts at closing down Orient House, Ehud Olmert's rancor spilled over into personal jibes at Faisal Husseini. When it was suggested to Olmert that he meet with Husseini to discuss the curricula for Arab schools in Jerusalem, he answered furiously, while pounding on his desk: "Have you lost your minds? Who is Faisal Husseini, anyway?" The soft-spoken Palestinian leader did not confront the mayor, but had he wished to, he could have defiantly told him something like: Who am I? It so happens that my grandfather, his brother, and his father and grandfather before him were all mayors of Jerusalem. And he could also have added, had he wanted to be cynical, that in fact it was only because of his having instructed the city's Arabs to boycott the municipal elections in November of 1993 that Ehud Olmert had succeeded in besting his opponent Teddy Kollek.

No direct confrontation between the Palestinian leader and the Israeli mayor took place. Each man's refusal to recognize the authority of the other precluded a dialogue between them, or even a polemical encounter. But for most Israelis, the fact that Husseini is the grandson, great-grandson, and great-great-grandson of Arab mayors of Jerusalem is not a neutral piece of historical data. As far as they are concerned, the history of the legitimate Jerusalem City Council began in 1948, or perhaps only in 1967. The Husseini forefathers' terms as mayor in the late nineteenth and early twentieth centuries are a distant echo from an era when a hostile foreign regime appointed Arab mayors to govern the city, the majority of whose residents were Jewish. That period came to an end the moment the people of Israel founded their independent, sovereign state and designated Jerusalem as their capital. References to the Arab mayors, and of course any attempt to resurrect the Arab municipal council disbanded in 1967, are considered rebellious acts threatening the status of Jerusalem as Israel's capital. The Jewish majority in Jerusalem jealously arrogates to itself the right to choose a mayor from its own numbers. It views the duly elected city council as the city's sole legitimate governing body and regards anyone challenging its authority as a provocateur and rebel.

One might think that this attitude was the exclusive province of nationalist groups, with only a weak influence on the mood of the general public. However, evidence of the deep-seated nature of the delegitimation of any authority with pretensions of representing the Arab public can be seen in the way Teddy Kollek—mayor of Jerusalem at the time of reunification—dismissed the mayor and elected council of the Arab municipality.

At the time of the Israeli conquest, East Jerusalem was governed by a municipal council that had been elected in September 1963. Mayor Rauhi al Khatib cooperated with the Israeli military government, and for three critical weeks not only strove to restore municipal services and get life back to normal, but also agreed to assist the Israelis with sensitive issues, such as calling upon the residents of the city to turn in their weapons. He even cooperated in the eviction of persons living in ruined synagogues in the Jewish quarter. This assistance, which provoked charges of "collaboration with the occupation," was no help to al Khatib. The day after the decision was made to annex East Jerusalem, the military governor, prompted by Teddy Kollek, summoned the Arab mayor and the members of his council and announced to them that "the Jerusalem Municipal Council is hereby disbanded." It was a hasty, disrespectful ceremony, and left the deposed mayor feeling bitter and offended, which surely sparked his later rebellious activities. He was eventually expelled from his home and country and lived in exile nearly until his death in 1993.

Attempts to induce Palestinian public figures to join the Israeli city council failed, both because the Arabs did not wish to lend legitimacy to the occupation and because the Israeli mayor was not enthusiastic about the idea, asserting that "they would interfere with my work." This did not stop Kollek from claiming that the Arabs were not imbued with a democratic tradition, and that their refusal to participate in the Israeli democratic process would only harm them, since it made it impossible for them to fight for their own interests. One wonders what might have happened if the Arab municipal council had not been disbanded and a way had been found for the two councils to cooperate in municipal government. However, this sort of cooperation was not possible under the conditions that prevailed after 1967, nor had it been possible prior to that. The sad history of the Jerusalem Municipal Council is a reflection of the unresolved ethnic strife in this torn city, and the Israeli attitude only mirrors that of the Arabs.

Israelis cannot imagine an Arab mayor, but Arabs too have always viewed the appointment of a Jewish mayor as robbing them of "the natural right of the Arabs of Palestine, . . . a post that has been held by a Muslim mayor for hundreds of years." According to a petition sent to the British authorities by Arab organizations from all over Mandatory Palestine in 1945, "Since Arabs constitute a majority of the inhabitants of Palestine, and Jerusalem is the capital of Palestine, the Arabs expect the government [the British Mandate] to protect the Arabs' rights, and not to appoint a Jewish mayor to the post that has been vacated." In 1945, there was a Jewish majority in Jerusalem, amounting to close to two-thirds of the city's population. Actually, there had been a Jewish majority in Jerusalem since the late nineteenth century. But this fact did not move the Mandatory government (which had the authority to appoint mayors from among the members of elected municipal councils) to transfer the right to govern to someone representing the majority of the electorate.

The British authorities behaved in this manner not only because they were colonialists, but also because they knew that the democratic principle of "one person, one vote" could not be applied to an ethnically polarized city. In a city such as this, the electorate is composed of monolithic ethnic blocs giving allegiance to their own communities. Should one of these obtain a majority of votes, the tendency would be to impose a "tyranny of the majority," depriving the minority of all influence. Those who occupy elected office (or appointees) are not chosen for their objective abilities alone, but largely according to their ethnic affiliation, and they therefore feel that they must act to further the communal interests of their respective constituencies. In cities where this polarization does not exist, the rules of the (democratic) game ordain that power is in the hands of shifting coalitions of citizen's groups. The ever-changing composition of these groups facilitates the smooth transfer of power from a democratically elected ruling body chosen by a majority of voters in one election to a different democratically elected body chosen by a different majority in a subsequent election. In polarized cities, these rules do not apply. In Jerusalem, as in all polarized cities, elections constitute a sort of census of ethnic affiliation, and the majority group, voting as a single bloc, "takes all." This is the situation that prevailed during the British Mandate, and that reappeared in 1967 in a different guise: Jerusalem elections became a means of legitimizing exclusive rule by the Jewish community, as well as an avenue for the expression of the Palestinian community's rejection of imposed Israeli rule.

Following the annexation of East Jerusalem, its Arab residents were granted the right to vote in city council elections. Their status was comparable to that of foreign Jews who had immigrated to the country but had not yet obtained Israeli citizenship; being Jordanian citizens, they did not have the right to vote in Knesset elections. The Arabs had not requested the right to vote, even in municipal elections. On the contrary, the overwhelming majority rejected this democratic gesture, which they viewed as another step in the illegal annexation of their city. As far as they were concerned, it was simply a way of covering up their enforced subjugation to the Israeli regime. This attitude was reflected in voter turnout; only a small minority participated in the elections. Those who did vote came mainly from the poor neighborhoods on the outskirts of the city, where the people were dependent on the Israelis for their livelihood, being primarily manual laborers for the municipality or for Israeli construction companies. In contrast, those with political consciousness, primarily residents of the more prosperous neighborhoods, boycotted the elections. The Arabs who voted were compelled to give their support to Jewish parties, since no Arab individual or political group ran for office. In Arab Jerusalem, thus, the norm was the opposite of that in most democratic societies: the greater the political consciousness, the less the participation in elections.

The elections held in November 1993 exemplified the convoluted nature of interethnic politics in Jerusalem and the inseparability of the local and national spheres. That year, for the first time since becoming mayor in 1965, Teddy Kollek found himself facing a serious contender for the office. The race between the veteran mayor and Knesset member Ehud Olmert was regarded not only as a competition between individuals, but also as a contest between opposing political cultures. Teddy Kollek was perceived as the father of peaceful coexistence between the city's Jewish and Arab populations. He was an advocate of patience and tolerance, fiercely opposed to Jewish attempts to take over Arab neighborhoods, and was the originator of a number of schemes designed to solve the problem of Jerusalem. In every election since 1969, Kollek had won a majority of the Arab votes which, though few in number, contributed to the establishment of his party as the central force in the Jerusalem municipal administration, determining its policies during an entire generation.

Teddy Kollek anticipated Arab support in his race against MK Olmert, a Likud man who championed rigid nationalist positions, was opposed to any political compromise on Jerusalem, and supported the efforts of Jewish fanatics attempting to squat in the heart of the Muslim quarter of the Old City and in other homogeneous Arab neighborhoods. In the latter stages of the campaign, capturing the Arab vote became crucial for Kollek, since Olmert had reached an agreement with the ultra-Orthodox parties, a subethnic bloc whose voting pattern was also monolithic. The extraordinary political significance of these elections was amplified by their being held so soon after the signing of the Israeli-Palestinian Declaration of Principles (September 1993); the political debate between Yitzhak Rabin's governing coalition and the opposition also had an influence on the municipal campaign.

The importance of the Arab vote was not lost on the leaders of the Palestinian community, and for the first time since 1967, serious consideration was given to the possibility of their actively participating in the elections. In a reversal of the traditional stance that the Arabs must boycott the municipal elections in order to demonstrate their nonacceptance of the annexation of East Jerusalem, a proposal was made to establish a slate that would run in the municipal elections and would support Teddy Kollek against Ehud Olmert. The arguments in favor of participation in the elections were based on the certainty that a victory by a coalition of the Right and the ultra-Orthodox would aggravate the situation of the Arabs of East Jerusalem, and that a list of candidates supporting the cessation of Jewish building in East Jerusalem and advocating its becoming the capital of the Palestinian State could be beneficial to the Palestinian national struggle. Hostile elements might plot the destruction of the Palestinian political institutions operating in East Jerusalem, the argument went, but it would be impossible to silence legally elected Arab members of the city council.

After extensive deliberations, the PLO leadership decided to adhere to the traditional position and did not take an active part in the election campaign. However, in contrast to past elections, prominent leaders made neither public declarations calling for a boycott nor threats against anyone who might dare to vote. The Palestinian leadership was of the opinion that the damage that would be caused by participating in the elections—thereby legitimizing the annexation—would outweigh the benefits. After all, the fate of Jerusalem would not be determined by the city council, but in negotiations between the Israeli government and the PLO. And in any case, the Arab caucus in the city council would constitute a minority. The Jewish majority, committed to a unified Jerusalem under Israeli rule, would impose a "tyranny of the majority" that would only be legitimated by the Arabs.

The 7,000 Arabs who voted in the 1993 elections (approximately 7 percent of the qualified voters, compared to 3 percent in 1989) did not succeed in preventing the defeat of Teddy Kollek. The Right–ultra-

Orthodox coalition lead by Olmert won an overwhelming victory, partly because most of the Arab voters abstained. The new mayor, who during the campaign had feared the Arab vote and had denounced Teddy Kollek for "courting terrorists who call for the division of Jerusalem," adopted an extreme nationalistic position after his election, which brought him into a head-on confrontation with Faisal Husseini, the man whose abstention policy had so greatly helped to get Olmert elected.

This paradoxical outcome was not the first of its kind in the complicated history of Jerusalem municipal elections. There was a similar instance in 1934, however with a reversal of roles. In 1993, the Arabs indirectly brought about the election of an Israeli nationalist, whereas in 1934 the Jews indirectly brought about the election of a Palestinian nationalist. The 1934 election campaign was especially fierce because of a mighty and prolonged struggle within the Palestinian community between the supporters of the Mufti Hajj Amin al-Husseini and those of the moderate opposition, headed by Raghib Bey Nashashibi, the incumbent mayor. This was both a power struggle for control of the political and economic resources of the Palestinian community and a manifestation of the rivalry between two aristocratic Jerusalem families. But it had an intercommunal political aspect as well. The Husseinis were the sworn enemies of Zionism and preached violent struggle against it and against the Mandatory government. The Nashashibis were more moderate and had both open and covert contact with the Jewish leadership. The 1934 elections were a face-off between Mayor Nashashibi and Dr. Hussein Fakhri al-Khalidi, the Husseini-led coalition's candidate. The two contenders were competing for a council seat in an electoral ward where 17 percent of the qualified voters were Jews. The Jewish leaders declared their neutrality, but in fact supported the Husseini candidate, as they wanted to punish Nashashibi for his corrupt management of municipal government. Thus, they contributed to the election of a nationalist candidate who, upon taking office, immediately took his place at the head of those agitating for rebellion against the authorities—and rebellion did indeed erupt in 1936.

How different that situation is from the atmosphere in 1898, described by Jewish educator and leader David Yellin in his diary. "The success of those desiring to be elected to the municipal council (be they members of whichever religion) is largely dependent upon a general agreement among the various sects, an agreement that—with God's help—has endured for decades in our city: such-and-such a sect votes for so-and-so from the other sect in order that the other sect will also vote for the first sect's choice." These words were of course written during the Ottoman period, before the nationalistic tensions between Jews and Arabs erupted, turning Jerusalem and its municipal council into the battlegrounds of an unending struggle. The Ottoman period may seem distant and irrelevant, but it is not by chance that the municipal system set up by the Turks in 1877 was not replaced until 1934, and that the Mandatory system that succeeded it survives, with certain changes, to this very day. Municipal government tends to be conservative in character, perhaps because its principal tasks, which are the provision of services and the planning and development of urban space, do not change. The chronicles of Jerusalem's municipal council, including the personalities of the city's mayors and the council's activities throughout the 140 years of its existence, provide a fitting backdrop for depicting the continuity and discontinuity, the proximity and remoteness, the hostility and neighborliness that have characterized the everyday life of the communities in this polarized city.

Jerusalem was one of the first cities in the Ottoman Empire in which a municipal council was established. Exactly when it was first constituted is not clear, but by 1867 a governing body was in operation. Its responsibilities and areas of jurisdiction were modeled on a similar authority set up in one of the neighborhoods of Istanbul in 1858. The institution of the municipal council, like the concept of the city itself, was different in the Muslim East than in Christian Europe. In Europe, the city grew up as a corporate body under the feudal regime, and the internal government of its citizens was defined by royal or ecclesiastical charter. The oriental city was made up of a variety of individuals and ethnic or religious groups. It formed a geographic unit which had undefined boundaries and was not clearly differentiated from its rural hinterland. The citizens' affairs were administered by the central government, with the assistance of "notables" and *mukhtars* (clan heads or representatives of ethnic or religious communities and neighborhoods). The municipal authorities that were established by the Ottoman regime were not independent but were administrative bodies subject to the central government, though they enjoyed a certain measure of budgetary autonomy. Only in 1877, with the promulgation of the Municipalities Law, were the fundamental principles of municipal governance, covering the election of municipal council members, the mayor's powers and responsibilities, and areas of authority set out.

David Yellin enumerates those entitled to participate in municipal elections (according to the 1877 law) as follows: "According to the laws of our exalted government, the right to participate in these elections is granted to all its subjects, regardless of religion. That is, every male Ottoman subject over the age of twenty-five, who owns land or a house for which the property tax levied is less than 50 [piasters] annually, has the right to vote; and every man thirty years of age or more, who has property for which he pays the government 150 piasters or more annually, has the right to be elected." The number of people elected to the council fluctuated between six and twelve, and they served for four years, with half of the members being replaced every two years. The number of those entitled to vote was very small. David Yellin recounts that qualified voters in the 1898 elections included 700 Muslims, 300 Christians, 92 Sephardic Jews, and 86 Ashkenazic Jews. At that time Jerusalem had a population of 55,000, of whom 35,000 were Jews, 7,000 Muslims, and 13,000 Christians. The meager Jewish representation on the municipal council—a total of one Sephardic and one Ashkenazic representative—and of course the minuscule number of Jews entitled to vote, reflected the inferior status of the Jews in relation to the other communities.

The "President of the Municipal Council" (the mayor's title, copied from France) was appointed by the Ottoman governor from among the council members, and the governor also had the authority to replace members of the council with other people. The mayor was the only elected official who received a salary, and his political and social status was high, although his importance was less than that of officials of the central government.

The political importance and social prestige attached to the mayor's office was such that well-connected Muslim families vied with one another to obtain the job for one of their relatives. The Ottoman regime knew how to make the most of their prerogative to choose the city's mayors, using it as a means of punishing the rebellious and rewarding the loyal. Most of the rivalry over the mayoralty involved the al-Khalidi and Husseini families. David Yellin recalls: "Among our Muslim brothers there are two well-connected families whose ancestry can be traced back to the beginnings of Islam in this country: the Husseini family and the al-Khalidi family; and there is always great rivalry between them, that is, 'whose is the country?'" During the years of Ottoman rule, five Husseinis and three al-Khalidis filled the office of mayor. But neither was the Alami family neglected; three of its members also were appointed to the coveted post. There was a quasi-dynastic character in the relationship of these families to the mayor's position; in the Husseini family a grandfather, father, and two of his sons held this office, in the Khalidi family, two brothers, and in the 'Alami family, a father and son.

The length of the mayor's term in office during the Ottoman period was one year. Some filled this role for one or two terms, and others for four terms. The longest period any mayor served was eighteen years. The mayor had a decisive role in all matters of municipal administration, and he received credit or blame for all the city's successes and failures. According to law, the municipality had many responsibilities, more and broader in scope than those of present-day Israeli cities. In addition to the usual obligations, including street and road construction, water provision, sewer maintenance, street illumination, planning and licensing of buildings and parks, and sanitation, Ottoman law also made the municipality responsible for population registration, local policing, municipal hospitals, for overseeing prices and weights in the market-places, and more. The list was long, but actual implementation was quite lax.

Not until the late 1880s was there improvement in municipal services. This improvement was a result of the accelerated process of modernization in Jerusalem, which was fostered by the growth of the European community (Jewish and Christian), and by the economic and social advances amongst the Arab population. These factors led to a building boom involving both large Christian institutions and the extensive Jewish neighborhoods outside the walls of the Old City. The improvements in the city and the expansion of municipal services can be credited to several mayors; Salim Effendi Husseini (1882–1897), Fidi al-'Alami (1906–1909), and Hussein al-Husseini (1910–1918). Historical sources single out the activities of Salim Effendi who, during his long years in office, developed the city for the benefit of all its inhabitants and earned the esteem of Christians, Jews, and Muslims. Jewish sources specify his paving of the area in front of the Western Wall and the access roads to it, and state that "Salim Effendi did great benefit by repairs [and] improvements to the city and its environs."

The career of Fidi al-'Alami is a tangible example of the exceedingly strong ties between the office of mayor of Jerusalem and the Ottoman governing system. 'Alami, son of Mayor Mousa 'Alami, was apparently born in 1881. He worked as a tax official for the district authority, was a member of the judicial committee that worked with the *qadi* (judge in the Islamic law court), was district commissioner of the Bethlehem subdistrict, was elected to the Jerusalem municipal council, and was appointed mayor. After serving for three years, he was appointed a member of the administrative council of the Sanjak (province) of Jerusalem, and in 1914 he was chosen to represent Jerusalem in the Ottoman Parliament. Fidi 'Alami also compiled a concordance of the *Qur'an*, and was for many years head of the 'Alami extended family, managing its extensive properties and endowments. He died in 1924.

Hussein al-Husseini, also son of a mayor, was appointed in 1910, after winning the highest number of votes in the municipal council elections (648 out of 1,200). He inaugurated a number of development projects, including a sewer system for the Jewish neighborhoods, but he is best known for conveying Jerusalem's declaration of surrender to General Allenby's army in December of 1917. Husseini, "middle-aged, well-educated, English-speaking," impressed Sir Ronald Storrs, the British military governor of Jerusalem, as someone who possessed both "honesty and weakness." Hussein Effendi did not have the privilege of serving under the new regime, as he died early in 1918. His brother, Mousa Kazzim Pasha al-Husseini, the governor of Yemen under the Ottomans, was home on leave in Jerusalem at the time and was appointed in his stead. Mousa Kazzim's appointment ushered in a new era in the annals of the institution of mayor of Jerusalem, one characterized by fierce political wrangling between Jews and Arabs. The Jerusalem Municipal Council and the mayor himself became the focus of a conflict between the Jewish and the Palestinian communities that extended far beyond municipal matters.

Intercommunal tensions had existed during the Ottoman period as well, but they were of a local-religious and municipal character and did not involve macronational conflicts. The Jewish community, despite its constituting a majority in the city, had uncomplainingly accepted Muslim hegemony; they made no protest over the fact that the mayor was always a Muslim Arab, or even that the administration of all municipal affairs was done in Arabic. The Arab mayors did not refrain from expressing political opinions. Mayor Sa'id al-Husseini, for example, publicly expressed his opposition to Zionism and attempted to prevent the sale of land to Jews in the vicinity of Jerusalem. But even these actions did not destroy the relatively relaxed atmosphere that prevailed in the municipal council chambers.

All of this changed completely after the British conquest, when the tensions between the Arab nationalist movement and the Zionists exploded into the open. The British military government appointed Mousa Kazzim Pasha (grandfather of Faisal Husseini) mayor with the explicit condition that he not take part in Palestinian nationalist politics. However, compliance with this condition was beyond the power of the head of a large and respected Jerusalem Palestinian family, and not only did he not refrain from involvement in politics, he took the lead in rowdy demonstrations against the British administration and the Zionists. At celebrations commemorating "Nabi Mousa" (the Prophet Moses) in the spring of 1920, the mayor marched at the head of a mob demonstrating against Zionism and then gave an inflammatory speech from a hotel balcony, after which anti-Jewish rioting broke out. The City Committee for the Jews of Jerusalem wrote to Governor Ronald Storrs: "We hereby protest against his lordship the mayor, who walked at the head of demonstrators and also addressed them. As mayor of the city he had neither the moral nor legal right to participate in a demonstration whose intent was to harm the majority of the city's residents. The Jews of Jerusalem no longer consider His Lordship Mousa Kazzim as their representative." The governor of Jerusalem did not require the encouragement of this protest. He sent for Raghib Bey Nashashibi—a member of a Jerusalem family that had accumulated power and influence during the second half of the nineteenth century, an engineer, and an officer in the Turkish army—and offered him the post of mayor. After Nashashibi consented, Storrs summoned Mousa Kazzim and informed him of his dismissal.

Raghib Bey ruled imperiously for fifteen years in office. Storrs commented that "his attitude toward the members of the municipal council was like that of a soloist toward a totally mute orchestra." His long term was distinguished by the improvement of municipal services, but also by unethical behavior. Raghib Bey was in the habit of bragging "that he was not terrified at the prospect of being brought to justice, since were he to be caught in a wrongdoing he would demand to be tried for all the wrongdoing and crimes he had committed throughout his term of office, and then all the judges in the land would not be sufficient to complete the task, even if they sat in judgment for the rest of their lives."

The Jews, with whom Nashashibi maintained friendly ties, did not succeed in obtaining much from him, with the exception of what he regarded as worthwhile in terms of furthering his personal and political objectives. In spite of their disappointment, the Jews supported Raghib Nashashibi's reelection in 1927, when the first municipal elections of the Mandatory period were held. Thanks to the Jewish vote, which went to the Nashashibi council candidates rather than to their hated foes the Husseinis, the mayor was enabled to continue his corrupt administration. Toward the end of Nashashibi's term in office (1930–1934), the Jewish members of the municipal council resigned in protest over his nonfulfillment of the promises he had made them during the 1927 campaign, which were "equalization of rights in both the creation and use of public works, equalization of access to posts in municipal administration and to appointments as officials, equalization of the basis for taxation, and full recognition of the Hebrew language in all areas of municipal activity."

In 1934, the Municipalities Law was issued, replacing Ottoman municipal legislation. According to the new ordinance, elections would be organized in a ward system. Six wards were allotted to Jews, four to Muslims, and two to Christians, with one council member representing each precinct. The Jews claimed that because they were the majority in the city, they deserved primacy on the council; even if they were to agree under pressure to only half the members being Jews, the division of representation on the basis of religious rather than national affiliation entitled them to a majority on the council, and therefore they deserved the job of mayor. The authorities rejected this demand, but they decreed that the Muslim mayor must confer senior status on his Jewish deputy: "The mayor must pay particular attention to the Jewish deputy mayor's position on all points affecting the Jewish half of the city's population." Even though the Mandatory authorities had initially agreed to the appointment of one—Jewish—deputy mayor, they later added a second, a Christian, thereby essentially negating the special status of the Jewish deputy.

The mayor appointed by the authorities in 1934 from among the twelve elected council members was Dr. Hussein Fakhri al-Khalidi, who had contested the seat held by Mayor Raghib Nashashibi in the Sheikh Jarah ward, and had defeated him because of, among other factors, the support of the ward's few Jewish voters. They chose to believe Khalidi's declarations of his willingness to work for the benefit of all the city's citizens, but their expectations proved to be unfounded. The new mayor adopted nationalistic positions and refused to cooperate with his Jewish deputy, Daniel Auster. Auster described the mayor's conduct thus: "The mayor did not assign me any portfolios; not even one piece of paper was handed to me for my comments." Of the five directors of municipal departments, two were British, two were Arabs, and one was a Jew, and only 28 percent of the municipal officials were Jews. The Arab mayor always made use of his double vote whenever Jewish and Arab council members were deadlocked. The Jews reacted by staying away from council meetings, a tactic that often resulted in there not being a quorum.

The principal matter that aroused the ire of the Jewish council members was the mayor's affiliation with the highest echelons of the Palestinian national movement. They had previously protested the nationalist activities of Mousa Kazzim and Raghib Nashashibi; however, Mayor Khalidi's participation in the Supreme Arab Committee and his prominent role in the provocation instigated by Hajj Amin al-Husseini, which led to the Arab Revolt of 1936–1939, resulted in a total rupture of their relationship. Dr. Khalidi was detained by the Mandatory authorities in 1937 and banished to the Seychelles Islands. Daniel Auster was temporarily appointed to take his place; he was replaced by Moustafa Khalidi, brother of the exiled mayor.

The political conditions that prevailed during the Arab Revolt, and afterward, in the wake of the issuing of the White Paper of 1939 (which drastically limited Jewish immigration and sale of land to Jews and called for the establishment of a Palestinian state at the end of five years, where Jews would not be allowed to exceed one-third of the total population) resulted in the municipal council effectively ceasing to function normally. These disruptions to the operation of the council were the outcome of actions by both its Jewish and Arab members. Any remaining semblance of a functioning municipal government collapsed in 1944 with the death of Moustafa Khalidi. In 1945, the British proposed that control of the municipal authority "be passed in turn to the municipal council members representing the Christian, Muslim, and Jewish religions." However, none of the parties accepted the proposal and the authorities disbanded the council, appointing in its place a committee comprised of British officials headed by John Webster.

With the commencement of hostilities in January of 1948, the Jewish office staff was transferred from the city hall close to the Old City walls to a building in the Mahane Yehuda neighborhood in the Jewish part of the city. Early in April the Jewish council members established a separate body, and the British district commissioner recognized its authority "in every place where a Jewish foot treads and in every place where it may be of service." The members of this municipal committee decided to change the committee's name to the Jerusalem Municipal Council (Jewish area). Thus was the Israeli municipal council established. In the Arab section of the city a municipal authority was also set up which was an administrative body without a council.

The Israeli council continued to maintain provision of municipal services to the best of its ability, but emergency conditions limited its opportunities to do so, and in addition there were serious frictions among various Jewish organizations over areas of authority and domains of activity. Only on December 31, 1948 was a municipal council finally set up, with seventeen members. The first elections for the Israeli municipal council were held in November of 1950; however, the functioning of the municipal government was far from satisfactory. The

fierce competition between the religious parties and the secular workers' parties resulted in constant disruptions. Two mayors affiliated with
religious parties did not endure long, and the council was eventually
disbanded and replaced by an appointed committee. In the 1955 elections, for the first time, a Labor party-led coalition was formed, which
remained intact in the 1959 elections as well. The coalition, under the
leadership of Mayor Mordechai Ish-Shalom, brought about the stabilization of the municipal government and also wisely established standard procedures for the governing of the city, and contributed to its
economic development. In the 1965 elections, *Mapai* (the Labor party)
was defeated, and Teddy Kollek succeeded in creating a wall-to-wall
coalition, which was in office at the time of the city's unification in
1967.

In 1949, a municipal executive committee was set up in the eastern
section of the city, headed by Anwar al-Khatib. He was dismissed by the
Jordanian authorities after a short term, and in his stead 'Aref al-'Aref,
a veteran leader and historian who had done research on Bedouin tribes
in the Negev, was appointed. July 1951 saw the first elections for a
twelve-member council. 'Aref al-'Aref won the largest number of votes,
but he was dismissed from office for irritating the Jordanians and
another mayor was appointed in his place. The constant turnover of
heads of the Arab municipality culminated in the appointment of Rauhi
al-Khatib in January of 1957. Khatib managed to remain in office
through the terms of three councils, and was still mayor in June 1967,
at which time he was ejected from his position, as previously recounted,
and later he was expelled from Jerusalem.

Teddy Kollek, who headed the Jerusalem municipal government
from 1965 until 1993, so thoroughly put his personal stamp on the
office of mayor that his predecessors have faded into historical obscu-
rity. From the time of the founding of the Jerusalem municipality to the
present, thirty or thirty-one public figures have served as mayor, of
whom twenty were Arabs, seven Jews, and three British. During the

7. Jewish and Arab employees of the municipality
(1930s) with the Arab mayor

Ottoman period (1867–1917) there were thirteen mayors, all of them
Muslim Arabs. During the Mandate (1917–1948), five Muslim Arabs,
three Britons, and one Jew filled this post. During the period of the
divided city (1948–1967) six Jews served on the Israeli side and on the
Jordanian side four Arabs served. Since the reunification of the city (and
until 1996), two Jews have carried this title.

Kollek became mayor almost by accident. He had served for fourteen years as director general of the Prime Minister's Office and was a
trusted aide of David Ben-Gurion. He left government service for the

private sector a short while before the 1965 municipal elections. In response to the urging of colleagues who had recently broken off from the Labor party and had set up a parliamentary faction headed by Ben-Gurion, Kollek submitted his candidacy for the Jerusalem City Council and went on to become mayor, again almost by chance. His slate had won an identical number of seats on the council to that headed by the outgoing mayor, but Kollek, unlike his Labor party counterparts, was not bound by the traditional Labor prohibition against forming a coalition with Menachem Begin's Herut party. He therefore could easily put together a coalition capable of ousting Labor from the mayoralty and installing him. Kollek quickly established a wall-to-wall coalition that endured throughout most of his tenure.

On the eve of the 1967 war, Mayor Kollek submitted a municipal budget on the order of $100 million, or approximately $500 per capita (in terms of the value of the dollar in 1992); at about the same time the mayor of the Arab city, Rauhi al-Khatib, submitted a budget of $5.3 million, or about $106 per capita (in 1992 dollars). The ratio of municipal expenditures between the two sections of the divided city reflects the large gap in the level of services between them (even though some of the services to East Jerusalem were provided and paid for by the Jordanian government). Sixty percent of East Jerusalem households were without running water and obtained their water from approximately 6,200 cisterns. There was no centralized sewer system. Only the Old City had sewers, and those dated from the time of King Herod. Garbage was collected by donkey-cart; government-run educational institutions suffered from a shortage of buildings; there were only 1,148 streetlights in the entire city, and many homes, especially on the periphery, were not connected to the electricity grid.

The hostile actions leading up to the conquest and annexation of East Jerusalem made a shambles of this already underdeveloped infrastructure. The Israeli authorities, who sought to integrate municipal services after the war, were faced with tremendous problems. They succeeded, however, within a relatively short time in repairing the damage caused by the war, and even in improving services to a large degree. The Israeli government put substantial budgets at the disposal of the municipality for this purpose, and not only because "equalization of services" was dictated in principle by the application of Israeli law to East Jerusalem, but also because it had great propaganda value. In sum, the annexation of East Jerusalem was presented by the Israeli government thus: "The measures adopted related to the integration of Jerusalem in the administrative and municipal spheres—these steps are aimed at improving the lives of the inhabitants." The more years went by, the more Israeli enthusiasm for "equalizing services" faded and was overtaken by indifference and neglect. The "mosaic principle," of "separation of and noninterference" in the Arabs' affairs became a justification and an excuse for discrimination in investment in infrastructure, welfare services, and housing.

In 1992, Teddy Kollek submitted the final budget proposal for which he was totally responsible (he was defeated in the 1993 elections). This budget totaled approximately $400 million (1992 dollars). Less than 6 percent was allocated to the Arab neighborhoods. The per capita expenditure in the Jewish sector was approximately $900, compared with about $150 in the Arab sector. The level of services per person, as reflected in municipal budgets, was nearly double that of 1967 in the Jewish sector, while in the Arab sector it had increased by only 50 percent (using equivalent dollar values).

The consequences were only officially revealed in 1995, after the ouster of Teddy Kollek and the election of Ehud Olmert. The new mayor, despite his rigidly nationalist stance, was interested in demonstrating that it was precisely Teddy Kollek's liberal and tolerant administration that was to blame for the long years of neglect and discrimination in East Jerusalem. In Olmert's opinion, "equalization of services" was not inconsistent with a struggle against expressions of Palestinian nationalism; on the contrary, "neglect leads to unrest and loss of confidence in the Israeli system," and one who wishes to preserve the integrity of Jerusalem "is obliged to improve relations between the Arab sector and the Israeli regime." He even went so far as to charge that the Israeli government was purposely refraining from investing resources in East Jerusalem, because "it intends to transfer portions of it to the Palestinian Authority."

The report, published in July 1995, reveals shocking neglect. East Jerusalem is short 150 kilometers of sewers, hundreds of kilometers of paved roads, tens of thousands of street lights, and 350 classrooms. There is no orderly system of garbage collection, and firefighting and rescue services are not up to standard. There is a serious lack of attention to the youth of East Jerusalem, a severe drug problem, and widespread truancy. There are also no institutions for mentally ill and retarded persons; poverty and deprivation are rampant, while the number of social workers is small. All of this is in addition to intolerable crowding in housing and the absence of approved town plans that would make it possible for additional homes to be built, a problem discussed in Chapter 5.

Discrimination is not confined to inequities in municipal services. Amongst the suppliers of the services themselves, that is, municipal workers, the disparities between Jews and Arabs are great. The proportion of Arabs employed by the municipality is not more than 17 percent. Two-thirds of these are manual laborers working in maintenance or for the sanitation department. An insignificant minority are employed in white-collar professions (not counting schoolteachers in the Arab sector), and even the few engineers, social workers, and physicians serve the Arab population exclusively. Only one or perhaps two Arab workers have reached senior positions where they supervise Jewish workers. The complete absence of Arab city council members and the decided inferiority of the status of Arabs in municipal administration has produced a municipal decision-making process that is not responsive to the demands and needs of the Arab sector. The dimensions of this neglect and discrimination were traditionally revealed shortly before municipal elections, when candidates were wooing the Arab vote, and when politically motivated persons and groups were publishing reports and research studies intended to embarrass the authorities or to win points in the debate over the future of Jerusalem.

Some Israelis—first and foremost Teddy Kollek—blamed the Arabs, maintaining that their political resistance was the principal reason for the lack of equality. Had they played the political game (so the argument went) they could have become a pressure group and worked, like other such groups, to further their material interests. This claim now sounds hollow and unconvincing. First, no one prevented the municipality from treating the Arab municipal workers—who did agree to cooperate with the authorities—well, from giving them promotions, or from admitting them to the circle of decision makers. Second, the discrimination against the Arab sector is structural, based upon dualistic-ethnic criteria. The Arab "pressure group" is not perceived as a legitimate community struggling for its slice of the public resources pie, but as a foreign element, whose demands impinge on basic Jewish interests. Were the Arabs to agree to participate in the political game, they would find themselves a minority group all of whose demands were rejected by the democratic majority on the city council—the representatives of the Jewish population. Third, the city is responsible for the provision of "street-level services" (basic municipal services such as garbage collection, sewers, etc.), and this level of services is defined according to quantitative, objective criteria. It takes a great deal of chutzpah to justify failure in fulfilling the obligation to provide these basic services with the claim that there is no "pressure group" fighting for the acquisition of minimal living conditions. Fourth, it seems that it is precisely the supposedly liberal argument that life in Jerusalem is based on a mosaic of ethnic groups and religious communities, and that it is necessary to refrain "from external intervention contrary to the traditional way of life of each group," that serves as the ideological basis for discrimination.

It is difficult to escape the feeling that the Arabs' refusal to play the political game provides many Israelis with a pretext for continuing the discrimination whilst feeling fair and liberal all the while. Since 1967 only Jews have sat on the Jerusalem City Council, yet they pretend to speak for all the residents of the unified city, Jews and Arabs alike. This pretense is based upon democratic principles. After all, they gave the Arabs the right to vote, and if the Arabs choose to boycott the elections on political grounds, the Jews may enjoy the benefits of that decision and even use it as an excuse for ethnically based discrimination.

The residents of East Jerusalem regard the unified Jerusalem municipality as a tool of the illegal Israeli occupation. They perceive the discrimination and unfair treatment they suffer as being a natural outcome of the occupation, which contradicts the principle of self-determination and is contrary to natural justice. They express their opposition to the imposed status quo in a variety of ways, from boycotting elections and staging demonstrations to perpetrating acts of violence. But even freedom fighters need water, electricity, and sewers. The independent mutual aid societies and educational and health care institutions they have set up provide for some of the community's needs, but haven't the capabilities that are necessary to sever East Jerusalem's connections with the central municipal infrastructure and rebuild from scratch the independent municipal system that was destroyed in 1967. Hence their political principles clash with the everyday needs that force them to maintain contact with the Israeli municipality, which they regard as illegitimate. The result is an ambiguous attitude toward the municipality. On the one hand, they denounce it as an Israeli tool of domination, and on the other, they criticize its negligence in the provision of services to East Jerusalem and demand immediate improvements. To prevent the contradiction from being too obvious, a division of labor exists. Political positions are voiced by political leaders, whereas demands for improvements in services come from persons whose roles are perceived as apolitical.

In any case, dialogue between the municipal authorities and the Arab population is unavoidable. The municipality needs liaisons to report on the mood of the Arab population and to act as channels for their demands and complaints; the Arabs need ombudspersons to pressure the municipality to improve services in their section of the city. Both sides need low-ranking mediators whose actions will not be regarded by the Arabs as collaboration with the occupation, or considered by the Israelis as constituting a competing municipal framework.

The most convenient method by which to obtain such mediators was found to be the revival of the institution of the *mukhtar*; the village elder, clan head, or leader of the religious community. His was an ancient role that had, as we have seen, been gradually superseded by the elected municipal council. During the Ottoman period, the *mukhtars* had retained some of their functions and areas of authority, and had competed with the members of the municipal council for official patronage. Under the British Mandate and Jordanian rule, the importance of the *mukhtars* had declined in every location where a municipal authority was introduced. Now, in the quasi-colonial situation that has prevailed since 1967, use has again been found for this archaic and anti-democratic institution. The job of the sixty municipally appointed *mukhtars* is to report to the office of the Mayor's Advisor on Arab Affairs—also a classic colonial post—bringing with them lists of requests, complaints, and proposals relating to their respective neighborhoods, extended families, or other constituencies. The *mukhtars* are also obliged to be present at official functions, where they are featured before the television cameras as "the representatives of the Arab population of the unified city."

Alongside the *mukhtars* work unofficial "liaison men." These are wealthy, well-connected, and well-educated members of Arab families with whom Israeli officials share a "common language." This ramified system of unofficial social and individual contacts between the mayor, some of his advisors, and members of the Israeli-Jewish elite, on the one hand, and the Arab traditional elite on the other, also creates an ongoing dialogue with benefits for both sides, although of course all of this contact is of a paternalistic nature; the Arabs are always the petitioners and the Jews are always the dispensers.

As mentioned earlier, the Israeli regime in East Jerusalem, including the municipal component, is based on coercion. Deprive the Israelis of their enforced supremacy, and the city will split along its ethnic seam. The Israelis' power and their willingness to use it have not decreased, but they have learned that inordinate employment of coercion arouses the resistance of the governed and may lead to the collapse of the regime. It is impossible to station a squad of soldiers in every classroom whose teacher refuses to use the Israeli curriculum, and it is impossible to imprison every Islamic preacher who calls upon worshipers to defend the holiness of Arab Jerusalem. When all is said and done, it is not the Jerusalem municipality's paternalistic dialogue with the *mukhtars* that has shaped the city's reality, but the "dialogue" of actions.

The guidelines for this dialogue are derived from cold—and not always conscious—calculations by both sides. The rulers must calculate what price they are willing to pay to keep the governed population within the system, and perhaps what conditions they are prepared to offer to prevent full-scale rebellion; the governed are forced to carefully consider their expressions of protest and rebelliousness so as not to expose themselves to harsh acts of repression, which would not only harm individual members of the group, but might even threaten its existence. Both ruler and ruled occasionally err in their calculations. Sometimes rulers lose control of or give in to extremist groups, but they quickly revert to the old dialogue of action and reaction, nonverbal but only occasionally violent, until they reach the conclusion that the time has come to replace it with a political dialogue aimed at reaching an agreed-upon political settlement.

The dialogue of actions between the Jewish and Arab communities has been going on for the past hundred years. The Jewish community's 1967 victory supposedly should have dictated the unconditional surrender of the defeated community, but this did not take place, much to the surprise of the victors. The vanquished Arab community managed to thwart a large number of coercive moves by the Israelis. The Arabs succeeded in maintaining their communal independence in the realms of education, religion, healthcare, and language. They had their own trade unions, professional associations, publications, economic system, and national symbols. These considerable achievements did not alter their status as a subjugated and deprived community, but they did guarantee the minimal conditions necessary for conducting communal life under occupation and for conserving strength until, at the end of 1993, the dialogue of actions between the Israelis and the Palestinians was finally replaced by a political dialogue.

The political dialogue—faltering and controversial within both communities as it is—has made the quest for a solution to the problem of municipal government in Jerusalem relevant. The history of efforts to come to an agreement regarding the administration of the municipality is as long as the history of the ethnic conflict over its control. Despite the failures and disappointments, there is a real common denominator, even if it is limited in scope: That is, the search for a formula for joint administration of Jerusalem's urban space embodies the aspirations of both sides to preserve the physical integrity of this space. Neither side is interested in seeing Jerusalem revert to being physically divided. All proposals, including Israeli ones whose objective is to guarantee Israeli sovereignty over the entire city (see Chapter 7), acknowledge the necessity of accommodating the interests and desires of all the ethnic groups living in Jerusalem, at least in the municipal sphere.

The problem of how to efficiently administer Jerusalem's urban space and to allow all its component ethnic groups to share control of its governance has always disturbed those concerned about the fate of the city. This problem has not been solved, and it has not changed in character for a century. It is no wonder, then, that despite the proliferation of proposals for a solution, all having various levels of sophistication and of detail, and despite the political changes that have taken place, there is great similarity among the solutions offered. They conform to several models, which repeat themselves with only marginal differences.

First Model: A centralized city council; elections by religious wards or seats on the council allocated by ethnic quotas. This model was applied under Ottoman rule and during the first decade of the British Mandate; it was later replaced by the system of voting by wards. However, the difference was not significant because each ward was demarcated in such a way as to secure a majority for the members of one community.

Elections were held according to this method during most of the British Mandate, and (with certain modifications) in East Jerusalem under Jordanian rule. Usually, this model is accompanied by strong interference on the part of the central government in the constitution of the city council. The Mandatory and Jordanian election laws gave the central government the right to appoint city council members and even the mayor. This right was necessary in order to correct "under-representation" of a particular community or to appoint a member of a group which would otherwise lack any representation at all. An amendment to the Israeli Municipalities Ordinance, enacted after the annexation of East Jerusalem, granted the Israeli minister of the interior similar powers.

This model secures the rights of the minority and protects it against majority rule. After 1967, various proposals and plans advocated it as a solution to the problem of Arab minority representation in the united city, which has a decisive Jewish majority.

Second Model: A centralized city council; council elections at large without communal quotas or voting by precincts; creation of neighborhood committees with limited powers, not secured by a binding law. The structure of the municipal government in Jerusalem since 1969 has followed this model, which ensures a decisive Jewish predominance and keeps the Arab minority from gaining an appropriate representation on the city council.

Third Model: Decentralized municipality composed of boroughs defined on a territorial-ethnic basis, and a supreme city council; division of powers between the borough councils and the supreme city council; elections for borough councils and representation of borough delegates in the supreme city council; rotation of the mayoralty or, alternatively, appointment of representatives of the majority and the minority as mayor and deputy mayor respectively.

This third model was initially proposed by the Jews at the beginning of the 1930s but was rejected by the British, who preferred the first model. In 1945, Supreme Court President Sir William Fitzgerald advocated this model (while leaving extensive authority in the hands of the central government), but the British authorities did not apply it. After the Israeli annexation of East Jerusalem in 1967, the idea of borough councils became popular among some Israelis, and others, who saw it as a substitute for satisfying the Palestinian national interests in the city. This model, combined with the division of sovereignty, is also favored by moderate Arabs.

Fourth Model: Limitation of the municipal government's authority and transfer of most of its functions to the central government; appointment of a nonelective commissioner; administration of the city as a direct function of the central government. This model was applied by the British Mandate, when Jews and Arabs could not cooperate in the management of the city. It was also adopted by the UN Trusteeship Council, combined with limited autonomy for the residents. Massive interference on the part of the central government in the everyday conduct of affairs was very common in East Jerusalem during the Jordanian era and in Israeli West Jerusalem during the fifties, due to frictions between the orthodox and secular residents. Teddy Kollek's suggestion to appoint "a minister for the affairs of Jerusalem" is in line with this model.

The problem of municipal government, like that of sovereignty and the holy places, has not yet been solved despite the abundance of plans and their sophistication. The magic formula has not been found because an intellectual effort, however well meant and impartial, is not sufficient. The real test of a formula for a solution is its ability to accommodate to changing circumstances, but even more essential is the willing cooperation of the parties to the conflict. Without this willingness, no plan, no matter how well balanced and inspired, can succeed.

Seventy-five years have passed since Mousa Kazzim al-Husseini left the small municipal offices opposite Jaffa Gate for the last time. Dismissed by the British district commissioner for political activism, al-Husseini left behind him a city suffering from a chronic shortage of water that required the trucking in of containers of water for sale on the street; a city with less than ten kilometers of paved streets, where one of the main jobs of the municipality was to wet the dirt roads to keep down the dust; a city with only 202 kerosene-fueled street lamps; and a city in whose hospitals dozens died each year of malaria for lack of a proper sanitary and storm-sewer system. Were Mousa Kazzim to be miraculously resurrected today, he would rub his eyes in wonder at the magnificent city hall from which a modern municipal government administers a 123-square-kilometer area within which close to 600,000 persons live—nearly ten times the population during his tenure. However, if he were to overhear the verbal blows being exchanged by his grandson Faisal and his successor Ehud Olmert, he would not be surprised. Mousa Kazzim Pasha would well understand both the content and the style of these verbal assaults. The seventy-five years that have gone by have totally altered the appearance of Jerusalem, but not the character of the relations between the conflict-embroiled communities. He might say that they haven't learned a thing and they haven't forgotten a thing.

CHAPTER FIVE

BLUEPRINT FOR CATASTROPHE

On April 8, 1918, when the front dividing the British and Turkish lines was within a few kilometers of the city and the end of the First World War was not yet in sight, Colonel Ronald Storrs issued a military order (Order 34) prohibiting the "demolition, construction, alteration, or repair of any building in Jerusalem." On June 9, 1967, the day after the Israeli conquest of the Old City—the streets were still littered with corpses—David Ben-Gurion called for "the demolition of the walls of Jerusalem because they are not Jewish." The British governor had sought to combat "the tendency to destroy everything interesting and beautiful [in Jerusalem] and to replace it with the cheapest and ugliest buildings," aspiring to "protect Jerusalem by preserving both the esthetic 'status quo' and the status quo in regard to religious worship and political status." David Ben-Gurion wished to destroy the city walls "so as to indicate continuity of Jewish control of the areas inside and outside them" and further demanded the construction of "thousands of huts" in all parts of Jerusalem in order to establish "facts" that would substantively alter the status quo.

The British governor represents one pole, preservation, and the veteran Zionist leader represents its opposite, the alteration of existing conditions. The holy city dangles between these two poles, the inherent tension between them shaping its physical form. The struggle between old and new, between the eternal and the mundane, between clinging to the past and adapting to the modern, is not exclusive to Jerusalem. But in Jerusalem, so polarized in its every aspect, this struggle is particularly acrimonious. The contrasting approaches of Ronald Storrs and David Ben-Gurion are manifestations of the power of this confrontation. Storrs—son of a vicar, student of the classics, esthete, orientalist, with a romantic affection for the East—had arrived in Jerusalem bearing the image of the Holy City as depicted in the engravings affixed to his Bible. He sought to preserve the silhouette of a city encircled by a wall and towers, with domes and turrets soaring overhead, surrounded by olive groves. This silhouette had become fantasy as early as the beginning of the twentieth century, and Ronald Storrs well understood that the very fact of his ruling as a representative of the European power that had replaced the archaic Ottoman regime heralded the end of this pseudo-biblical image of Jerusalem.

Farsighted persons predicted even then that the modernization of Jerusalem would destroy the city's biblical character: "Were the choice mine," one individual stated, "I would rather that the city remained in Turkish hands and did not turn into an English town." However, these people did not live in Jerusalem and were not required to grapple with the other face of this eastern city: the dirt, the neglect, the lack of paved roads and sewers, uncontrolled building, the use of cheap building materials such as tin and mud, the lack of municipal services, and the chronic shortage of water.

Ronald Storrs himself was aware of the tension between preservation and development: "The city's inhabitants are not exhibits, to be preserved in a state of romantic wretchedness just so the sentimental tourist can experience the thrill of observing the romance of Jerusalem." He, like many who came after him, sought to balance the two poles by instituting a system of town-planning statutes. The objective of Jerusalem's first town-planning scheme, which he commissioned in 1918 was "not necessarily to plan, but to put in place regulations that would preserve Jerusalem's special flavor and character." Schemes for the planning of Jerusalem began to accumulate.

In no other city in the world has such vast financial and human capital been invested in the creation of planning schemes and have planners made such extensive use of phraseology and demagoguery in attempting both to bridge the gulf between the contradictory values of preservation and development and to justify megalomania and greed. Only in Jerusalem could a huge construction project, threatening to destroy the skyline of the Old City and dwarf it with grandiose exhibitionism, be proclaimed "a modern echo of the Old City, in dialogue with the Temple Mount." This gigantic hotel was "planned," according to its designers, "deductively, with a great deal of attention to the specific character of Jerusalem, . . . the hotel's concave tower facing the Temple Mount creating a clear orientation toward the city."

Plans produced during the Mandatory period were grounded in the liberal ideology that reigned in those distant days, according to which the rights of the individual were to be restricted only if they impinged upon those of the public. This point of view has not entirely disappeared, and supreme importance is still attached to a series of maps and regulations setting out developers' rights regarding their land and its allowable uses with the objective of ensuring preservation of the urban public's quality of life. As time passed, however, it became clear that passive regulatory planning was not sufficient and had to be supplemented by "developmental planning" that would not only address land use but would also determine the resources required for the implementation of the plans. The individualistic approach was replaced by one that emphasized the physical, economic, social, and cultural needs of the community and that set guidelines and restraints according to which the planner was required to organize the entire area of the city; this organization would dictate the limits of an individual's rights with regard to the land.

The definition of "public needs" has always been more complex in Jerusalem than elsewhere. Its status as a city sacred to hundreds of millions of "citizens in spirit" has meant that Jerusalem does not belong to its tax-paying residents alone. The British were clearly cognizant of these spiritual considerations and perceived their ultimate role in Jerusalem as fulfillment of "a sacred trust of civilization." They laid down principles regarding the preservation of the Old City—its varied architectural elements and textures, its building tradition, and scale. These principles found their way into plans prepared after the British ouster, but they were transformed into mere "principles for determining the form and appearance of the city," which one must "endeavor not to harm" when implementing the new objective of planning, namely, development. As one plan expressed it: "to direct and guide future development so that irreparable damage is not done to that which makes Jerusalem unique."

In Israeli eyes, British planning principles were not universal, but "Christian." "The British," states the Jerusalem Master Plan prepared by the Israelis in 1968, following the city's "reunification," "decided to preserve Jerusalem in a form that approximated as closely as possible that of the Crusader city. . . . Surprisingly, it turns out that the position taken by the British on the shaping of the city's image struck deep roots in the consciousness of the Israeli public . . . just as the romantic sentiment with which the British (and most Europeans) regard the exotic East has taken hold in Israel."

The Israelis' disparagement of the British planning legacy was a way of declaring that the definition of "public needs" in modern Jerusalem would not be limited to the quality of life of its inhabitants and the spiritual requirements of the multitudes who hold the city sacred, but would be particularly aimed at expressing Israel's emotional, religious, and national attachment to the city. The Jewish people's prerogative supercedes the rights of the Muslims, who (states the Master Plan) "at least in recent generations, have allowed the city to degenerate," and certainly those of "the Christians, who were faithfully represented" by the departed British colonial regime. By contrast, today "the renewal of Jewish independence in Israel is being consummated in Jerusalem; for the Jewish people Jerusalem is a patrimony, whose image they are entitled to mold in conformity with the requirements of their collective life and the city's special significance for them."

The planning and development of Jerusalem became, then, a Jewish national undertaking. Organization of the urban space ceased to be a question of planning aimed at guaranteeing optimal quality of life; the physical space came to be perceived as a battlefield to gain control of and to defend against the Muslims and Christians. Building homes is seen not merely as a way of satisfying people's needs but as a strategic component of a national struggle. Mundane matters such as the building of roads and hospitals and the laying of water and electricity lines are charged with symbolic, almost spiritual meaning. The consummation of the Jewish attachment to Jerusalem is expressed in the rapid building and settlement of additional Jewish neighborhoods on formerly Arab land, on the principle that the establishment of physical and demographic "facts" is the only way to "redeem the land"—to take possession of it physically and thereby make it Jewish. David Ben-Gurion's demand that thousands of huts be erected immediately in Jerusalem is an example of this approach. The primacy of demographic considerations was implied in the words of an Israeli government minister during a debate over the implementation of a construction scheme in 1970: "To me, houses inhabited by Jews and Jewish children playing in the streets are more beautiful than bare hills; at any rate, this is more important than anything else."

There is nothing new in any of these attitudes. They reflect the classic Zionist viewpoint that the boundaries of the Jewish collective are determined by the extent of settlement, and that "facts on the ground" have far-reaching political significance. This imperative decrees development and construction at all costs.

The interesting thing is that the cult of development has long coexisted with its opposite—the cult of ancient relics, of nature and greenery. Archeological digs, afforestation and a deep sensitivity toward the landscape and the environment, and even "romantic affection for the Orient" are intermixed with the surveying of roads, the laying of foundations, and the building of industrial plants. The conflict between preservation and change in Zionist ideology is only apparent: both preservation and development are mobilized for the realization of national goals. Just as homes inhabited by Jews ensure possession of space, so do forests planted by the Jewish National Fund. Just as the construction of roads and water pipelines facilitates the flow of Jewish domination, so the preservation of the environment and the recovery of relics of the past are acts that assert ownership. Wildflowers and eagles' nests are also Jewish national property, and caring for these "national" natural assets is a test of Jewish ownership of the land. After all, who takes the effort to nurture the property of another?

The cult of development was not motivated by ideological and political imperatives alone. The necessity of absorbing millions of immigrants and building an economic infrastructure to provide them with a livelihood was bound to subordinate every other consideration. However, patriotic arguments also served to camouflage greed. Plans that had been rejected on esthetic or professional grounds were approved as soon as their promoters trotted out political arguments to justify them. In these circumstances, considerations of environmental quality and preservation had little chance of overcoming the pressures of development.

When these considerations were stood against each other and a probing debate took place over the need to find a balance between them—a contentious issue in planning circles—it still amounted to a family quarrel. The basic assumption shared by both sides in the debate was that the "environment" was vacant land belonging to no one, virgin territory awaiting its Jewish redeemers, who were simply arguing about what to do with it. The right of the Arab landowners, as individuals or as a collective, to make use of it or to participate in the urban planning debate was not taken into consideration.

The planning decisions that determined the shape of Jerusalem for many generations to come were made not at the drawing board but around the cabinet table. Political responses to the needs of the hour, real or imagined, had far-reaching implications. Entire environments were created or altered as the result of a decision to map out a road; to grant or withhold building rights; to determine land values; to locate a theater, a shopping center, a parking lot, or an industrial or entertainment area; or to populate a neighborhood with religious or secular residents of a certain ethnic origin. Politicians, out of insecurity, out of vanity, or perhaps simply by nature, wish to believe that their decisions are readily reversible. With a word they decide the creation of a neighborhood, and they believe that with a word they can do away with it when they find they have erred. They rely on professional planners to explain their mistakes and to provide them with ways to cover up one mistake with the help of a new one. Patriotism—the refuge of scoundrels, charlatans, and the greedy—provides a cover for acts of folly and corruption.

For the past thirty years, political decision makers have set as their objective the wholesale alteration of the image of Jerusalem, and they have succeeded in fashioning it into an environment consonant with the desires of the Jewish collective. In so doing, they have altered Jerusalem's character to such a degree that it is no longer the city that has for generations been etched on the imagination and consciousness of hundreds of millions of people. The character of this once-distinctive urban entity has been so blurred that those entering the city do not feel they have reached their destination: the compact city, perched on a hilltop and bordered on all sides by deep valleys, its houses and walls composing a single block, standing out from the surrounding pastoral scene. That city is no more. Suburbs now sprawl from the approaches to Jericho, in the east, to the hills bordering the coastal plain, in the west, and along the watershed from Ramallah, in the north, almost to Hebron, in the south.

The pressures of development threaten to obscure two vital components of the city's image: its mountainous topography and its distinctive skyline. The old practice was to permit construction on hillsides and ridges only, leaving the valleys as open spaces, so that the city would not be transformed into one flat carpet of buildings. This principle is no longer observed, and the Old City skyline has been marred by the erection of several high-rise buildings. The authorities were impelled for a time to refrain from granting additional permits, but this policy too was changed, and office and apartment towers of dozens of stories are slated to go up not far from the Old City walls. The excuse offered is a shortage of building space and the necessity of revitalizing downtown Jerusalem. The price of this unbridled development is becoming increasingly obvious.

Each generation and each regime has left its imprint on the city, and together these imprints have created the wondrous mosaic of Jerusalem. So broad and deep was the city's absorptive capacity that these contrary influences were incorporated into an organic part of its fabric. Jerusalem was capable of assimilating the physical manifestations of the Israeli connection as well. These need not have copied the monuments of the past, but should have reflected a sense of proportion and reverence for the city as it was when it fell into Israeli hands. The Israelis should also have respected the Palestinians' attachment to the city whose urban space they were to share, and regarded them as a legitimate constituency, whose needs must be met. However, in their speedy development to create irreversible "facts on the ground" in Jerusalem, they forged a reality that is hard to reconcile with the profound emotion experienced by the pilgrim entering the portals of the Holy City.

Is this the inevitable price of progress and the unavoidable consequence of the urge, in itself understandable, to give concrete expression to the Jewish affinity for the city of their longings? The answers to these and other questions relating to Jerusalem depends on the identity of the person giving them. But anyone who wishes to understand the reality that has been created here must delve into the past, and especially must follow the twists and turns of "political planning"—or the politics of planning—in Jerusalem over the past 150 years.

In all likelihood, the very establishment of Jerusalem was itself an act of political planning. After all, the founding of Jerusalem on this particular site is very difficult to explain in physical-geographical or functional terms. The city's topographical features do not correspond with those of other ancient cities. Why was it situated on a steep slope surrounded by hills, on the border between desert and sown land; inaccessible and far from trade routes, river, and sea? Many solutions to this mystery have been proffered, and their sheer number indicates that none is satisfactory. Some say the condition that determined the location of the first settlement was the presence of a freshwater spring, but similar springs are found in many places. Others hypothesize that it was the site of an indigenous cult, but the Bible describes many of these in the vicinity of Jerusalem.

Whatever the reasons for the establishment of an urban center and place of worship in the period preceding King David, there is no doubt that the decision to designate this site as his capital and the center for the worship of the One God was political. David, who strove to unite the tribes of Israel into one kingdom, chose a site located on the border between the southern and northern tribes but held by neither of them. The decision to make Jerusalem David's capital was, then, based on the same considerations behind the choice of Washington, D.C., as the capital of the United States 2,700 years later.

This political decision necessitated planning decisions, the most crucial being the establishment of the Temple to the God of Israel on Mount Moriah, rising above the slopes of David's city. King Solomon, and the kings of Judah after him, built a number of monumental structures in the city, which was fanning out to the north and west, and encircled it with walls and towers. But all of these were essentially an integral extension of the Temple. The whole city functioned as a provider of services to the tens of thousands of pilgrims who thronged its streets during the thrice-yearly religious festivals. This is the reasoning behind the half-shekel Temple levy paid by every Jewish male in the land and abroad to be applied to the maintenance of "the aqueduct and the walls of the city and its towers and all the needs of the city."

The Temple and the whole city with it were destroyed and rebuilt, and reached the peak of their splendor and size a few years before again being destroyed, by the Romans. The Roman emperors, who were well aware of Jerusalem's political importance to the Jews, sought to create irreversible planning "facts" that would preclude the rebellious nation's restoring its religious and national center. They rebuilt Jerusalem according to classical Roman planning principles, which determined the form of the city for 1,600 years. Walls followed a four-cornered pattern, and there were two straight main thoroughfares, intersecting in the city center near the forum and the Temple of Venus (which was to become the Church of the Holy Sepulchre). The Temple Mount became a heap of ruins and garbage, and this too was a political decision.

The Jewish people, powerless to rehabilitate their Holy City, expressed their longings in dreams of a "celestial Jerusalem." However, the restoration of the earthly Jerusalem was perceived not as a task for God alone, but as an undertaking within human capabilities. Year after year, for nearly 2,000 years, Jews vowed, "Next year in Jerusalem," mourning over its destruction and longing to work for its rebuilding. Time did not diminish their yearning, and it burst forth with irresistible force when the political conditions necessary for its fulfillment were attained. And until then, others were at work: Christian and Muslim heirs to Judaism's tradition of belief in the sanctity of Jerusalem.

Seeking to compete with their rivals on the Arabian Peninsula, the Omayyad caliphs built the Temple Mount mosques, the Dome of the Rock (A.D. 691) and el-Aqsa (A.D. 710-15), as an alternative pilgrimage site to Mecca. They forbade the local population to fulfill the religious obligation of the hajj (pilgrimage to Mecca), fearing that pilgrims would be influenced by their stay and, upon their return, would revolt against the rulers in Damascus. The Dome of the Rock was intended to rival the rotunda of the Church of the Holy Sepulchre (which was part of the giant edifice built by Emperor Constantine); hence, the dimensions of the domes and other details are identical in the two structures. Political decisions such as these yielded one of the most impressive gems of planning in Jerusalem. They also signaled the beginning of the scramble for control over the physical territory and skyline of Jerusalem. The Crusaders, who converted the Temple Mount mosques to churches, chose to symbolize their dominion over the city with an enormous construction project that utterly transformed the Church of the Holy Sepulchre. It was rededicated on the fiftieth anniversary of the conquest of Jerusalem, July 15, 1149. Thirty-eight years later, the products of the grandiose Crusader planning ventures were all reduced to rubble or transformed into places of worship for their enemies, the Muslims—except for the Church of the Holy Sepulchre, which mostly fell into the hands of the Greek Orthodox, from whom it had been usurped during the Crusader occupation.

The period between the thirteenth and eighteenth centuries demonstrated that destruction and neglect can also serve as agents of political planning. Although the Mamluks and the Ottomans executed public construction projects in the city, notably the impressive wall around the Old City, such structures could not conceal the deliberate neglect. This picturesque wall, with its formidable appearance, gives an indication of the decline in Jerusalem's importance during that period: this was the last city wall built to withstand an attack with bows and arrows. The Ottomans, themselves masters in the use of firearms, built the walls of Jerusalem to fend off attacks by rebellious Bedouins and peasants, and not shelling by the cannons and mortars of a regular army.

For hundreds of years, Jerusalem remained shut away behind its walls. Neither its inhabitants nor its rulers seemed motivated to take action of any kind. Some have argued that this was the result of a passivity of character and the absence of a tradition of action and develop-

ment, as well as a lack of financial means. However, as far as the
Ottoman rulers were concerned, Jerusalem was nothing but an insignificant provincial town on the edge of the desert. According to travelers'
accounts, the city was a collection of half-ruined buildings with herds
grazing in the vacant lots between them. It was filthy, with no sewers or
running water. The magnificent edifices of a bygone era were mini-
mally maintained, and the few pilgrims who dared to visit returned
appalled by the forlorn state of the Holy City.

The 1830s ushered in a new era in city planning, and within fifty years
Jerusalem would be altered beyond recognition. The opening of the
Ottoman empire, including Jerusalem, to competing European interests led to a prolonged contest over Jerusalem's physical space, with the
guiding principle "faster, higher, bigger." The aim for each party was to
fill the space in the city and its skyline with towering masses of stone
before others could; the minaret must rise higher than the belfry and
the dome of the synagogue higher than the vault of the church. Each
competitor—English, French, Russian, German, Sephardic Jew,
Ashkenazic Jew, Greek Orthodox, Muslim—made an effort to muster
the best architects and builders. Consequently, the buildings of
Jerusalem in the late nineteenth century represented the tradition, culture, style, mythology, vanity, tribalism, and uniqueness of each group.
The inevitable result was a medley of styles that created an eclectic
landscape, emphasizing the centrality of the Holy City and infusing it
with a cosmopolitan character.

The result of these planning decisions represents, of course, the wisdom of hindsight. The initiators of the competition over the physical
expanse of Jerusalem did not aspire to contribute to a magnificent
mosaic whose details would blend into an integral whole. On the contrary, they sought to accentuate their own handiwork, to overshadow
the works of their rivals, and to focus the observer's attention on their
own buildings and to divert it from all the rest. It was the British who
started the race. In 1841 they built Christ Church, the first church to

be erected in Jerusalem for hundreds of years. In the next twenty years, no fewer than twenty-five church and public buildings went up in the Old City, built by Catholics, Armenians, Greeks, Russians, Germans, Austrians, the French, the English, and the Jews.

It quickly became clear that these structures—massive, lofty, and impressive as they might be—could not make a significant imprint on the Old City. The crowding of the buildings, the enclosure of the court-yards within stone walls, and the limited perspectives caused the indi-vidual buildings to become lost in the landscape. What is the point of domes and towers if they all merge in a uniform panorama?

Perhaps the international competitors realized that, in the rivalry over the visual symbols of the Old City, they had lost before even begin-ning: the works of the "backward natives" would endure eternally as the symbols of the Old City. No individual or nation would ever succeed in obscuring the image of the Dome of the Rock, the walls and gates of the city, or David's Tower, even with the construction of higher domes and thicker walls.

Only the open spaces outside the walls of the Old City afforded the opportunity to emphasize a nation's uniqueness and to erect structures that would display the flag. Following relatively modest beginnings (by the British, of course), the Germans and Russians embarked on gar-gantuan building projects in this territory. In 1860, the year when con-struction of a huge center for Russian pilgrims and a German orphans' home was started, the first Jewish building project outside the Old City walls was begun.

Competition over space outside the walls increased throughout the 1870s and continued unabated until the British conquest. The volume and height of a building were the central architectural guidelines. The steeples of the Church of Notre Dame de France (now Notre Dame de Jerusalem) were planned to be higher than the "Russian Compound," situated on a topographically superior spot; the tower of the Augusta Victoria Hospital on Mount Scopus competes with that of the Church of the Ascension on the Mount of Olives for dominion of the eastern skyline (later the planners of the Mount Scopus campus of the Hebrew University sought to impose an exclamation point of their own on this skyline and built a "Jewish" tower).

Who was the victor in this competition? Not three years had passed since the Russians (who undoubtedly built the largest and highest structures of all) completed their last building when the Bolshevik Revolution effectively ended their presence in Jerusalem. The British learned their lesson. First, they endeavored to halt the competition and, as we have seen, to impose an "esthetic status quo." Second, during the three decades of their rule (1917–48) they erected only three governmental structures in Jerusalem: a post office, a municipal building, and the high commissioner's residence. Plans to build an office complex for their ramified administration were never implemented.

The Jews also learned a lesson: Dominion over the physical space of the city must be accompanied by demographic superiority. Church domes and buildings to house pilgrims will not determine the identity of the Holy City; homes for people will. Any group that wishes to establish political "facts" must bring the members of their community to the city. Since the mid-nineteenth century the Jews have been engaged in this effort, which continues to this day. At first they accomplished this without the benefit of power of enforcement; in recent generations they have employed all the power at the disposal of their sovereign state. The Jews wholeheartedly entered the competition over the city's skyline, seeking to erect buildings no less beautiful or massive than those built by the Germans and the Russians. However, their primary efforts were focused on planning, building, and populating neighborhoods. The first Jewish neighborhoods outside the Old City, Nachalat Shiv'a and Mea She'arim, were erected on the same hill on which the Russians, Germans, and French had built. The neighborhoods were crowded and poor but were self-sufficient. Their builders had no urban infrastructure to rely on, since the Ottoman authorities provided neither urban planning, roads, sewers, nor police protection. Residents of these neighborhoods carried on an intensive social and religious life, financed in most cases by contributions from the diaspora. Although efforts were at first sporadic and dependent on isolated private initiatives, a pattern gradually emerged: Every house built and every tree planted came to be seen as a quasi-military stronghold in the national struggle for spatial and demographic dominance.

The Arabs too emerged from the Old City and built homes that gradually gave rise to neighborhoods. However, for them this was an individual and family effort. They took care to build fine, spacious houses surrounded by gardens; these were homes that were pleasant to live in and not barrack-like neighborhoods. These houses in Sheikh Jarah, Talbiyeh, Katamon, and the Greek Colony proudly bore their owners' names. Most of these architectural gems, however, were eventually seized by Jews. The Jews' ability to mobilize the resources of an entire people for the creation of physical facts, even without a government to depend upon, ultimately defeated the aristocratic individualism of the Arabs.

The city outside the walls spread to the north, west, and south. The British, who imposed modern planning principles and provided a relatively advanced urban infrastructure, sought to keep the press of urban development from the visual basin of the Old City. But it was beyond their power to remove Jerusalem's principal business center from the area adjacent to the Jaffa Gate and abutting the western wall of the Old City. The urban space grew fuller, with houses touching one another. The pattern of ethnic separation between Jews and Arabs was not clear-cut at first, and many neighborhoods were mixed. However, the intercommunal riots that culminated on the eve of the Second World War brought about a rupture, and at that time both the old and new cities became a patchwork of ethnic neighborhoods (except for the center of the new city).

The Jews' political and security-oriented planning and the community's total mobilization stood the supreme test of war and triumphed, while the Arabs' chaotic individualism led to their downfall and desertion of their homes. July 1948 witnessed a political fact of utmost significance for future planning: The city was officially divided between Israel and Jordan, and the two sectors perforce resigned themselves to the reality of geographical partition.

In the Jewish section of the city there was a long-standing tradition of centralized planning, as well as established administrative institutions that the state assumed control of in 1948. In addition, planners and powerful governmental agencies with competence in making and carrying out decisions were operating there. As a result of the partition of the city, its urban center of gravity was shifted westward from its traditional location near the Old City walls. Government offices and institutions were located west of the built-up area, and Jewish Jerusalem turned its back on the Old City and faced west, toward the "corridor," the narrow lifeline connecting it with the coastal plain and Tel Aviv. Development emphasis was placed on the new neighborhoods in the western hills. The neighborhoods of the old center, some of which now bordered no-man's-land, were neglected. No effort was made to expand the historical center of the new city, to step up construction in the vacant spaces remaining in the built-up area, or to rehabilitate the neighborhoods along the seam with East Jerusalem, which had been sparsely populated before the war and now had become slums.

The Jewish planners were not to blame for the westward orientation of West Jerusalem's development. This was dictated by the Israeli city's being surrounded on three sides by areas under Arab control. However, rather than attempting to check this process, which fostered the perpetuation of the partition of Jerusalem, the planners actually encouraged it. Their acquiescence with the partitioning was also reflected in their choice of locations for public, governmental, and municipal buildings. Continuation of this process would result in a complete split between the two sectors of the city, leaving a deserted no-man's-land between them, bordered by a wide expanse of deteriorating and largely abandoned slums.

The housing projects that more than doubled the Jewish population of Jerusalem—from approximately 80,000 at the close of the 1948 war

8. Hebrew University, on Mt. Scopus, and the Old City

to some 190,000 in 1967—were built mainly on land abandoned by Arabs during the war. In fact, according to various (controversial) calculations, more than 60 percent of the area of the Israeli city belonged to Arab refugees.

In East Jerusalem too, now under Jordanian control, strong trends toward political planning were operating. However, in contrast to the Israeli sector, where the goal of political planning was to reinforce the city's status as the capital of Israel and as a vigorous population center, political planning in East Jerusalem was directed toward preventing development. The Jordanian regime worked persistently and aggressively to consolidate the status of Amman as the sole economic and political center in the kingdom, and deliberately hampered Jerusalem's growth and progress. The jurisdictional area of Jordanian Jerusalem was not expanded, and large areas at the edge of the built-up section remained undeveloped because the government did not permit building on the slopes of Mount Scopus and French Hill. This facilitated the Israeli expropriation of these areas after the 1967 war and their use for construction of Jewish neighborhoods. Meanwhile, the development taking place in the East Bank (formerly Transjordan) attracted emigration from Jerusalem, and the city's meager public budgets prevented urban development, limiting construction activity to areas of moderate size to the north and south of the Old City.

The Jordanians adhered strictly to the British planning tradition and prohibited massive construction in the visual basin of the Old City, preserving the esthetic value of the landscape that the Israelis later inherited and boasted about, as if they had designed it.

Thus, on the eve of the Six-Day War, East Jerusalem's "historical character" was still intact. Planner David Kroyanker describes the scene in his book *Jerusalem: Conflicts Over the City's Form*: "In the Old City within the walls, building was dense and crowded. Surrounding it, valleys with meager greenery, on whose upper slopes were scattered homes and churches. Beyond, to the West, a concentration of residential neighborhoods and administrative-cultural centers, and to the East and North-East, sparse residential construction. On the surrounding desolate hills, a smattering of thickets of cypress and pines and a few religious buildings" (Tel-Aviv: Zmora-Bitan, 1988 [Hebrew], 58).

The partition of the city, which resulted in the diversion of construction away from the city's historical center (now bisected by barbed wire), the paucity of development in the Arab section, and the westward shift of the Jewish demographic center all contributed to the preservation of Jerusalem's traditional visual texture. The city, which had become accustomed to aristocratic assault by the builders of churches and erectors of public edifices and had successfully withstood the more modest schemes of the politicians, was now threatened by the relentless thrust of bulldozers fueled by national imperatives and abundant resources.

Even before the din of the Six-Day War had subsided and the government had managed to address the political future of East Jerusalem, demands were being made for Jewish settlement in the territories recently conquered. All political groups and state authorities were seized by the urge to establish physical and demographic "facts." The mess created by the multiplicity of declarations and plans, and especially by the creation of faits accomplis by private interest groups, forced the government to intervene. From the moment the prime minister took over responsibility for "the acceleration of the building up and populating of greater Jerusalem" in August 1967, planning and development were nationalized and made subject to the supreme political authority of the state. Municipal authorities, regular statutory planning bodies, and considerations with regard to quality of life, landscape, and urban functioning all became secondary. The ultimate arbiters of the character of the Holy City were not the mayor, the municipal council, town planners, architects, and historians, but government ministers aided and abetted by omnipotent officials and clandestine teams who actually carried out the work.

The quasi-military style of planning that gained ascendancy actually pursued the objective of dominion over the urban space using methods similar to those of a military operation. The first political planning decision in the "reunified" city concerned plans not for construction but for the geopolitical determination of borders. The decision regarding these borders had far-reaching urban planning implications, although those responsible for drawing them were not guided by such considerations. The outcome was disastrous. The arbitrarily created urban space encompassed areas and population centers that were difficult to weave into the urban fabric, excluded some settled areas, created an immense expanse that was extremely expensive to connect to the physical infrastructure, and, above all, paved the way for the disintegration of the compact structure of the historic city. However, the determining consideration, "a maximum of vacant space with a minimum of Arabs," laid down as the basic tenet in the delineation of the borders, made possible the planning and implementation of the principal political objective: the creation of physical and demographic faits accomplis.

The political planners encountered a serious problem: Where would they find the land reserves required for construction of the Jewish neighborhoods? A survey revealed that there were several thousand dunams (four dunams equal one acre) of land that had been the property of the Jordanian government (which the Israeli government hastened to take possession of), but of this amount only several hundred dunams were suitably situated for Jewish settlement. The government rejected suggestions that houses occupied by Arabs be seized (except in the Jewish quarter of the Old City), and it was therefore clear that the planners must set their sights on the vacant areas on the outskirts of the city and surrounding it. These areas would have to be expropriated from their Arab owners. The legal instrument at the disposal of the Israelis for this purpose was the Land Ordinance (Expropriation for Public Purposes) of 1943, which grants the treasury minister the authority to expropriate private land when there is a "public need" for such action—with the definition of "public need" left to the minister himself. The Israeli government, whether Labor- or Likud-led, has made wholesale use of this Mandatory ordinance in Jerusalem: between 1967 and 1995, five major expropriation orders were issued, affecting a total area of about 23,000 dunams (5,600 acres), or over one-third of the area annexed to the city since 1967.

These expropriations were presented as being politically neutral: "for the purpose of construction, development, and settlement in Jerusalem—so as to provide a land base adequate both for meeting the need for massive construction of residential housing, including the accompanying infrastructure and public buildings, and for the purpose of laying out a suitable road system for the city and the new neighborhoods." But no one was deceived by the designation of these "ethnically colorblind" needs; the expropriated areas were being taken from Arabs and handed over to Jews. This was an extraordinary interpretation of the word *public*: The only legitimate public was Jewish, and therefore only Jews were entitled to benefit from the expropriation. The Arabs, a "haphazard collection of individuals," were to have their private property confiscated so that the Jews could settle Jerusalem and create geopolitical "facts" there.

A document authored by Israeli town planners defines the principle behind the choice of areas to be designated for expropriation: "Any area in the city that is not populated by Jews is in danger of being cut off from Israeli jurisdiction and coming under Arab rule. Hence the administrative delineation of the municipal boundary must be translated into the language of deeds by building throughout the entire area, especially its farthest reaches. Jewish neighborhoods must not be left isolated; this consideration dictates the drastic reduction of open spaces in the city."

The location of areas to be designated for expropriation and the subsequent construction of Jewish neighborhoods was based on political considerations, and this was inconsistent with urban planning considerations. Since the planners too accepted the macronational imperatives, it is not surprising that the image of Israeli Jerusalem was shaped by the same people responsible for drawing the maps presented to the treasury minister for his signature: the prime minister's representative, an official from the Israel Lands Administration, and a local housing ministry director.

Following the signing of the expropriation documents, teams of professionals got together to prepare detailed construction plans. But even the detailed plans were arranged to suit political guidelines. When criticism increased over the slow rate of "creation of facts" in East Jerusalem, the housing ministry utilized plans that had been prepared for a neighborhood near Tel Aviv, merely adding "traditional Jerusalem motifs"—concrete arches and ceramic tiles—to the buildings' facades. When a plan for the resolution of the Israeli-Arab conflict that did not appeal to the Israeli government was aired, the housing minister responded by ordering the immediate addition of two or three stories to already tall buildings situated on French Hill, overlooking the Old City.

The first piece of land expropriated in 1968 was dubbed "the northern door-latch." It was the fulfillment of a dream: "abolishing the vacuum" between West Jerusalem and Mount Scopus and erecting a "physical defense line" in northern Jerusalem. For nineteen years the university campus on Mount Scopus had been cut off from the Jewish city, and the small Jewish enclave had survived thanks to convoys that made the biweekly trek under Jordanian escort. The Israelis sought to wipe out the memory of this protracted shame by the establishment of Jewish neighborhoods that would end the campus's isolation. The same aspiration, to learn the lessons of the last (1967) war, motivated the authorities and the Hebrew University administration to construct an enormous extension to the campus on Mount Scopus, which would become the university's principal campus, replacing the new one that had been built in West Jerusalem when the city was still divided. The gigantic structure erected on the mountain—almost one-third of whose summit was first shaved off—expresses the spirit of that period better than any other building. It is a massive edifice—resembling a fortress with its towers, embrasures, glacis, and moat—rising above the biblical landscape of the Judean desert to the east and the Old City to the southwest. This extravagant and pretentious megastructure was eminently suited to the Israelis' sense of omnipotence in the wake of their glorious victory in the Six-Day War. The location of the campus in the visual basin of the Old City—for whose preservation so much effort had been expended—and its designation as a "Temple of the Israeli spirit," of all things, underscored the dangers inherent in political planning.

The "northern door-latch" neighborhoods (whose construction, ironically, was possible only because of the prior Jordanian prohibition on building in this area) were absorbed into the fabric of the city because they were so nearby. Despite their hasty planning and the political imperatives that had motivated their construction, quality of life there was good. This success was regarded as proof of the validity of the approach espoused by the professional planners: that Jerusalem must be planned as a compact city and the empty areas between the scattered western and eastern neighborhoods must be filled in. However, these urban planning considerations had in fact been outweighed by political ones.

In August 1970, the government issued expropriation orders for large tracts of land to the north, northwest, and southeast of the city and in southern Jerusalem. All the areas designated were, of course, across the armistice line, and their choice was explained in terms of "strategic considerations." The timing of this massive expropriation was not accidental. It was a direct response to the diplomatic initiative known as the Rogers Plan, after its originator, the American secretary of state at the time. Rogers stated that U.S. policy on Jerusalem was that the city must remain unified, but that a Jordanian presence must be reestablished there. Israel rejected the entire plan, but the state's response was not expressed only in words: The aim of the new expropriations was to encircle the city with huge dormitory suburbs "that would obviate any possibility of the redivision of Jerusalem."

The government decided to plan 25,000 apartments at once and to continue building them at a rate of 6,000 to 8,000 per year. To speed the process of detailed planning, an interministerial committee was set up, and it in fact appropriated the powers of the regular planning authorities. A thick curtain of secrecy shrouded the building plans. Teams of architects were instructed to prepare "rushed plans" and not to show them to anyone. The architects quit their jobs in protest over these political guidelines, and a public furor ensued. According to one expression of public sentiment at the time, "After a three years' wait, a hasty decision was made regarding expropriation, planning, and construction, in order to create a Jewish presence. If the result is an ugly stain on the face of the city, it is not a Jewish presence, and is even bad politics—not taking into consideration the esthetics of Jerusalem."

The principal objections revolved around structural details as well as the location of the Ramot neighborhood. This giant neighborhood was planned for the area north of Nahal Sorek, and its construction threatened to destroy one of the chief visual principles of Jerusalem. Planners had always sought to preserve its image as a walled city standing on its historical site, bounded on the north by Nahal Sorek and on the south by Nahal Rephaim. They had warned that construction on the Nebi

Samwil ridge, on the far side of Nahal Sorek, would lead to the spread of the city in a northwesterly direction, would upset the balance of population distribution, and would necessitate the building of a huge road network. As long as the debate was restricted to esthetic issues, there was still some chance of introducing meaningful changes to the plan. However, the urban planning issue was immediately linked to the political one, and there was foreign intervention in the debate. Once the spokesman for the U.S. State Department expressed concern over the building plans, all hope for their alteration was lost: approval of the plans became a patriotic duty, and they were therefore approved unanimously. The planners accepted the verdict; the Ramot neighborhood was incorporated into the city's master plan, and the politician-planners turned their attention to other areas where they could create physical "facts."

Exactly ten years after the approval of the decision to establish Ramot, and under similar circumstances, the politicians forced through another far-reaching planning decision. In March 1980 the Security Council passed a resolution calling on Israel to withdraw from "the occupied Arab territories, including East Jerusalem." In reaction to this resolution, the minister of housing brought before the government a proposal to expropriate an area of 4,000 dunams (1,000 acres) northeast of the city, which was approved. The new neighborhood was to be situated between Neve Ya'acov and French Hill, with the aim of "creating Jewish territorial continuity between these Jewish neighborhoods." Once again, the location of the neighborhood contravened a new master plan, approved only six months previously, in which the area had been designated as an "open landscape area" because "it is typical of the edge of the Judean desert, a pastoral environment, unchanged since the days of the Bible—and all possible measures must be undertaken to prevent the spread of extensive construction to this area."

As if it were not enough that the planners had acquiesced to the political decision and sacrificed the "pastoral landscape," they also changed the designation of Jerusalem's basic character as being that of

9. Jerusalem's new skyline

a "walled city" and began speaking in terms of "historical corridors."
According to this new conceptualization, "with the development of
construction outside the walls, the gateways to the city were transferred
from the walls to the new construction boundary—therefore planning
in Jerusalem must be based upon, among other things, the development
of these three historical approach corridors." The gates to the city were
thus transformed by the planner-politicians into an elastic concept.

The expropriation policy designed to determine political "facts" has
continued into the 1990s. In May 1991 a large area on the border of
neighboring Bethlehem was expropriated, it too in order "to complete
the ring of Jewish presence around the city, thereby preventing its partition." Plans for additional expropriations (including one that had
already been announced) were suspended in the face of vigorous
protests by the Palestinian Authority, the pressure of world public opinion, and threats by Arab Knesset members from parties supporting the
coalition government to precipitate a parliamentary crisis. Past experi-

ence suggests that these expropriations will be carried out at the politically opportune moment.

"Political rationales" helped in obtaining approval for a number of construction plans that severely damaged the landscape, and also in promoting various ostentatious building projects. Just as development pressures threatened to destroy the city's skyline with office towers and massive hotels, the construction of a stadium, parking garages, industrial parks, multilane highways, and residential neighborhoods have violated the fundamental planning principle of building only on hilltops and leaving the valleys as open spaces. Political considerations also were behind the establishment of large urban settlements in the West Bank, outside the city's municipal boundaries. Ma'ale Adumim, which started out as an industrial area, has grown to a city of more than 20,000. It is connected to Jerusalem by a major highway, and in 1994 its municipal boundaries were extended to the border of Jerusalem. In a similar manner, "the Jewish presence" is creeping toward the edge of Jericho and tentacles are radiating northward and southward, deep into the heart of the West Bank.

Political planning has supposedly achieved its declared purpose: between 1967 and 1995, 64,000 apartments went up in Jerusalem, of which 38,000 were built on expropriated land. By 1994 the Jewish population of the parts of Jerusalem that were Arab prior to 1967 was larger than the Arab population. But this success has exacted a heavy price. The compact city, situated in its historical location, has disintegrated; the development at the periphery has resulted in the weakening of the historical center; the migration of well-to-do elements of the population to outlying neighborhoods has weakened the socioeconomic structure of the inner city. Moreover, the new neighborhoods were planned as dormitory suburbs—without sources of employment, or commercial or entertainment areas—and thus are dependent on the city center. Their residents' frequent automobile commuting has put an intolerable burden on the road system, which has not been developed fast enough to keep pace with the growing use. And the hasty planning did not augur well for the quality of life of many of those living in the new developments; municipal services are overburdened, with the need for them to reach vast areas taxing their ability to function efficiently.

All of these undesirable consequences have failed to diminish the pride of the Israeli people in their successful shaping of Jerusalem, "a patrimony they are entitled to mold to suit the requirements of their lives and (the city's) special meaning for them." Those responsible for town planning in Jerusalem do acknowledge the heavy price the city has paid for bowing to the exigencies of political planning. However, they hasten to point out their achievements: rehabilitation of the Jewish Quarter of the Old City, renovation of the old marketplaces, establishment of a park around the walls of the Old City, planting and maintenance of a number of public gardens, founding of cultural institutions forming a "cultural mile" in the western part of the city, erection of public and administrative buildings, preservation of old neighborhoods and buildings of historical or architectural importance, revival of the old commercial center of the city, construction along the seam between East and West Jerusalem, and development of high-tech industries.

Jerusalem has undoubtedly undergone a major revolution since the 1967 war. From an inward-looking provincial town it has been transformed into a huge metropolis, Israel's biggest city, with a population of almost 600,000. The massive building venture that made this possible is credited to Mayor Teddy Kollek, who earned the appellation "the second Herod." For twenty-seven years this man presided over a municipal authority within whose jurisdiction a construction enterprise was implemented that some compare with the one undertaken by the first-century B.C. Edomite king, who rebuilt the Temple and public buildings and expanded the city walls. In Herod's day, it was said that "He who has not seen Jerusalem in all its glory has never seen a truly lovely city." Kollek was not pleased with the title because Herod "built

10.   A new Jewish neighborhood

primarily magnificent buildings, palaces and structures for military purposes," while in Kollek's opinion, "the main thing is not external
grandeur . . . [but] to construct a network of relationships that builds
bridges among the varied populations of Jerusalem." He rejected the
criticism over the destruction of the historical image of Jerusalem,
viewing it as reflecting a nostalgic and utopian attitude that did not take
the needs of the city into account. "'Facts' have been created in the city
by virtue of a realistic approach characterized by sober evaluation of the
tremendous difficulties and recognition of the importance of patience,
tolerance, and time," he wrote. In Kollek's opinion, the critics are not
free of hostile intent. "Many are lying in wait, hoping to find deeds that
can be presented in a distorted manner as justification for non-accep-
tance of our rule." As he sees it, the Israelis have succeeded "in preserving the historic city and implementing plans that others had only
dreamed of . . . despite the mighty scale of development and the pressure of time, which compelled us to plan hastily."

Teddy Kollek is the father of the "mosaic theory," with which he explains the expropriations and the establishment of homogeneous Jewish neighborhoods in East Jerusalem. "This is part of the traditional character of Jerusalem, and the new neighborhoods will certainly not change this," he stated. The model of the Old City divided into religious and ethnic quarters—Jewish, Christian, Armenian, and Muslim—is presented as a successful means for creating coexistence based on the separate, undisturbed cultural and ethnic development of its constituent communities. According to the mosaic theory, the pattern of homogeneous neighborhoods diminishes the tensions that arise when people of differing cultural backgrounds live side by side.

Kollek saw no contradiction between "separate development and peaceful coexistence" and aggressive intrusion into Arab areas via the construction of Jewish neighborhoods on expropriated land; "reunification of the city" is the most important consideration. "The supreme principle in the planning of Jerusalem is to secure its unity," declares the city master plan of 1978. This principle requires "building up the city in a manner that will prevent the bipolar consolidation of two national communities, in order to prevent the possible redivision of the city along the dividing line between them. The objective of building a city which is an unpolarized mosaic of national communities greatly influenced the locations of the new Jewish neighborhoods."

These principles, purporting to create "an unpolarized mosaic," have in practice produced extreme polarization, since they served as a basis for blatant discrimination between Jewish and Arab areas. This discrimination was not concealed at all; if the aim of political planning is to determine physical and demographic "facts" that will ensure Israeli rule over the unified city, it follows that efforts must be made to prevent the growth of the Arab population or the expansion of its living space. Teddy Kollek reaffirms this official policy when he quotes certain government officials in his recent book (*Teddy's Jerusalem*, [Tel-Aviv: Maariv, 1994], 105 [Hebrew]): "[It is necessary] to make life difficult for the Arabs, not to allow them to build. . . ."

The Jerusalem city engineer and chief planner confirms the connection between demography and political planning with her statement that "there is a government directive to preserve the ratio between the Arab and Jewish populations of Jerusalem at 28 percent Arabs and 72 percent Jews. The only way to manage this is [through manipulation of] housing potential. On this basis the growth potential [of construction programs for Arabs] is delimited and capacity is determined." The principles and details of implementation of the planning process in the Arab sector are laid bare in the following description provided by Teddy Kollek: "Planning [for northern Jerusalem] was based on the calculation of the rate of Arab population growth. It was determined that Arabs would be permitted to build 17,000 additional apartments in the area. . . . The plan was rejected and revoked. The official reason was 'violation of the demographic balance'—so once again the municipal experts appeared before the planning committee and again they explained how many apartments were vitally needed by the Arabs. The longer the deliberations continued, the more clearly I recognized the harsh reality that the question of the Arabs' needs and how it was possible to satisfy them was of no concern to the senior government officials. They were interested in only one thing, what was it possible *not* to give the Arabs."

Ultimately, a "compromise" was reached: of the 17,000 apartments, only 7,500 received approval, and even those housing units were not planned in accordance with accepted planning principles. In response to a demand from the ministry of housing, the area to be built upon was reduced and large sections of the planning map were colored green, denoting open spaces. The planners were motivated not by the desire to guarantee space for parks, but by the following consideration: "It could be that we will want to expand the industrial zone, or maybe we will build another Jewish neighborhood on that side." The classification of broad expanses as open space makes it possible to freeze their development and then free them for construction once the decision is made to establish a Jewish neighborhood. As a result, no more than 10,000 dunams, or 14 percent of the area annexed in Jerusalem in 1967, have been left available for the construction of Arab neighborhoods.

However, strict limitations on building apply even to this small remaining area. First, the general plans have not been elaborated in detailed plans, although it is only in reference to the latter that building permits are granted. Second, no neighborhood infrastructures (schools, roads, sewers, lighting) have been planned, and no public budgets have been allocated for implementation. Third, the planning authorities responsible for granting building permits operate according to rigid bureaucratic procedures. Fourth, the real estate market in the Arab sector is based not on supply and demand, but on ownership within the family. Therefore, families whose plots of land are not included in an area zoned for residential housing are not able to solve their housing problems.

Is it any wonder, then, that between 1967 and 1995, only 9,000 apartments were built for Arabs (as opposed to some 65,000 for Jews), of which only a few hundred received government incentives? In (formerly Arab) East Jerusalem, by 1995 there were 38,000 new Jewish residential units, compared with only 21,000 Arab residences. An indication of the housing shortage among the Arabs is the fact their average housing density is twice that of Jews: 2.2 per room versus 1.1. One-third of the Arab population lives in overcrowded conditions of more than three persons per room, in contrast to 2.4 percent of Jews. According to expert estimates, in 1995 the accommodation shortage in the Arab sector reached approximately 21,000 apartments; in other words, the number of homes must be doubled.

This policy of polarization and discrimination is presented as creating an "unpolarized mosaic" that contributes to peaceful coexistence. In practice, it brings about a deepening of hostility and an exacerbation of ethnic conflict. Individual anger over the seizing of family land is combined with collective rage over the plunder of the homeland. Such political planning courts disaster; indeed, it is nothing short of a blueprint for catastrophe.

It is the height of irony that Israeli planning has not actually achieved its goal. For one thing, massive development turned out to be a decisive factor in the phenomenal growth of Jerusalem's Arab population. This "paradox" stems from the fact that the labor force that built the Jewish neighborhoods was nearly if not completely Arab. The livelihood provided by the Israelis and their investment of billions of dollars in Jerusalem transformed the city into an "employment magnet," attracting tens of thousands of Arabs.

Although the Israelis have succeeded in more or less preserving the "demographic balance" that gives them a majority in the city, this balance is a fiction. As noted in Chapter 2, it was achieved by means of gerrymandering and the imposition of severe restrictions on the construction of Arab housing within the city limits. However, the Arabs who were drawn to Jerusalem built houses outside its municipal boundaries but within the metropolitan area. Soon the Arab dormitory suburbs were no less populous than those of the Jews, and the ratio between the numbers of Jews and Arabs within commuting distance of Jerusalem reached parity.

In the past, the creation of physical and demographic faits accomplis was an important means of establishing political "facts." However, under the conditions that prevail as we approach the end of the second millennium, houses inhabited by Jews are not necessarily the determining factor in the conflict; the political struggle over the urban space of Jerusalem has not yet been decided. Political planning has merely contributed to its exacerbation; only negotiations can determine its outcome.

One might claim that all town planning is a political act, since the planning of space—the scarcest resource in urban life—involves, first and foremost, the making of value judgments, which is the essence of politics. Professional know-how, pragmatic solutions, and even esthetics merely give concrete form to a series of value-oriented decisions based on political, social, and cultural perceptions as well as material constraints. One can therefore maintain that there is nothing wrong with planning in Jerusalem being political in nature. However, town planning in Jerusalem is political in an additional sense. Its objective is not to reconcile the claims of all the city's inhabitants or to manage the inevitable and natural dissension resulting from their conflicting interests. Rather, it is to impose the interests of the Israeli community on the entire city at the expense of the collective and individual interests of the Arabs. Israeli intentions even overshadow any willingness to take into account the interests of Jerusalem's hundreds of millions of "citizens in spirit" throughout the world.

After a whole generation of political planning that has fueled the fires of intercommunal hatred, what is needed is an entirely different brand of community planning: planning that will organize the urban space in an egalitarian manner, for the benefit of all the citizens and not of just one ethnic group. Jerusalem has enough space to accommodate the needs and aspirations of all its inhabitants.

CHAPTER SIX

A MARKETPLACE OF DISCORD

Acensus held by the Ottoman authorities in 1905 counted approximately 7,500 family units whose permanent place of residence was Jerusalem. About half of these were Jewish, some 30 percent were Muslim, and about 20 percent were Christian. The numerical ratio was, of course, very important, but no less important was the categorization of the families according to religious and ethnic community. The Ottoman census was carried out not only to obtain statistics, but also to define the personal status of Jerusalem's inhabitants for various administrative purposes, including the issuing of the Ottoman identity document called the *Nafus*. Therefore, the recording of ethnic affiliation was an indication that the authorities recognized these communities as independent and as having authority over internal religious matters. The multiplicity of communities listed on the *Nafus* gave an accurate picture of the diversity of Jerusalem's population.

The Jewish community was subdivided into Ashkenazim, Mughrabis (North Africans), Sephardim, Yemenites, Kurds, and Georgians, as well as former residents of Allepo, Urfa, and other cities, who were included in the Sephardic community. The Muslim community was divided into "locals" (i.e., natives of Jerusalem), Blacks (i.e., those of African origin), Gypsies, Mughrabis and, for some reason, Copts (Egyptian Christians). The Christian community was divided along denominational lines: Armenian Orthodox, Armenian Catholics, Greek Orthodox, Greek Catholics, Protestants, Roman Catholics ("Latins"), Maronites, Russian Orthodox, Chaldeans, and Assyrians (Syrian Orthodox). The census also enumerated foreign nationals, including Germans, Americans, Greeks, Turks, Uzbekis, Afghans, French, and many others.

Ottoman records reveal the extreme degree of communal segregation characteristic of Jerusalem, including residential segregation. Most of the Jews lived in the Jewish Quarter of the Old City, and the overwhelming majority of the city's residents who dwelt outside the walls were Jews. The Christians were concentrated in the Christian and Armenian quarters, and the Muslims in the remaining parts of the Old City. Only 10 percent of the "new" city's residents were Muslim.

The compulsive recording of the ethnic and residential fragmentation of the city's population has not been confined to the distant past. In 1939, the Jewish Agency carried out a survey and census of the residents of Jerusalem in which the affiliation of the members of the Jewish community was broken down as follows: 38,256 Ashkenazim, 10,067 Sephardim, 3,632 Yemenites, 2,419 Mughrabis, 1,727 Aleppans, 209 other Syrians, 3,730 Babylonians (Iraqis), 1,473 Urfalis, 4,289 Kurds, 5,556 Persians (Iranians), 1,092 Bucharans, 547 Afghans, 60 Indians, 998 Georgians, and 19 Karaites.

In the 1960s, a classification was made of the Jewish neighborhoods of Jerusalem according to the ethnicity of their residents. Nine of them had a clear majority of Jews of European origin, in nine most of the residents were of Oriental (i.e., Sephardic and other non-European) background, and in only six neighborhoods was there a mixed Jewish population. And the residential segregation within Jerusalem's Jewish population was nothing in comparison to that between the Jewish and

11. Mea She'arim neighborhood

Muslim populations. According to a survey carried out by the British authorities on the eve of the 1948 war, only four Jerusalem neighborhoods were mixed, and even then, each had a majority of one group or the other large enough to determine the Jewish or Arab ethnic character of the neighborhood. According to the same survey, 88 percent of the Jews and 90 percent of the Arabs (both Muslims and Christians) lived in ethnically homogeneous neighborhoods. The 1948 war resulted in absolute Arab-Jewish separation. Thereafter, all of the Jews (plus an insignificant number of non-Jews) lived in West Jerusalem, whereas all of the Arabs—Muslim and Christian alike—lived in the eastern part of the city.

The straightforward division of Jerusalem's urban expanse, with the Jews in the west and the Arabs in the east, was altered in the wake of the Six-Day War by the construction of large Jewish neighborhoods in East Jerusalem. But the pattern of segregation changed not at all. Although many Jews have settled in sections of East Jerusalem, these neighborhoods are inhabited exclusively by Jews and, despite their location, have no contact or interaction with the adjacent Arab neighborhoods. This spatial polarization is accompanied by socioeconomic polarization. The differences between the Jewish and Arab populations in terms of all of the parameters relevant to urban, economic, and societal analysis are huge. They are so great that any general statistics or average figures for economic level, poverty and dependency ratio (i.e., ratio of dependent children and elderly persons to breadwinners), education and services, population density, house size, infant mortality, or employment for the city as a whole are meaningless. The customary comparison between Jerusalem and other cities in Israel, which appears in all official statistical reports, not only uses facts that are not equivalent, but is misleading, and deliberately so. For example, a table comparing the extent of poverty in Jerusalem with that in other large cities in Israel (and with the national average), states that the proportion of the Jerusalem population defined as "poor" (i.e., those living below the poverty line) is more than double that in Haifa or Tel Aviv. Close to 40 percent of the children in Jerusalem live in poverty, as opposed to 15 percent in Tel Aviv and Haifa. However, these figures do not differentiate between Jews and Arabs. If the percentage of non-Jews below the poverty line were reported, the fact that poverty is three times more prevalent among Arabs in Jerusalem than in the Jewish community would be revealed.

In light of the extreme differences between the Jewish and Arab ethnic groups, one must regard general statistics on Jerusalem as a political statement rather than a reliable measure of the pertinent parameters that can stand up to analysis, since statistics can be mobilized in support of certain political positions. The utilization of numbers, which are by nature "objective," lends credibility—ostensibly scientific—to data that are actually shaped by the values held by those publishing them, and these value-laden data are in turn used to provide confirmation and backing for politically-dictated positions.

The Israelis, cognizant of the importance of statistics and proficient at manipulating them, invest a lot of effort in their publication; and the fact that it is they who are in control and who have access to scientific institutes with great stores of experience and expertise forces Israel's political opponents to rely on the statistical data they provide. Few realize that the tendentious statistics with which they are furnished are actually derived from large quantities of objective raw data, which they, if they so desired, could employ in presenting a less biased picture. But Israel's opponents, too, are interested only in statistics that support their positions. Thus, statistics, especially demographic statistics, serve as ammunition for the ultimate argument in the debate over Jerusalem. After all the emotional, religious, and historical arguments are exhausted, the demographic assertions are trotted out. "We are now and always have been the majority in Jerusalem, and therefore Jerusalem belongs to us," say the Jews. "You achieved this majority only because you flooded Jerusalem with illegal immigrants, expelled the Arabs, and manipulated the city's boundaries," say the Arabs.

Indeed, the debate over the demographic balance between Jews and Arabs in Jerusalem began eighty years ago and has gone on ever since with undiminished intensity. Pro-Israeli sources state with satisfaction that there has been a clear majority of Jews in Jerusalem since the beginning of the twentieth century, and perhaps even earlier. Pro-Arab sources discount this view and express doubts concerning the reliability of the statistical data. But their principal argument has to do, of course, with the definition of Jerusalem's boundaries, which arbitrarily created this Jewish majority. If certain nearby areas were included within the city's boundaries, claim the Arabs, the Jewish majority would become a minority. It is hard for them to blame the Ottomans for arbitrarily defining Jerusalem's boundaries, but they do not hesitate to assert that the British purposely created the impression of a Jewish majority by artificial means.

There was a Jewish majority in Jerusalem before the beginning of the British Mandate, which continued to grow throughout that period, reaching 55 percent in 1922 and 60 percent in 1946. "A more generous drawing of boundaries," according to Palestinian scholars, "would have created a more balanced picture, which is something that the British government did not want. The deliberate exclusion of the Arab communities on Jerusalem's periphery from the reckoning inflated the relative size of Jewish population figures—and this policy must be examined in the light of Britain's commitment to its 'Jewish National Home' policy." Examination of the data, however, proves this to be an empty claim. Even had the Arab villages been incorporated into Jerusalem, the Jews would have remained a majority, albeit by a slightly smaller margin. In any case these villages were not interested in being part of Jerusalem just for the sake of bolstering the Arab political-statistical argument.

Claims that boundaries were being drawn with the objective of improving the city's demography from the Israeli point of view had a firm basis, though, following the 1967 war. The boundaries fixed by Israel were drafted explicitly so as to ensure that the proportion of Arabs in the population would not exceed 28 percent, and maintenance of this ratio (i.e., 28:72) was defined as an Israeli demographic goal. In reality, the proportion of Jews fell from 74.2 percent in 1967 to 71.7 percent at the end of 1993 (in 1993 the population of Jerusalem was 570,000, of which 161,000 were Arab). This small decrease was achieved only with great difficulty; the government invested enormous sums in the construction of apartments in the Jewish neighborhoods of East Jerusalem and in subsidies to purchasers. The large-scale immigration from the former Soviet Union, upon which many had pinned their hopes, did contribute somewhat to the growth of the Jewish population, but on the whole not many of the new arrivals were attracted to Jerusalem. Meanwhile, the Arab population of the city had tripled since 1967, thanks to migration from the immediate vicinity and especially to a very high rate of natural increase. The crude birth rate of the Arab population in 1993 was 35.4 births per thousand, compared to 26.3 per thousand in the Jewish population (a rate far higher than the Jewish-Israeli national average, as an outcome of the extremely high birth rate of the *Haredi* [ultra-orthodox] population). As a result, the Arab population was very young: over half were less than eighteen years of age.

According to official predictions (based on optimistic assumptions regarding Jewish migration to Jerusalem), by the year 2010, Jerusalem will have a population of 800,000, approximately one-third of which—or about a quarter million people—will be Arab. These figures paint a picture that is comfortable for the Israelis, and relate only to the territory within the artificial boundaries fixed in 1967. In the metropolitan area surrounding Jerusalem, however, the Arab population is growing at a tremendous rate, and, as previously mentioned, demographic parity between Jews and Arabs is already a fact in this region (including Jerusalem). The Arabs will soon have a numerical majority because of their high birth rate.

Except that, as already noted, statistical analyses are political statements. Complete data with a population breakdown for Jerusalem including its metropolitan area do not appear in official publications, and anyone attempting to calculate them will encounter many difficulties. Israeli officialdom hides behind the claim that Jerusalem is part of the State of Israel, and its statistics are for that reason included in the Israeli data, whereas the metropolitan area outside the boundaries of what was annexed in 1967 are under "a different authority." The

Palestinians, for their part, do not recognize the annexation of East Jerusalem and, in calculating the city's population, they subtract the 180,000 Jewish residents of the neighborhoods that were established on their side of the armistice line.

Thus, each side can interpret selectively chosen data to suit its political and propaganda requirements. Nor are the interpretations always consistent. Sometimes the Israelis present the virtually undiminished Jewish majority as evidence of the success of their unceasing efforts to reinforce the city's status as "unified Jerusalem, the capital of the Jewish people," and sometimes they represent the same figures as signaling the danger of the imminent loss of this majority. The Palestinians sometimes interpret the data as evidence of their success in preserving the Arab character of Jerusalem—despite immense efforts on the part of the Israelis, the demographic balance in the city has hardly changed at all, and that little was in the Arabs' favor—and sometimes they present the same figures as proof of "the Judaization of Jerusalem," a dangerous process against which the "Arab world" must rally its forces. In any case the choice of data and their interpretation depend on the political and ethnic perspective of the observer, and shed less light on the prevailing reality of Jerusalem than on the polarization of the city.

It appears that the difficulty in arriving at reliable and objective socioeconomic data regarding Jerusalem stems from the fact that official statistics treat the city as a single geographic, social, and economic unit, whereas in actuality it is a city so divided that characterizing it as unified is in itself a political, economic, and social fiction. True, there no longer are impassable physical barriers between Jewish and Arab neighborhoods, and there is some interaction between the two ethnic groups. But one may nevertheless define the most obvious characteristics of the city thus: Two distinct societies live within its bounds, each of which has its own "normal" system of social stratification and cultural cohesion. These two "normal" societies, living in close proximity to each other, have a very "abnormal" set of mutual relations. The existence of the neighboring society is perceived by each as a threat, and thus the level of ethnic exclusivity as well as the degree of alienation from the other group is increased.

There is an additional dimension to this ethnic polarization. These "normal" societies, which have found themselves living side-by-side, do not have equal political or socioeconomic status. All of their interrelationships are influenced by the fact that one of them enjoys higher status in terms of every socioeconomic indicator, to such a degree that there is a clear correlation between ethnic affiliation and class. The depth of this polarization obliges the person seeking an understanding of the social reality of Jerusalem to study the Jewish and Arab societies separately, and only then to attempt to understand the connections between them.

On the eve of the Six-Day War, West Jerusalem had a population of 200,000, all Jews. A population whose composition already had been quite heterogeneous (as shown by the 1939 census) had become a mix of immigrants from some 100 countries. These immigrants came in several waves, but most arrived between 1948 and 1951, during which time some 50,000 settled in Jerusalem, increasing the city's population by 65 percent in the course of only three years. Statisticians lost no time in cataloguing the newcomers according to their continent of origin: Asia and Africa (replacing the category "Sephardim"), Europe and the Americas (replacing "Ashkenazim"). Then, of course, there were "the native-born." This last group made up approximately half the city's population, and was extraordinary in that one third were third generation Jerusalemites. This was three times as high as in the rest of the country (17 percent of the city's overall population as opposed to 6 percent in other population centers), a result of the fact that Jerusalem had had a sizable Jewish population for much longer than had the other towns and cities.

A quarter of Jerusalem's (Jewish) 1967 residents were born in Asian and African countries and a similar number came from the West. However, if the parents of the native-born Jerusalemites are included, the proportion of Sephardim reaches 45 percent. By 1980 this figure had risen to an estimated 60 percent of the total Jewish population. Until the mid-seventies there was a noticeable socioeconomic gap between the Sephardi and Ashkenazi populations of Jerusalem, which was reflected in all the relevant indicators: income, residential density, educational level, illiteracy, employment. The genuine hardship and the sense of deprivation that pervaded the "Oriental" community led to outbreaks of violence organized by radical protest groups like the Black Panthers. These groups focused not only on their own economic adversity, but also on the arrogant Ashkenazi establishment, whose leaders frequently offended the honor of the Orientals and denigrated their cultural heritage.

In the Orientals' feeling of impoverishment there was clearly a component of "relative deprivation"—that is, a sense of the gap between their expectations and their ability to realize them. There are and always have been pockets of extreme poverty in Jerusalem. On the other hand, the city contains some of the richest, most prestigious neighborhoods in the country. But the gap between those in the highest and lowest positions on the socioeconomic scale is smaller there than in the country's other large cities. This is the result of the peculiar pattern of employment in Jerusalem. Approximately half of the city's Jewish breadwinners are employed in the public services, working for the government or for national, religious, educational, or cultural institutions. This is more than double the percentage of similarly employed people in Tel Aviv and reflects Jerusalem's status as Israel's capital. In contrast to this substantial population of clerks and officials, the percentage of Jerusalemites employed in business and finance is less than half that of Tel Aviv; Jerusalem's standing as a commercial and financial center is markedly inferior. The prevalence of a relatively narrow range of income in the public sector influences Jerusalem's economy and has shaped its citizens' relatively modest lifestyle.

Government efforts to expand "productive activity," (i.e., manufacturing and commerce) in Jerusalem have not gone well. Even though productivity has increased, the number of Jews employed in industry and as craftspeople has declined. These characteristics have not changed significantly since 1970, nonetheless there has been a substantial decrease in the magnitude of the socioeconomic gap between "Orientals" and "Westerners" and in the sense of relative deprivation experienced by the former. Many native-born Israelis of Oriental extraction have escaped the cycle of poverty and hardship and have become financially successful. One important indicator of this phenomenon has been the exodus of tens of thousands of people from the old, poor neighborhoods of the inner city and from miserable immigrant housing projects to the newer neighborhoods across the armistice line. The sense of relative deprivation has also diminished because in the wake of the political upheaval that brought the Likud to power in 1977 (an upheaval explained in part as a clear-cut expression of rage against the Ashkenazi establishment), the way was opened for the Orientals' integration into the government bureaucracy. Although pockets of poverty remain, and politicians have not ceased using ethnic sensibilities as a means of recruiting supporters, hardship is no longer the exclusive lot of the Orientals. They have been joined by a myriad of new immigrants, including Ashkenazim from the former Soviet Union.

By 1994, native-born Israelis made up two-thirds of the population of Jerusalem; immigrants from Asia and Africa constituted 11 percent and from Europe and North and South America 23 percent. The intercommunal tension that had characterized relations within the city's Jewish community since the middle of the nineteenth century gave way to tension of another sort—between the secular and ultra-orthodox factions. As residential segregation along ethnic lines became less clearly defined, segregation dictated by lifestyle—between groups of people following a closed, traditional way of life, as close as possible to the one they had led in the shtetl of the diaspora, and those leading a modern, western-style life—became increasingly common.

The chasm dividing secular and ultra-orthodox Jews is supposedly not an ethnic one, since neither of the two groups identifies itself as a separate ethnic unit. An ethnic unit is a group of people that perceives itself as culturally and socially unique on the basis of real or imagined kinship ties. The ultra-orthodox do indeed regard themselves as culturally and socially unique, however this uniqueness is not based on kinship, and therefore they welcome any Jew who wishes to join them, provided he or she is willing to observe the religious commandments and behave as directed by the leaders of the sect. Nevertheless, the split between this group and the secular community has an ethnic quality about it to a far greater degree than does that between Oriental and Western Jews, even though the latter is ostensibly inborn.

The residential self-segregation of ultra-orthodox Jews is a permanent feature of Jerusalem. When the ultra-orthodox (who were called the "old 'Yishuv'") emerged from the Old City around the turn of the century, they built themselves separate neighborhoods in the north of the city. From their "fortress" (the Mea She'arim neighborhood), they went forth and conquered a wide area in the northern end of the city, where Haredi homes and religious institutions were concentrated around major intersections and along main streets, from which they spread into surrounding areas. Their rate of natural increase, twice that of the non-orthodox community, along with the large number of ultra-orthodox immigrants, has led to an increasingly insatiable demand for housing. Once the solidly ultra-orthodox section in the northern part of Jerusalem filled up, gigantic neighborhoods were established much farther from the city center, with the activity of ultra-orthodox real estate entrepreneurs extending deep into the West Bank. In the five years between 1990 and 1995, the ultra-orthodox population of Jerusalem grew from 110,000 to 130,000, at which point they made up 31 percent of the Jewish population. By 2010 they are expected to reach 40 percent.

The survival of the ultra-orthodox as a unique population group is conditional on their voluntary segregation in residential "ghettos." In this they differ significantly from the "modern orthodox." The latter do not close themselves off in ghettos—they are not fearful of contact with secular culture and do not need to protect themselves from it in this way. Many of them live by choice in well-to-do mixed neighborhoods, exhibiting openness to modern culture and pursuing a way of life more similar to that of their secular neighbors than to that of the ultra-orthodox (while, of course, observing the religious commandments). The ultra-orthodox, by contrast, regard the secular city as a threat to their very existence as a "holy community" and to their most fundamental values. They have therefore created a protected space, where they are guaranteed the fulfillment of the most basic needs of any ethnic or cultural minority: protection from external threat and a secure place where the group's identity is guarded from alien influences and where contact with the external world is minimized. This voluntary ghetto also serves as a base for the community's struggles with other groups and as a sheltered environment where an ultra-orthodox person can feel comfortable and unthreatened by an alien and sometimes hostile world. It is also a defined space, which makes possible an optimal degree of control by the leaders of the community and facilitates its mobilization for political and religious battles.

The Haredi community's internal life, its composition and organizations, and political activity within the ghettos are not of interest to us here, aside from the fact that the ultra-orthodox community is composed of both Ashkenazim and Oriental Jews who have paradoxically adopted the way of life of the eastern European diaspora, including the mode of dress. This is additional evidence that the Haredim are a heterogeneous group behaving as if it were ethnically homogeneous.

The relationship of the ultra-orthodox to the external, secular world is dualistic. On the one hand, they reject the secular political system because it is not based on the principles of Jewish religious law (halacha). Their absolutist principles should also oblige them to repudiate the government, to refrain from influencing it, and to forgo the favors it bestows on its political supporters. This is, in fact, the approach of the most extreme members of the community. But they belong to a small, if vociferous and aggressive, faction. Most ultra-orthodox community leaders are well aware that without their participation in the never-ending haggling over public resources that goes on in the political arena, the interests of the ultra-orthodox community as a whole and of each and every one of its individual members would be seriously compromised.

Thus, paradoxically, the ability to pursue and preserve the Haredi way of life is conditional on being actively involved in the political and public life of the secular community. Without this involvement, they would not be assured of continued control of their physical space, of receiving a hefty slice of the welfare and education budgets, which are vitally important to them, or of safeguarding their cherished religious practices, such as strict observance of the Sabbath and of special dietary requirements.

The compromise between absolute principles and everyday needs is achieved, first of all, by minimizing the Haredi population's exposure to alien influences by ensuring that their ghettos function as homogeneous, self-sufficient units, while at the same time carrying out the massive mobilization of the community during municipal and general elections. Haredi candidates are determined by the community's Ashkenazi and Sephardi rabbinical authorities (called the Council of Torah Greats and the Council of Torah Wise Men, respectively). The primary (or perhaps sole) concern of representatives of the Haredim on the municipal council and in the Knesset is to procure the biggest possible slice of the public pie while foiling any attempts to interfere with the pursuit of their segregated way of life. Their involvement in government is in general limited. They have no desire to take it over, and they leave to others the responsibility of reconciling the conflicting interests of the various sectors of the urban and national communities. They will support candidates from the Right or the Left, depending on the cold calculation of who will give them the greatest return for their effort. This opportunistic approach has caused many in the secular community to view them as a bunch of power brokers whose sole objective is to rob the public purse and impose their religious practices on the general population.

The appetite of the Haredim has kept pace with their increasing numbers. In the 1993 Jerusalem municipal elections, their monolithic vote decided the contest between the incumbent mayor, Teddy Kollek, and Ehud Olmert. Haredi voter turnout approached 90 percent (compared to less than 50 percent in the secular community), and the 43,000 Haredi voters (over one third of the total turnout) voted as a bloc for the right-wing candidate. The newly-elected mayor, totally beholden to the ultra-orthodox for his victory, handed them key portfolios that enabled them to bite off huge chunks of the public pie, to impose what they call "prevention of desecration of the Sabbath" in large areas of the city, and to obtain additional land for the construction of Haredi neighborhoods.

Tension between secular and ultra-orthodox Jews intensified, and this was reflected not only in violent verbal and sometimes physical confrontations, but also in the growing exodus of young secular Jews from the capital because the Haredim are "suffocating" them. People concerned for Jerusalem's future as a secular, modern, open city point to official forecasts indicating that the secular public will soon be a minority in the city. According to these forecasts, by the year 2010 there will be approximately 550,000 Jews living within Jerusalem's current boundaries, of whom some 270,000 will be secular, 210,000 Haredim, and 70,000 modern orthodox. In addition, there will be 250,000 Arabs living in the city by then.

Secular Jews are worried about the effects of intra-Jewish tension on their way of life, but despite all this tension, the Jewish community functions as a "normal society," the authority of whose institutions is generally respected and whose internal conflicts are reasonably well handled through political channels. The sense of Jewish communal and national unity is strong and is not likely to weaken because of the close and palpable presence of "the others"—the Palestinian Arab community with whom the Jews share the urban space. The differences that divide secular and ultra-orthodox Jews cannot even be compared to the yawning chasm separating the Jewish and Arab collectives, although secular proponents of peace and the "brotherhood of nations" would be appalled at this idea. In their opinion, the ultra-orthodox threaten their way of life far more than do the Arabs, whose only desire is to be free of the Israeli occupation. That is, until the blast of police sirens is heard in the city, or the radio reports some act of political violence in which a Palestinian harms an Israeli. Then the inherent ethnic polarization becomes more acute and the "abnormal" mutual relationship between the two peoples is exposed.

Up to and including the year 1994, residents of Israel (and of Jerusalem) were designated as members of one of two categories in official publications, Jews and non-Jews. This negative designation of anyone who did not belong to the majority was sometimes criticized as being politically colored, or perhaps even tainted with a hint of racism—as if one who was not a Jew lacked an identity. These objections were not given serious consideration in light of the difficulties created by any other method of categorization. Only in the case of the Jews were religion and nationality identical, whereas the Arab people included both Christians and Muslims. And designation according to citizenship would be complicated because on the one hand, there are "Israeli Arabs," while on the other, most Palestinian residents of East Jerusalem are Jordanian citizens.

Even classification according to religion would not preclude accusations of political bias. The Arabs of Jerusalem have always accused the Jews of choosing this way of categorizing in order to separate Muslims and Christians and to thereby artificially create a Jewish majority. And although it is true that most of the Christians living in Jerusalem are Arabic-speaking and regard themselves as belonging to the Palestinian Arab people, not all of them are. Some 2,000 Armenians should be deducted from that total, as well as several hundred foreign nationals. Matters have been further complicated in recent years in the wake of the arrival of large numbers of mixed Jewish-Christian families among the immigrants from the former Soviet Union. These Christians are also included in the general enumeration of members of that religion.

In the year 1995, Israel changed the method of classification, and now non-Jews are classified as "Arabs and Others." In the past, this classification would have caused difficulties in the statistical analysis of the characteristics of the Arab population of Jerusalem, since it would have lumped together two groups that differed in their socioeconomic characteristics—the Muslims and the Christians—and combining them could have distorted the data. However, the dramatic thinning-out of the Christian community has given the Muslims an overwhelming majority in Jerusalem. Suffice it to say that in 1922, the number of Christians in Jerusalem was greater than the number of Muslims, and even toward the close of the Mandatory period they made up close to 40 percent of the city's Arabic speakers. In the wake of the 1948 war, their numbers decreased to 16 percent. A similar proportion was reported following the commencement of the Israeli occupation. By the early 1990s, the Christian presence had fallen to less than 8 percent of the Arab population (and 2.5 percent of the total population of the city). The Arab part of Jerusalem is, then, practically homogeneous from an ethno-religious point of view, but this does not mean that the Muslim Arab community is all of a piece. It is, of course, impossible to compare this indigenous population with the immigrant community of the Jews, but even so, the differences within the Muslim community are rather great, reflecting the stormy history of Jerusalem over the past hundred years.

In the Ottoman census referred to earlier, the overwhelming majority of the members of the Muslim community were designated as "locals." The remainder were a small number of Muslim pilgrims who had settled in Jerusalem and members of exotic groups such as Gypsies and black African slaves that had been freed. The indigenous community, called in Arabic *Maqadsse*, included families who had settled in Jerusalem at the time of the first Arab conquest (638) and others who had come with Salah-al-Din (Saladin) in 1187, but most of the Muslim population (about 4,500 souls at the beginning of the nineteenth century and 11,000 at its end) had come from villages in the vicinity.

Several large families with close ties to the Ottoman regime, and others, members of the Muslim religious-legal establishment, capitalized on the political and societal changes that were taking place in the Ottoman Empire in the mid-nineteenth century, amassing considerable economic assets as well as religious and political power. Some parlayed their positions as tax collectors to gain control of vast tracts of land, while others used the leverage conferred on them by religious posts in the Holy City to accrue political power, on the municipal level as well as within the Ottoman imperial establishment itself.

Little by little, a local aristocracy took shape in Jerusalem, whose might was greater, even, than that of the Turkish governors. The influence of the *qadis* (Muslim religious judges) was far-reaching, since throughout most of the Ottoman period, civil cases involving non-Muslims were heard by Muslim courts according to *sharia* (Muslim law). The directors of the *Waqf* (Muslim religious endowment), too, became quite powerful, as did those in charge of the Temple Mount mosques. The wealth accumulated by members of these prominent families enabled them to send their sons abroad to obtain higher education or to become entrepreneurs—whose chances of success increased considerably during the last half of the nineteenth century, with the opening of Jerusalem to western influence and the city's consequent rapid development.

Contention was fierce among these prominent families, and the curse of divisiveness and cutthroat competition eventually brought an end to their hegemony. The wealth of the few stood in sharp contrast to the poverty and miserable conditions in which most members of the Muslim community lived, and this wide gap between the strata of Muslim society in Jerusalem remains one of its conspicuous characteristics to this day.

The economic opportunities that opened up toward the close of the nineteenth century attracted large numbers of migrants from the villages in the vicinity, especially from the Hebron highlands. The flow of Hebronites to Jerusalem increased during the 1920s and 30s, and they became a very important component of the city's population. Longtime Jerusalem residents had a disdainful and arrogant attitude toward the *Khalyleh*, as Hebronites are called (from the Arabic for Hebron, *al-*

Khalil (the friend), after "Abraham, the friend of God"). They could not, however, ignore the newcomers' positive traits: diligence, skillfulness, frugality, business acumen, deep commitment to religion, and loyalty to their families and their leaders. These traits helped the Hebronites prosper in their adopted city.

The conquest of Jerusalem by the British did not put an end to the dominance of the city's well-connected families. On the contrary, their power increased because the regime needed them and the political power they wielded as leaders of the Palestinian national movement. There was also a cultural aspect to the Britons' wooing of these Jerusalem families. A number of top people in the British administration and in the military found they had a great deal in common with some of the heads of the leading families, whose lifestyle and manner appealed to them far more than did those of the ideologically-driven Zionist leaders with their Eastern European aggressivity. British efforts to cultivate the aristocratic families did not fare well, however, and a number of the latter, in fact, stood at the forefront of the violent anti-British struggle. In the end, the authorities were forced to crack down on them and to exile many of their leaders from the country.

But ultimately, the decline and fall of the families came not as the result of persecution by foreign occupiers, but as the outcome of a combination of two other factors: the challenge placed before them by the Zionists and their alienation from the common people. On the one hand, they incited the masses against the British and the Zionists, but on the other, they regarded them essentially as contemptible rabble whom they could manipulate as they wished. Thus, when it became truly necessary to rally the entire community to their cause, they were unable to depend on any solid popular support. They were also incapable of comprehending the essential nature of the power embodied in the Zionist enterprise, its "plebeian" pioneering ethos, and its preoccupation with building one house and then another.

When the aroused masses forced their leaders into a life-and-death struggle with the Jews and the moment of truth arrived, long-standing

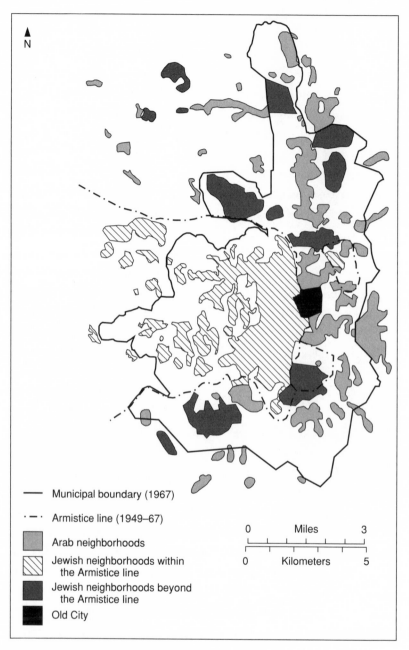

N

Municipal boundary (1967)

Armistice line (1949–67)

Arab neighborhoods

Jewish neighborhoods within
the Armistice line

Jewish neighborhoods beyond
the Armistice line

Old City

| 0 | Miles | 3 |

| 0 | Kilometers | 5 |

MAP 4.   Arab and Jewish neighborhoods of Jerusalem, 1991

antagonisms surfaced, and all were engulfed by an ocean of blood—most of it the result of cruel intergroup fighting among the Arabs themselves (1937–39). In the 1947–48 war, the Arabs of Jerusalem paid the ultimate price. The Arab community was incapable of standing up to full-scale warfare, and had the Bedouins from Transjordan not rescued the survivors, Arab Jerusalem would have been totally destroyed. The first to flee in terror from the war were the members of the city's leading families, and many of those who remained were persecuted by the Jordanian regime, which regarded some of their number as a political threat.

The 1948–49 war was a traumatic blow for Jerusalem's Arab community. Some 28,000 refugees from parts of the country conquered by Israel crowded into East Jerusalem, and within three years about half of the city's post-1948 Arab population had left. In 1952 the population of the Arab section of Jerusalem was approximately 45,000, of which a very high proportion were recent immigrants from Hebron who joined the veteran Hebron migrant community. During the nineteen years of Jordanian rule, the Arab population of Jerusalem grew more slowly than might have been anticipated from its birthrate. The main reason for this was the continuing exodus from the city, particularly to the capital city of Amman, where the Hashemite kingdom's economic development efforts were focused. On the eve of the 1967 war, about 30 percent of Arab households in Jerusalem had at least one child living outside of Palestine. This number, of course, does not include the many whole families that pulled up stakes and left the city.

These extreme oscillations in population number, and especially the departure of so many of the city's more prosperous and educated residents, Christian and Muslim alike, led to far-reaching changes in its social fabric. The absolute control exercised by the highest social strata crumbled as the concentration of economic and religious power slipped from their hands. As a result, the prevailing hierarchical social system was undermined, leading to greatly increased mobility. No longer was membership in a well-connected family synonymous with high socio-economic class, education, and political power. Members of ordinary families and migrants from the villages amassed considerable wealth, which brought with it political influence. Higher education reached even formerly illiterate families. Above all, a new political elite emerged and was cultivated by the Hashemite regime.

Despite the increase in social mobility, Arab society was still based on definite and rigid stratification and privilege acquired through wealth or in return for political services rendered to the regime. The structure of the extended family also remained intact. Seeking election to the municipal council or, especially, to the Jordanian Parliament was, even more than a way of obtaining political influence, a means of reaching a position of status from which access to the patronage of the regime was conveniently accessible.

The Hashemites suppressed every aspect of Jerusalem's economic life, and this had a devastating effect on the Arab community and on its demographic and economic development. But there was one field of endeavor that the Jordanians were unable to harm: tourism to the Holy City. This was something that could flourish only in Jerusalem, and indeed, the development of tourism was what kept the Arab economy going. However, because of the sensitivity of this sector of the economy to political tensions, and the resulting security concerns, the city's economy rested on a very unstable base. Every tense situation that brought about a reduction in the flow of tourists would cause an economic crisis, and there was no shortage of tension between 1949 and 1967. One indication of the shaky economic situation was the fact that twelve thousand persons with refugee status (dating from the 1948 war) were supported by international welfare organizations throughout that period, and 28 percent of households received assistance from relatives who worked abroad. Approximately one-third of the population was part of the workforce, of whom only 15.7 percent were engaged in commerce, as compared to 33 percent in the service industries, primarily tourism.

A comparison of standard-of-living indicators in the divided city on the eve of the 1967 war is enlightening. The average number of persons per room in East Jerusalem was 2.4, compared to 1.6 in West Jerusalem.

Approximately 60 percent of East Jerusalem dwellings lacked running water and about 30 percent had no electricity, whereas in West Jerusalem water and electricity were universal. Seventy-seven percent of families in West Jerusalem had electric refrigerators, compared to 22 percent in East Jerusalem. In West Jerusalem, 30 percent of an average family's expenditures went for groceries compared to 50 percent in East Jerusalem, and for durable items, fourteen percent as opposed to five. The large disparities in spending on groceries and durable items are clear signs of the great difference in standard of living. And indeed, just preceding the 1967 war, the average annual per capita income in Israeli West Jerusalem was four times that of East Jerusalem, East Jerusalem's illiteracy rate was two-and-a-half times that of the Jewish section of the city, and the percentage of Arab university graduates was one-fifth of that in the Jewish population.

The political and psychological consequences of the Israeli conquest of East Jerusalem were more severe than those of the 1948–49 war; however, its demographic and economic effects were less so, and in some senses were even positive. Although around one-fifth of the city's Arab population fled the city immediately before and during the Six-Day War, most returned home within a few weeks of its end. And in fact, the Israeli occupation ushered in a period of unprecedented Arab demographic expansion: the number of Arab residents of East Jerusalem doubled in the course of nineteen years, reaching 136,000 in 1987. During the nineteen years of Jordanian rule, by comparison, the population grew by only 50 percent. In contrast to the Jordanian period, when the number of migrants leaving the city was equal to half the community's natural increase, with the Israeli conquest not only had the out-migration ceased almost entirely, but the in-migration from adjacent areas had increased as well. The growth of the Arab population under Israeli occupation would seem even more impressive were we to add to the official statistics—which include only those parts of Jerusalem annexed to Israel—the rapid growth that took place in the areas just outside the city's municipal boundaries.

There were two principal factors behind this sizable demographic expansion: employment opportunities and Israel's extension (in a limited manner) of its welfare state system to the annexed territory. This enabled the Arabs, paradoxically, to enjoy the fruits of the Israeli government's efforts to entrench the "Jewishness" of Jerusalem, and to take advantage of its massive investment in building Jewish suburbs to strengthen their own grip on the city. For years massive government budgets went into the construction of tens of thousands of housing units and of the physical infrastructure serving them, and most of the workers in the building trades were Arabs. Moreover, the government's ambition to prove that Israeli law and administration applied to East Jerusalem meant that all its Arab residents were covered by Israeli welfare provisions; notably, they were eligible for inclusion in the National Insurance system. Although their coverage was limited in comparison to that enjoyed by Jews, what they did receive was sufficient to make the Israeli identity card a coveted document whose loss they were unwilling to risk. Thus, when the Arabs of East Jerusalem were called upon to register to vote in the elections for the Palestinian National Authority, many refused out of fear that by so doing they would forfeit their right of residency in Jerusalem.

The social welfare benefits offered by the Israeli regime were important, but even more important was the openness of the Israeli marketplace to the employment of Arabs, which was linked to the desire to prove that the annexation of East Jerusalem was beneficial to the Arab population. And indeed, the flow of Arab laborers from East Jerusalem into West Jerusalem began immediately after the annexation and soon involved just under half the city's Arab workforce (the other half being employed in the Arab sector). Workers holding Jerusalem identity cards were joined by thousands from the occupied territories adjacent to Jerusalem. Together they numbered—in peak years—some 20,000, or more than 15 percent of the total workforce in West Jerusalem, and were employed in a variety of sectors. About 40 percent were employed in blue collar occupations in the construction and other industries, while some 20 percent held unskilled and semiskilled positions in the services. Over the years, many Arab workers earned tenure and social benefits, but the essential picture remained unchanged: Arab workers populated the lowest rungs of the employment ladder, working in low-paying, low-prestige fields.

The employment of so many Arab family heads in the Jewish economic sector had far-reaching implications for Arab society. On the one hand, their standard of living rose as a result of the higher wages customary in the Jewish community, but on the other hand, what was taking place was the proletarization of the Arab population. Those at the bottom of the socioeconomic pyramid doubled or even tripled their income in real terms, compared to only a modest rise in the income of the members of the Arab middle class employed in the East Jerusalem economic sector. But the competition between the two economies was on unequal terms; rather than continuing to develop, the Arab economy began to concentrate on industries that supplemented the Israeli economy and served a subcontractor function.

By the mid-seventies the real per capita income in East Jerusalem had doubled, and it continued to rise until 1987, but the feeling of deprivation increased as well. The Arabs of East Jerusalem stopped comparing their situation at that time with what it had been prior to the Israeli occupation, and began contrasting it with that of their Jewish neighbors; what is more, the economic circumstances of their relatives in Amman had also improved more than had theirs. Indeed, the economic gap between the two halves of Jerusalem grew greater and greater. All of the socioeconomic indicators showed a clear correlation between economic condition and ethnicity. The political dominance of the Jewish community was reproduced in the economic sphere, imposing an inferior social and economic status on the Arab community. Thus, political polarization, ethnic alienation, and residential segregation were accompanied by socioeconomic polarization.

Many Israelis believed that improvement of the economic circumstances of the Arabs was the key to peaceful coexistence in Jerusalem.

They were convinced that people who enjoyed a high standard of living would tend not to rebel against foreign rule, and that the economic advantages brought about by the unification of Jerusalem would persuade the Arabs that continued Israeli rule was in their interest. In other words, they emphasized the importance of the continued economic and social progress of the Arabs simply because they saw this as compatible with their desire to retain exclusive political control. These Israelis not only made a serious miscalculation (or were deluding themselves), but also neglected to further the realization of even this materialistic vision, and so Jerusalem remained a classic example of a city where ethnic and class divisions go hand-in-hand.

The economic realm can serve as a point of departure for an examination of the interaction between Jerusalem's two vastly disparate societies because economic ties and worker-employer relations require their members to have direct daily contact. Every day thousands of Arab workers cross the invisible but very real dividing line between the two parts of the city, and scatter to their jobs in the industrial parks, hotels, hospitals, and construction sites. Movement of Jewish workers from West to East Jerusalem is limited to officials and office workers employed by Israeli institutions that deal with the Arab population (banks, the post office, healthcare and municipal institutions) or in government ministries located in East Jerusalem for political reasons—as symbols of Israeli sovereignty. No Jew is known to be employed by Arabs. Many Jews provide counseling and advisory services to Arabs, but this, too, is a one-way street: Arabs hire Jewish professionals (lawyers, tax consultants, architects) because of the latters' access to the Israeli bureaucracy and familiarity with the seats of power in the municipal and national governments.

Hebrew is the language of the workplace. Every Arab employed in the Jewish sector has become proficient in Hebrew, whereas only a miniscule minority of Jews have learned Arabic. Many years of work have rendered the Arab workers experts at their trades, but neither this expertise nor the seniority they have accumulated has advanced them to positions in management or opened up white collar occupations to them. They are paid the same wages as Jews in equivalent positions, but there are relatively few Jews in the so-called "Arab" trades, and those who are so employed are soon promoted. Work relations in general are good, but the ethnic distinction is always present, and relationships are confined to the workplace with little, if any, socialization after hours. A widespread and noteworthy phenomenon is that of Arab workers using their Jewish employers, workmates, and even casual clients as intermediaries between themselves and the Israeli authorities, most frequently for assistance in obtaining building permits for family homes, or visitor's permits for relatives from abroad, or for intervention with the police.

Workers and employers evince a mutual loyalty that is put to the test each time violent incidents take place or when a hostile atmosphere prevails. Throughout the years of the Intifada, most Arab workers from East Jerusalem never failed to show up at their West Jerusalem jobs each morning. Jewish employers often protected their employees from threats of violence on the part of Jewish hooligans preaching harm to Arabs in revenge for terrorist acts, intervened in cases of arbitrary arrest or harassment by the Israeli security forces, and drove them home on particularly tense days.

How characteristic it is that worker-employer relations, which are by nature built on a clear hierarchy, have been the most intense interactions between Jews and Arabs in Jerusalem. These are relationships of expediency for both sides: the Arabs need to make a living and the Jews need cheap labor. But even here the interdependence is not symmetrical. The Arabs cannot find alternative employment since their own economic sector can neither absorb them, nor pay the wages customary in the Israeli sector. In contrast, the Jews can easily find other workers, and there is, indeed, fierce rivalry between Arabs and new immigrants from the former Soviet Union, for example, and even guest workers "imported" for the purpose from abroad.

A closely related domain is that of wholesale and retail commerce. In wholesaling, and in contacts among manufacturers, importers, and providers of financial services, the same hierarchy exists as in the workplace: the Jews are dominant and the Arabs are dependent on them. These relationships are stable, however, unlike those in retailing, which are greatly influenced by security-related tensions and the political climate. On the whole, consumers in Jerusalem prefer to patronize stores owned by members of their own community, with three exceptions: Jews who live on the border of Arab neighborhoods and shop at Arab stores that are open on Saturdays (and whose prices are lower), well-off Arabs visiting high-class Jewish shops or modern West Jerusalem shopping malls, and Jews who combine a stroll through the alleyways of the Old City with the purchase of Oriental food and Arab handicrafts. The human element in these essentially "antiseptic" contacts only serves to emphasize the distance and mutual alienation of the two populations.

Following a brief period of renewed Jewish interest in exploring the Old City in the early days of the occupation, most Jewish Jerusalemites stopped going for walks there. The Intifada put an end to the last vestige of retail commercial relations—eating in Arab restaurants. With the recent improvement in Jewish-Arab relations in the wake of the peace agreement between Israel and the PLO, the stream of Jewish tourists visiting the Old City has increased once again. However, it is interesting to note that most of these visitors are Jews from other cities, and not Jerusalemites. Once, the business center of East Jerusalem—open on Saturdays, when the Jewish business sections are closed—thronged with Jews paying visits to inexpensive Arab dentists, purchasing clothing and household appliances, and filling prescriptions at the pharmacies. The Intifada imposed on the business sections, which had generally remained "neutral territory," the dominant pattern of Jerusalem: functional and spatial segregation.

This double-barreled form of segregation is typical of all bi- or multi-ethnic cities, and the degree of separation is a reliable gauge of the severity of the prevailing ethnic, cultural, and societal tensions. In fact, one may construct a segregation-conflict continuum ranging from separation based on differences of lifestyle or economic class to hermetic segregation, with snipers positioned along barbed-wire fences, and from voluntary segregation to segregation imposed by force of arms. Jerusalem lies very close to one extreme of this continuum, at the voluntary end. The removal of the barbed wire fences and sniper positions in 1967 created an urban expanse free of physical barriers, but scarred by other impassable barriers, those of animosity, fear, and alienation. The borderline that once split the city down the center had disappeared; however, in its place other lines had arisen, which had become even more concrete and dramatic than the physical manifestation had been. A quick visit to the border area between the Jewish and Arab neighborhoods today is sufficient to convey the understanding that Jerusalem is not a "unified city" except for sloganeering purposes.

Belfast, the capital of Northern Ireland, is known as a city where strict spacial segregation reigns. But in Belfast there are mixed neighborhoods where Protestants and Catholics live side by side, and one business section that functions as a common commercial center. In Jerusalem, there are barely two mixed streets, and the two ethnically homogeneous business sections function separately. In Belfast, there is no visible physical difference between the separate ethnically and religiously uniform neighborhoods. Therefore, the two communities have developed mechanisms to identify the borders between them, and ways to visually emphasize the ethnic character of the various areas: flags, graffiti, slogans, parades. In Jerusalem, there is virtually no need for visual symbols of identity. The differences between the congested Arab neighborhoods, most of them neglected and lacking a modern infrastructure, and the Jewish neighborhoods, most of them with high quality housing and advanced infrastructure, are conspicuous and impossible to mistake. Nevertheless, in Jerusalem too, considerable effort has been expended in emphasizing the separation by various means: graffiti, placards, the powerfully-amplified call-to-prayer of the muezzin, a "Sabbath fence" (a thread symbolizing that within the area it encircles,

Jews are permitted to carry light objects from place to place on the Sabbath). But these boundary markers and symbols of identity are not employed in order to warn outsiders away; rather, their objective is to strengthen the sense of ethnic affiliation of the area's inhabitants and to mark it as their exclusive "turf."

The need to preserve the ethnic "purity" of their neighborhoods impels both groups to struggle to prevent incursions by tenants from the other community, especially their purchase of homes and lots. Many Israelis refuse to rent apartments to Arabs, and special clauses in long-term lease tenancy contracts in the new neighborhoods built on state land (much of which was expropriated from Arabs) forbid the owners to transfer titles to anyone who "is not a veteran of the military" (i.e., to Arabs).

The Jordanian government imposed the death penalty on anyone convicted of selling land and buildings to Jews. Jews who have tried to rent apartments in Arab districts have often been forced to leave because of the atmosphere of hostility that surrounds them. Groups of Jewish fanatics seeking to penetrate the heart of the Muslim Quarter of the Old City and to "Judaize" it have succeeded in taking over several buildings, but only after receiving massive assistance from the government to, among other things, finance an extensive system of armed guards to protect them day and night, and hire armed escorts for their children anytime they go out into the streets.

The ethnic boundaries are clear to all Jerusalemites. They have the "tribal map" stored in their heads, and know which areas are "safe" and which are "dangerous." Jews driving to the Hebrew University campus on Mount Scopus, for example, will choose a "Jewish route" taking them through areas inhabited by Jews, over the shorter, more direct route through Arab sections. In the asymmetrical reality of Jerusalem, only the Jews can steer clear of potentially hostile areas. The Arabs, though just as fearful, cannot allow themselves the luxury of avoiding Jewish areas; they must spend time there in order to make a living. But the Arabs have their own map of safe and dangerous areas, taking routes that allow them to sidestep the police roadblocks and humiliating surprise checks carried out by young women soldiers looking for West Bank and Gaza residents in Jerusalem without the requisite permits.

The mutual seclusion that has characterized Jerusalem since the 1967 war was at its height during the Intifada (1987–1993). Commercial strikes, stone-throwing, attacks on passersby, stabbings and hatchet murders, car torching, demonstrations, slogan-painting, and flag-flying—all took place with great frequency and knew no geographical or ethnic boundaries. The Israeli security forces reacted with counter-attacks: arrests, beatings, imprisonment, brutal house-searches, humiliations. The Intifada dispelled the illusions of those Israelis who believed that Jerusalem's ethnic segregation constituted a "mosaic" of homogeneous communities and was essential to peaceful coexistence. The direct relationship between the degree of segregation and the depth of the conflict became clear even to the most naively well-meaning. Moreover, the fiction of peaceful coexistence between cultural communities in unified Jerusalem had been exposed for what it was. People were no longer ashamed to express their longing for a day when they would wake up and find that "the others" had disappeared altogether. This desire to cut ties paradoxically united them all: Arabs seeking to be free of Jewish rule and the physical presence of Jews in their midst, chauvinistic Jews who preached expulsion of the Arabs, and moderate Jews who regarded segregation as a prerequisite for the establishment of an independent Palestinian state. "We must create a buffer, restrict contact, separate us from them" said the Jews, while the Arabs replied, "Get out from among us."

This wish for separation, "to rid ourselves of the Arabs (or the Jews)" was the motivating force behind the Israeli-Palestinian peace process. It was mutual, but the power relationship was not balanced. A segregation that reflects the hierarchy of horse and rider protects the interests of the dominant community at the expense of the dominated. Its forcible imposition exacerbates the alienation and the powerless hatred of the weak and dispossessed.

Spatial and cultural segregation reflect the fundamental needs of the two communities for physical security and preservation of their collective identities. But segregation in Jerusalem was imposed unilaterally. Indeed, a "mosaic of homogeneous neighborhoods" does exist in the city, but the Jewish neighborhoods and the other areas designated as "Jewish" encompass most of the urban space of the city and turn the Arab neighborhoods into isolated enclaves separated one from the other. The asymmetric economic relationship enables the Jews to rid themselves of the Arabs, but for the latter to be cut off from the Israeli economy would sentence them to lives of poverty and want. This sense of strangulation is what causes the Arabs to denounce the "Judaization of Jerusalem."

In mid-1968, the Jewish population of Jerusalem was surveyed regarding their attitudes toward Arabs. The results so shocked the Jerusalem municipal council, which had ordered the survey, that it decided to suppress them and to burn all copies of the questionnaire. One of the questions asked respondents to rank a series of statements according to which ones best described the Arab population. These statements and the order in which the respondents ranked them are as follows: "a people with many cowards"; "a people most of whom are poor"; "a cowardly people"; "a primitive people"; "there are quite a few educated people amongst them"; "they want peace with the Jews"; "an educated people."

From these and the responses to other questions, the following picture emerged: 55 percent of Jews were not prepared to have their children study with Arab children; 62 percent were not willing to work in a business whose proprietors were Arab; 58 percent did not agree that Arabs should be allowed to live in Jewish sections of the city; 89 percent agreed that Jews should be allowed to live in the Arab part of the city.

The survey revealed hostility, fear, prejudice, and a desire for complete separation. Although a similar survey was not conducted of the Arab community, it can be said without a doubt that their positions too were hostile and reflected a similar degree of fear and prejudice. These were the foundation data upon which ethnic coexistence in Jerusalem was to be built. Twelve years later, another survey was conducted of a representative sample of the Jewish population of Israel. It showed that time had not improved inter-ethnic attitudes. Forty-two percent of those surveyed stated that Arabs were "primitive," forty-one percent agreed with the statement that Arabs are "violent," fifty-two percent said that Arabs hate Jews, fifty-two percent would not live in the same building with Arabs, and only forty-two percent agreed with having mixed schools. Empirical studies undertaken in later years revealed that hostility had not disappeared, and that during the Intifada it had intensified. Expressions of Arab hostility, scrawled on the walls or printed in widely-distributed leaflets, were extreme.

However, an additional phenomenon has recently come to light. The hostility and prejudice each side feels have become dormant and have been replaced by increased mutual avoidance, apathy, and lack of interest concerning the activities of the other. In interpersonal encounters—in the workplace, in neighborhoods on the dividing line and in chance meetings in markets and buses—Jews and Arabs avoid bringing up controversial subjects. Actions such as the flying of Palestinian flags, which used to arouse anger and hostility among Jews, have gained legitimacy since the government has legalized them. Perhaps the most encouraging sign is that there is a growing willingness to transform spatial, cultural, and functional segregation into political separation. The likelihood of finding a mutually satisfactory formulation for political separation in Jerusalem will be addressed in the next chapter.

CHAPTER SEVEN

UNRAVELING THE ENIGMA

A s May 1996—the designated date for the commencement of
the Israeli-Palestinian negotiations on the final status of the
occupied territories—approached, the volume and variety of
writings dealing with proposals for a solution to the "Jerusalem problem" increased. Teams of researchers of various nationalities, but particularly Israelis and Palestinians, diligently engaged in simulated
negotiations and professional deliberations with the objective of arriving at a formula that would finally bring about the solution of the
Jerusalem problem in all its aspects. Conferences and meetings of various sorts were held with the aim of mobilizing public opinion behind
positions either supporting the status quo or advocating radical change.

There was nothing remarkable about this intensive level of activity;
over the past few years, dozens of similar schemes had accumulated on
the shelves, the fruit of research carried out by a variety of working
groups and academic institutions. The novelty lay in the fact that, for
the first time in the annals of the conflict over Jerusalem, the parties
directly involved—the Israelis and the Palestinians—had agreed to discuss the city's fate in the context of official, binding negotiations. The
Declaration of Principles signed in September 1993 states, "It is understood that those negotiations (on the permanent status) shall cover

remaining issues, including Jerusalem, refugees, settlements, security arrangements, borders, relations and cooperation with other neighbors and other issues of common interest" (Art. 5:3).

In the past, debate over the situation had been considered a purely theoretical matter and had even encountered opposition from advocates of the prevailing Israeli view that "the Jerusalem issue is not amenable to negotiation." Now, however, it was perceived as an activity whose time has come, and as useful in assisting the official negotiators in identifying and analyzing options. The precedent of Oslo, where negotiations had begun as unofficial discussions among academics and progressed to a historic agreement, became a model for emulation: if two young academics could succeed in setting the wheels of history in motion, why not others? Despite the multiplicity of approaches and motivations, the teams have all been striving for a mutually agreeable and comprehensive solution. Therefore, all of them stress the seriousness of the problem, the urgency of the need for a solution, and the fact that it is in the interest of all parties to participate in the attainment of this goal.

The search for a solution to the Jerusalem problem is indeed an undertaking of vital importance, and those engaged in the search do not doubt that one will be found. A precondition for any viable solution is, of course, that neither side feel it is the winner or the loser. Thus, in the words of one team, "The thinking is based on a positive-sum approach, which aims at securing a solution from whose implementation both Israelis and Palestinians will benefit."

How the needs of and benefits to the respective parties may be balanced such that both sides are satisfied depends on the working assumptions of the teams. Each team claims to understand the political, economic, cultural, and symbolic desires of the Israelis and the Palestinians, and each has its own "model" to propose. The most commonly accepted approach to achieving this balance is to break down the problem into its component parts: sovereignty, holy places, symbols, the economy, municipal administration, planning, and so on. This compartmentalization allows for flexibility, since one side's dissatisfaction in a given area can be "balanced" by its satisfaction in another. For example, a proponent of full sovereignty for one side might propose extensive concessions to the other in the realm of economics or municipal rule. The theoretical point of equilibrium depends, of course, on the assumptions held by the party making the proposal concerning the relative importance of each issue. These assumptions are, in turn, based on a party's official stance regarding their value. One side will always inflate the importance of "concessions" in areas it perceives as less crucial, presenting them as fair compensation for its exclusive control in areas that are important.

The "Jerusalem problem" is perceived as a complex crossword puzzle, whose solution depends upon correct responses to a large number of "horizontal and vertical" clues, and where only fully-matching responses will allow its completion. This puzzle is unique in that the correct answers are determined not by the clues, but by the positions held by the person solving it, so that the answers are seeking questions and not the other way around, as is usually the case.

As with any serious piece of research, the prelude to discussion of the Jerusalem question is devoted to a survey of previous proposals and their comparative analysis. Here a surreptitious competition is going on among the teams: Who will unearth and analyze the most solutions to the problem? One research team has published analyses of forty-two plans, while another team has uncovered eighteen others in obscure periodicals. And an industrious scholar claims to have discovered no fewer than ninety plans. The logic underlying this competition is similar to that which guides researchers in the natural sciences: a profound knowledge of the professional literature and an analysis of earlier cases provides a solid basis for new experimentation. However, in this instance, competition has resulted in the blurring of distinctions between agreements and unilateral statements, between official plans and the ruminations of anonymous theoreticians, between detailed proposals and those that pertain to the problem in a general way only. The emphasis has been on the analysis of the previously proposed solutions, and the problems and historical conditions that prevailed at the time of their proposal have not been considered.

The Jerusalem problem is perceived as being static, and proposals for its solution that were written as early as the beginning of this century are still regarded as deserving of attention as the century draws to a close. A plan for the reorganization of Jerusalem's municipal administration, proposed by a Mandatory judge as a solution to a crisis in the management of an ethnic conflict–riven municipal council in 1945, is perceived as relevant to the situation prevailing in the late 1990s. Plans and proposals for regularizing the status of Christian holy places, submitted by international experts with the aim of ensuring that foreign interests would not be endangered by the "natives," are being represented as models for the solution of the national-religious conflict among the natives themselves. Proposals made by one party to the conflict, which served its interests at the time, have been adopted by its rival now that the tables are turned, even though they were abandoned by their original advocates. Solutions that were imposed by force of arms and that only exacerbated the problem are being trotted out alongside utopian programs that deliberately disregard reality.

The fact that none of these plans was ever implemented, at least not successfully, does not deter today's planners. On the contrary—the failure of a plan only prompts them to come up with more sophisticated versions. A previous proposal for a division of sovereignty has led to one for a whole redefinition of the concept of sovereignty itself, along with the division of the city into three areas under three sovereign authorities, two national and one universal-religious. Whereas once two municipal councils were proposed, now it seems necessary to propose ten "spatial-functional" municipal entities.

The proliferation of plans, with their increasing level of sophistication and degree of detail, is quite impressive. However, once these proposals are stripped of their veneer of rhetoric, fancy formulation, statistics, and argumentation, what remains are the same three models, repeated over and over: (1) Jerusalem as the undivided capital of a geopolitical unit encompassing all of Mandatory Palestine (or most of it), along with provisions necessitated by the city's unique character with regard to the holy places and the multi-ethnicity of its population; (2) Jerusalem as a divided capital, as required by the division of Mandatory Palestine into two separate geopolitical units, with provisions ensuring the continuation of its functioning as a shared urban unit; and (3) Jerusalem as a distinct geopolitical enclave, administered apart from the separate sovereign domains of the former Mandatory Palestine.

Choosing one of these models or attempting to combine them is not a decision free of value judgments or political influence. Paradoxically, one might say that the preoccupation with searching for a solution to the Jerusalem problem is more a reflection of the extent of that problem than a contribution to its solution. Indeed, the rate at which "solutions" are being contrived can be seen as increasing in direct proportion to the intensity of the conflict—to such an extent that the number of plans for resolving the conflict serves as a reliable gauge of its gravity, comparable to the proliferation of statistics concerning acts of violence.

The Jerusalem problem is perceived as sui generis and is represented as a tangled skein of national, religious, and ethnic problems, making it a particularly challenging "case" and consequently attracting anyone with pretensions to a concern for conflict resolution. But this medium-sized, highly provincial city does not, in fact, have some terrible eternal curse hanging over it. Even the problem of the holy places, which caused so much bloodshed in the past, has in recent generations become a secondary aspect of a broader conflict common to many of the world's cities: the dispute between two national communities seeking to control the country and the city that they share.

The Israeli-Palestinian conflict over Jerusalem—a municipal, ethnic dispute with an interreligious flavor—includes a macro-national dimension, which intensifies existing local antagonisms. But such conflicts exist in many parts of the world. Jerusalem's fame (and thus the obsession with its "resolution") is due primarily to the fact that its conflict is being played out on a historical stage decked with powerful symbols and myths and pervaded with an air of sanctity. Take away Jesus, Muhammad, David, Jeremiah, Omar, and Godfrey de Bouillon, and the preoccupation with Jerusalem shrinks to the level of a petty family quarrel among cousins vying for their inheritance.

However, this reductionist (and perhaps somewhat irreverent) definition of the Jerusalem problem enrages those who are working on solutions, inducing them to emphasize the "universal character" of the problem and the global interests at stake, as well as the peril to world peace it represents. Thus, every survey of the Jerusalem problem and of the proposals for its solution begins with a description of the international conflict over the holy places.

But territorial control over the city itself was not a key factor in the conflict over the Church of the Holy Sepulchre and the other Christian holy places in the city and vicinity of Jerusalem. Only when the Allied powers—Britain in particular—arrived at a conclusion sealing the fate of the Ottoman Empire and commenced to divide up the spoils, did the issue of control of Jerusalem assume an international dimension. The Sykes-Picot Agreement of 1916, the first international pact to deal with the geopolitical future of Jerusalem, heads every list of solutions for the Jerusalem problem. This accord, the parties to which were Britain, France, Russia, and Italy, divided the Middle East into spheres of influence directly or indirectly controlled by these nations. The only part of the Sykes-Picot Agreement pertinent to this discussion is the article that states, "In the brown area there shall be established an international administration the form of which is to be decided upon consultation."

According to the map appended to the Sykes-Picot Agreement, the international zone was to encompass that portion of Palestine extending from the Acre–Sea of Galilee line in the north to the Beersheba-Rafah line in the south. It is noteworthy that, although the agreement refers to many cities by name (Damascus, Aleppo, Haifa, Acre, and others), mention of Jerusalem is conspicuous in its absence; French documents indicate that the purpose of the "international administration" was supposedly to "assure the independence of sacred places" throughout the holy land, and not necessarily those in the Holy City itself.

The real basis for the agreement on internationalization of the holy land was not a desire to protect universal interests, but the necessity of arriving at a compromise between French and British claims there. France, viewing itself as successor to the Crusaders, aspired to control the entire eastern coast of the Mediterranean Sea, from Antioch to Gaza. The British sought control of Palestine as a way of securing their grip on the Suez Canal. Neither saw the Sykes-Picot Agreement as the final word on the matter: the French attempted to circumvent it by colluding with the Russians, while the British, with Prime Minister Lloyd-George in the lead, connived to use the Zionist movement to help them secure a grasp on the holy land. Britain's imperialistic interests were mingled with an honest desire, the legacy of a profound belief in the Bible, to bring about the fulfillment of the prophecy regarding the Jews' return to Zion.

In the end, the fate of Palestine—and with it, that of Jerusalem—was determined by force of arms. It was the British army that conquered the country, and this belligerent occupation was quickly transformed into de jure rule: on December 1, 1918, Premier Clemenceau of France asked Lloyd-George, "What [part] of the Middle East do you want?" "Mosul [the oil-rich region of northern Iraq]," he replied. "Anything else?" "Palestine." "You shall have it," stated Clemenceau. This too was perceived as a "solution" to the Jerusalem problem.

Four years later, the British Mandate was ratified by the League of Nations. Palestine became a separate geopolitical unit with Jerusalem as its capital. Thus, as the capital of the land over which Jews and Arabs were fighting, the Holy City became the focus of that conflict. The British, who believed in their ability to rule this conflict-riven land and to mediate between the Jews and the Arabs and arbitrate their national claims, soon discovered that they had deluded themselves. What's more, they were largely responsible for the intensification of the conflict, having dispensed contradictory promises to the two national movements.

Within fourteen years of taking control of Palestine, the British came to the conclusion that the Mandate could not work. The report of the Peel Commission (1937) recommended the partition of the land into two states, one Jewish and one Arab. According to the commission's recommendation, Jerusalem should become an enclave permanently under British mandatory rule. The logic behind these recommendations was clear: As long as the Land of Israel remained a single geopolitical unit, the capital of this unit would be subject to the sovereign rule of the entity that controlled the country as a whole, and arrangements for dealing with the problem of the holy places and municipal rule would not impinge upon this sovereignty. But with the decision to partition the land, it became necessary to decide who would acquire control of the capital, the Jews or the Arabs.

Dividing sovereignty over the city itself was regarded as unreasonable and unworkable. And the Peel Commission had another important reason for leaving Jerusalem under British rule. True imperialists, they did not believe the "natives"—the Jews and the Arabs—capable of preserving the sacred character of the city; only a European power could guarantee this "sacred trust of civilization." "This trust," stated the Peel Commission's report, "does not belong to the people of Palestine alone, but to the multitudes of people in other lands for whom one or both of these places [Jerusalem and Bethlehem] is sacred." Since its intention was to remove Jerusalem from the arena of Jewish-Arab conflict, the Peel Commission sought to guarantee the independent existence of the "sacred enclave" by including in it a long corridor leading to the shores of the Mediterranean Sea and the port of Jaffa. This was the first time anyone had attempted to extend Jerusalem's cloak of sanctity to expanses of territory beyond the city. As noted in Chapter 2, many others were to utilize the same stratagem.

Even though the Peel Commission determined that the Mandate could not cope with the situation, Britain was in no hurry to rid itself of

Palestine. The clouds of the Second World War were gathering, and because of the country's strategic importance as the central crossroads of the Middle East, the British did not carry out the Peel Plan or any other plan. Instead, they attempted to improve the functioning of Jerusalem's municipal administration, which suffered severely from the perpetual strife between Jews and Arabs.

The most famous plan for revamping Jerusalem's municipal administration, about which numerous studies have been produced and whose principles have been proposed to this day as part of nearly every plan for the solution of the Jerusalem problem, was the Borough Plan, authored by Judge Sir William Fitzgerald in 1945. Sir William defined the problem as follows: "The problem . . . appears to me a twofold one: to preserve those traditions which the city enshrines, an obligation dictated by conscience and imposed by the mandate, and to provide the amenities of modern city life. . . . Can a solution be found that will satisfy the just claims of both [Jews and Arabs]?"

His unequivocal conclusion was that there was no possibility of Jewish-Arab cooperation within the framework of a single municipal council; therefore, he concluded, the city must be divided into two separate municipalities. However, Fitzgerald could not recommend an absolute partition of the city since, in his eyes, the "Jerusalem of tradition . . . conjured by millions of Jews, Christians and Moslems who have never even seen its towers and minarets, is indivisible." He therefore proposed a two-tier administrative structure that would preserve the unity of the city physically while dividing it along ethnic lines administratively: "Jerusalem should be treated as an administrative county under the control of an administrative council. [The county would be divided] into municipal boroughs as [is] the county of London. . . . One borough will be Jewish and the other will be predominantly Arab."

Judge Fitzgerald went on to enumerate the administrative powers of the borough councils. Although seeking to grant them the greatest possible measure of autonomy, he left no doubt that the supreme authority rested with the county administrative council, nor did he attempt to hide the latter's ties with the British regime. This council was to be composed of a chairperson appointed by the high commissioner, four representatives elected from the residents of each borough, and two other members, "neither Jews nor Arabs," also appointed by the high commissioner.

The division of Jerusalem into boroughs was meant to solve the problem of ethnic strife in the city, but Judge Fitzgerald neglected to address one vital issue: the macro-national conflict over the political future of the land as a whole. He assumed that the central government would remain in the hands of an external power that would oversee the operation of the autonomous ethno-municipalities. In the absence of such a power the entire complex structure would collapse; after all, the conflict was not over the management of the water supply and sewage, but over sovereign control of Palestine itself. The Fitzgerald Report was not implemented and was relegated to the growing pile of similar proposals and solutions.

Two years after the submission of the Borough Plan, other teams were hard at work on another proposal for Jerusalem, the Corpus Separatum Plan. This partition plan was intended to replace the British Mandate, and its authors, members of the UNSCOP (United Nations Special Commission on Palestine), were faced with the same dilemma that had confronted the Peel Commission ten years earlier. As soon as they reached the conclusion that Jews and Arabs could not live together in a shared state, the partition of Palestine became inevitable. But that did not solve the problem of to whom the Holy City was to be given. One could divide the country along any given set of boundaries, but the question remained of what to do with the capital, the focal point of the two rival peoples' national interests.

Possible alternatives were (1) to include Jerusalem in the Jewish state because of the city's Jewish majority—but then there was the question of how to maintain a geographical link between Jerusalem and the Jewish state via the Arab state; (2) to include Jerusalem in the Arab state—but then something would have to be done about the city's

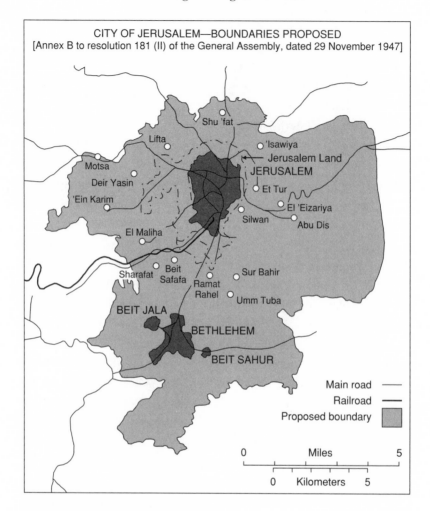

MAP 5. Proposed "corpus separatum," 1947

100,000 Jews (one-sixth of the total Jewish population of Mandatory Palestine); and (3) to create a Jewish-Arab condominium in the city— but if it was unlikely that Jews and Arabs could coexist in one state, how could they coexist in one city?

The least complicated of these impossible alternatives appeared to be that of removing control of the city from the hands of the two rival

sides. What's more, theoretically, additional interests could be satisfied—those referred to as "the religious interests of the three monotheistic religions and of the civilized world, to [all of] which Jerusalem was
sacred"—through the internationalization of Jerusalem, making it a
"corpus separatum."

The majority recommendation of the UN commission (ratified by
the UN General Assembly on November 29, 1947) did not address the
question of the administrative structure of the international city, except
for the provision that the governor of Jerusalem should be appointed by
the Trusteeship Council and should be neither a Jew nor an Arab, and
that "a legislative council elected by adult residents of the city on the
basis of universal and secret suffrage and proportional representation
shall have the power of legislation and taxation" subject to the "governor's right of veto." The makeup of the executive, legislative, and judicial
bodies in Jerusalem was to be determined by the Trusteeship Council.

The General Assembly ratified the Partition Plan, including the proposed boundaries of the "corpus separatum," which encompassed
extensive territory outside the municipal boundaries of Jerusalem,
including Bethlehem. Various committees worked diligently on the
preparation of a statute for Jerusalem, which was ratified by the
Trusteeship Council in April 1950. This is an especially impressive document that specifies a detailed and efficient governing mechanism;
guarantees civil rights and basic freedoms; lays down requirements for
residency and citizenship; establishes regulations regarding elections,
internal security, official languages, the educational system, radio and
television, the economy, taxation and tariffs, and foreign relations; and
addresses the protection of the holy places and antiquities, national
symbols, and flags. The legislative council of international Jerusalem
was to be made up of twenty-five elected members and "no more than
fifteen appointed members." The twenty-five were to be chosen by four
electoral colleges—Christian, Jewish, Muslim, and "a college which
shall be composed of the residents who declare that they do not wish to
register with any of the other three colleges."

The Jews, Muslims, and Christians were to have equal representation (eight representatives per community), despite the fact that Jews constituted two-thirds of the population. The city was to be neutral, and no military units or maneuvers would be permitted within its boundaries, with the exception of a "special police force." Regrettably, this elaborate structure never got beyond the drawing board. It did not even obtain the approval of the UN General Assembly. It is difficult to ascertain whether its authors knew that the plan they were designing was purely theoretical and had no chance of being implemented—not because it wouldn't be ratified by the United Nations, but because the fate of Jerusalem had already been sealed two years before, on the battlefield.

The vast chasm separating the formulation of elaborate plans and their implementation is particularly conspicuous in the case of the internationalization of Jerusalem. Representatives of scores of nations have sat down to deliberate the international governance of Jerusalem down to the tiniest detail, but no one has been able to impose even an effective cease-fire. The United Nations sent their municipal commissioner to Jerusalem to begin preparations for implementing the Partition Plan. However, Commissioner Harold Evans, a Quaker, declined to accept a military escort, and so remained in Cairo "till peace came."

By the time a cease-fire was finally concluded, Jerusalem had already been divided between Israel and Jordan, who collaborated in resisting the UN's efforts to internationalize the city. Although they succeeded in thwarting the scheme, the idea underlying it survived: every time future authors of solutions to the Jerusalem problem encountered insoluble conflicts between Israeli and Palestinian interests (such as that over the Old City), they would cite "universal interests" that required the "removal of the area [i.e., the city] from the cycle of nationalist strife" and its internationalization. After all, the planners were not responsible for implementation, just for coming up with creative ideas.

During the nineteen years that the city was divided (1948–1967), the amount of attention devoted to plans for the solution of the Jerusalem problem diminished. The de facto division of sovereignty over Jerusalem between Israel and Jordan never won international acceptance, but the existence of this fait accompli meant that "functional" as opposed to "territorial" proposals began to appear. Most proposals from this period were for the "functional internationalization" of the holy places. The best-known of these was a plan authored by the Swedish government, according to which territorial control would remain in the hands of Israel and Jordan, while a UN commissioner would oversee the holy places and access to them only. The commissioner was supposed to "request" of the states that controlled the Jerusalem area that they change, suspend, or repeal laws, regulations, and administrative measures that, in his opinion, interfered with the protection of the holy places or with freedom of access to them. The commissioner was also supposed to ensure the extraterritoriality of the sites and the privileges and independence of the religious establishments.

Israel enthusiastically supported the proposals for "functional internationalization," since this support did not cost the state a thing: all of the holy places were located in territory administered by the Kingdom of Jordan. These proposals also came to naught, although the idea of functional internationalization itself was not forgotten and expediently provided the basis for proposals that Israel made after 1967, when forced by changing circumstances to exhibit signs of flexibility.

The 1967 war totally altered the geopolitical status quo in Jerusalem. The fact that one national state had taken control of the entire area of the city once again raised the question of sovereignty. The bitter national conflict, which had supposedly been resolved with the partition of Jerusalem in 1948, broke out anew. The Israelis knew well that, even if the occupation of East Jerusalem was justifiable as an act of self-defense, its annexation was clearly illegal and unacceptable to the international community. This unilateral move evoked an unsympathetic response in many quarters, increased tensions in the city, and sabotaged all efforts to arrive at a peaceful settlement. Politicians and scholars applied themselves to proposing new plans for the solution of the problem, both to contribute what they could toward the achievement of peace and to reduce political pressures.

The proposals advanced by the Israelis were marked by their classification of previous plans based on new ways of defining the problem. Almost every one of their schemes opened with an identical categorization of the "various aspects of the Jerusalem question," which included "sovereignty" (or "national aspirations"), "holy places," and "municipal administration." The problem's subdivision into these three subproblems is not devoid of logic, nor is it artificial; these problems are indeed intertwined. However, they are not identical, and solving one does not guarantee the solution of the others. Finding a solution to the problem of sovereignty would not solve the problem of the holy places and the squabbles over their maintenance. And even if everyone were to agree on geopolitical and religious arrangements, the ethnic communities would continue to wrangle over public resources and to vie for positions of dominance in municipal government in a city whose physical integrity is important to all.

The choice of this manner of categorization was not accidental, but was the result of the fact that the majority of Israelis do not dare to deviate from the "national consensus" on the preservation of Israeli sovereignty over all of Jerusalem. "Sovereignty" in this instance is perceived not in its legal, constitutional sense, but as encompassing such basic elements as identity; awareness of national worth; and control over one's own fate, welfare, and security. Sovereignty thus perceived is the distillation of the legal, administrative, economic, social, and cultural being of the nation. This concept of sovereignty does not allow for breadth of interpretation or flexibility. However, flexibility is achieved by assigning the issues of the holy places and municipal administration a value equal to that of sovereignty. Thus, generous and flexible proposals regarding municipal and religious autonomy may be posited that supposedly counterbalance the inflexibility on the issue of sovereignty, autonomy in these areas not being incompatible with the principle of national sovereignty.

A typical Israeli or pro-Israeli proposal includes some or all of the following components: (1) Jerusalem is to remain undivided and under Israeli sovereignty. (2) The holy places are to be fully under the control of their respective religious communities, with guaranteed access and the status of either extraterritoriality or diplomatic immunity. (3) The religious courts are to enjoy judicial authority as under the "millet" system (a system allowing for autonomous administration by the religious communities, which existed under Ottoman rule and to some extent survives to this day). (4) Municipal government is to be decentralized, with ethnically homogeneous boroughs governed by bodies responsible to an umbrella municipal council. These autonomous boroughs would enjoy a large measure of independence. However, on central issues such as town planning, they would be subject to the authority of the municipal council, which would reflect the decisive demographic weight of the Jewish community.

"Sovereignty" being an expression of national aspirations, the assertion that exclusive Israeli sovereignty will prevail in Jerusalem is tantamount to claiming that the Palestinians do not have legitimate national aspirations with regard to the city or, if they do, they must sacrifice them in the face of stronger or more just Israeli claims. Religious or communal autonomy is perceived as being sufficient to fulfill the Palestinians' collective longings.

The recognition of Palestinian collective interests is itself considered a radical stance, since any acknowledgment of the existence of a collective Palestinian presence in Jerusalem has been perceived by Israelis as opening the door to "the redivision of Jerusalem." Thus, any proposal regarding the establishment of a separate Palestinian borough, or even the granting of Muslim extraterritorial status to sites sacred to that faith, was sure to encounter a hostile political response. Considering the political climate, it is no wonder that these proposals were viewed by their creators as important and courageous contributions to the solution of the Jerusalem problem.

A few Israelis, understanding that proposals that did not acknowledge the legitimacy of Palestinian national claims were worthless, augmented their contributions with recommendations for functional autonomy in such fields as education, the economy, citizenship, and the right to vote for representatives on legislative bodies outside of Israel (Jordan, the Palestinian National Authority). Others sought to solve the sovereignty problem by extending Jerusalem's boundaries and placing this additional territory under Arab (Jordanian or Palestinian) sovereignty, leaving Jerusalem proper (including the parts annexed in 1967) under Israeli sovereignty.

The latter approach was, of course, nothing but an evasion of the problem. The handing over of areas that never had been considered a part of the city to Palestinian control in an attempt to justify Israeli dominion over the whole of the city proper could never constitute a solution. In the opinion of the Arabs, even the inclusion of the annexed territory (i.e., parts of the West Bank arbitrarily placed within the boundaries of East Jerusalem when the latter was annexed by Israel in 1967) was artificial since these areas had never been part of the Holy City. Only a few isolated Israelis, on the extreme left of the political spectrum, had the temerity to propose the division of sovereignty over the city itself and the creation of a symmetrical relationship of the two national movements, Israeli and Palestinian, to their common capital.

Demands for the geopolitical partition of Jerusalem were first raised, of course, in the context of solutions proposed by Arab or pro-Arab elements. For many years following the 1967 war, this was not couched in terms of a "peace plan" but was simply put forward as a demand for a return to the conditions preceding the Israeli occupation. According to the Arab position, Jerusalem is an integral part of the occupied territories, and Israel is obligated "to withdraw from all the territories occupied in 1967, including East Jerusalem." When queried as to how such a requirement could be regarded as part of a "peace plan," the Arabs responded that it in fact represented a painful concession—they were not demanding West Jerusalem as well.

Little by little the Arabs have refined their position. They have made it clear, for instance, that a return to the 1949 borders need not mean the physical partition of the city, but only "a division of sovereignty accompanied by arrangements for coordination on the municipal level." They also have promised members of the Jewish faith freedom of access to holy places. Arab plans proposed in the early 1980s included an additional component: the designation of East Jerusalem as the capital of the Palestinian state. An example of a recent Palestinian peace plan is the following proposal by Prof. Walid Khalidi (1988): "the designation of West Jerusalem as the capital of Israel, East Jerusalem as the capital of Palestine. Exterritorial status and access to the Jewish holy places would be assured, and a grand ecumenical council would be formed to represent the three monotheistic faiths (with rotation of chairmanship), to oversee interreligious harmony. Reciprocal rights of movement and residence between the two capitals with agreed-upon limits would be negotiated."

Concerning municipal government, Khalidi proposes that "a joint interstate great municipal council could operate and supervise certain municipal common services, while residual services would fall under the separate municipalities of each sovereign state." This proposal does not address the demographic "facts" that Israel has established in East Jerusalem, with the exception of a hint at "a reciprocal right of residence," regarding which negotiations would be conducted. Also, the reference to the Old City as simply an issue of "freedom of access to Jewish holy places" ignores Jewish ties to the Old City and to the Jewish Quarter. Some Arab public figures and others have dealt with these issues by proposing the reduction of the amount of the city regarded as "sacred" and the designation of the Old City as neutral territory.

According to an April 1992 proposal by a Jordanian official, Adnan Abu Odeh, the walled portion of Jerusalem would not be part of the domain of any state, nor would the Old City come under the political sovereignty of any state. The Old City would be administered by a council of representatives of the Muslim, Christian, and Jewish religious authorities. The area outside the walls, which would be divested of all religious significance and symbolism, would be partitioned into

Arab and Jewish sections, to be called Al-Quds and Yerushalyim, where the flags of Palestine and Israel, respectively, would fly. The Jewish neighborhoods of East Jerusalem would be subject to the same arrangements as those applying to the settlements in the occupied territories.

Whereas those Israelis who advocate the partition of Jerusalem into two sovereign sections propose first expanding the boundaries of the area considered a part of the Holy City, Abu Odeh is proposing the opposite strategy: reduction of the area identified as Jerusalem to its ancient core, and its removal from the realm of the Israeli-Palestinian national conflict. However, just as the artificial expansion of Jerusalem is a form of evasion, so too is its contraction. And while the stratagem of expansion is unacceptable to the Palestinians, that of contraction is acceptable to neither the Palestinians nor the Israelis. After all, the efforts to internationalize Jerusalem have failed because both the Israelis and the Arabs refuse to differentiate between religious and national control and regard the Old City as a symbol of both national and religious identity, whose components are inseparable.

With the commencement of the peace process, and especially following the signing of the Declaration of Principles with the PLO ("the Oslo Accords") in September 1993, the influx of plans for the solution of the Jerusalem problem again increased. What was new this time was the fact that Israeli and Palestinian teams collaborated in the discussions and benefited from the open assistance of university-affiliated bodies, which had previously avoided getting involved because they regarded it as a politically sensitive issue. This collaboration led to a more objective evaluation of the various plans and the drawing of ideas from both Israeli and Palestinian sources. A typical plan contained proposals for the massive expansion of the boundaries of the city and its partition into sovereign Israeli and Palestinian areas; the designation of Palestinian and Israeli capitals in Jerusalem; and the division of the metropolitan region into ten Israeli and ten Palestinian uni-ethnic municipalities, whose administration would be overseen by a body of representatives of the Israeli and Palestinian central regimes as well as of the various municipal councils such that each national community would have equal representation, and headed alternately by a Jew and an Arab. Demographic balance between Israelis and Palestinians would be achieved by having the city's boundaries drawn in accordance with demographic factors and by the introduction of a policy limiting the number of people allowed to move into the city. The Old City would be administered as a separate municipality, and each religious community would exercise administrative independence in its holy places.

There was nothing new in these proposals, except for their joint formulation. The deliberations, though, had a less theoretical air than those that had preceded them, since the problem of Jerusalem was now on the verge of being discussed officially, in the context of the final status negotiations. Nevertheless, the solutions produced in this climate suffered from the same logical flaw as had earlier plans and, like them, were fated to remain on the drawing board: their framers were working under the assumption that the proposal of definite, comprehensive solutions was the proper approach for tackling the conflict over Jerusalem. They were guided by the presumption that every problem can be resolved and that reaching a solution is contingent only on the opposing parties exercising reason and demonstrating the same goodwill and openness to compromise as the proposal's authors.

Peacemakers, once they "objectively" analyze a problem, proceed to determine the desired conditions, also objectively. Since they are convinced of their own objectivity and professional skill, they regard the two sides' attitudes toward the problem and its solution as obstructions to a settlement, as immature and irrational, and as sheer stubbornness—all qualities that must be overcome. These champions of objectivity are outraged by the suggestion that their optimistic and somewhat arrogant views might be baseless, and that the conflict might not be amenable to permanent resolution at all because of its chronic-endemic character and its unique, complex origins. As far as they are concerned, it is useful to debate the pros and cons of a given proposal, but any questioning of the general intellectual/theoretical exercise of formulating solutions is considered tantamount to spreading defeatism and a paralysis-inducing pessimism, and to lending legitimacy to the status quo.

It is no accident that every solution proposed thus far has dealt with the design of political structures and has concentrated on functional-bureaucratic arrangements. The proposals are couched in legal language and the terminology drawn from the vocabulary of political science. "Sovereignty," "autonomy," "demilitarization," "annexation," "municipal administration," and other such concepts are perceived in an abstract sense. "Sovereignty," for example, is understood in legal-theoretical terms, as political authority, exclusivity of rule, and the employment of means of coercion—rather than in its popular/emotional sense of full expression, of fulfilling basic needs such as identity, and of being in control of the collective fate. One can find legal formulations that define the concept of sovereignty in less absolute terms, but the fact remains that the concept is more difficult to deal with in its nonrational aspects. One may, on paper, manipulate a group's sense of belonging to a given space by expanding its administrative boundaries and renaming the parts of the expanded whole. But these manipulations, constructive and rational all, can hardly influence the emotions that lie deep within a community attached to the physical site of its homeland.

The Jerusalem situation involves more than the sum of its parts that are amenable to rational analysis. Indeed, despite the existence of real and measurable conflicts of political, economic, and other interests, the problem is irrational at its core. When it is presented in rational and objective terms (in order to fit it to a rational solution), one can categorically state that it is insoluble. It also might be said that the preoccupation with theoretical solutions is aimed not at facilitating real political progress, but rather at nurturing the hope that a solution is indeed attainable and that salvation lies right around the corner.

The conflict over and within Jerusalem is not so much a problem as it is a condition. That is the typical case with intercommunal conflict, which arises from the daily friction between two ethnic groups living in intimate proximity and competing for urban space, public resources, and the preservation of their respective ways of life. To this local-municipal aspect of the conflict are added national frictions over the fulfillment of competing aspirations for self-determination, independence, and sovereignty. This conflict is not purely political but pervades every level of private and collective life; it is organic in essence, endemic, and resistant to political "solutions." Conditions have no solutions; there are just solutions to some of the problems they cause. Even once solutions are found to the political problems, the ethnic groups will continue to quarrel over key positions in municipal government; even if they agree on a joint political framework, they won't totally succeed in channeling the conflict through the political system, and the threat of violence will remain beneath the surface.

In any ethno-national conflict, an agreeable solution can take only two alternative forms: vertical partition and horizontal partition. Vertical partition refers to geopolitical separation; horizontal partition refers to the devolution of powers to the ethnic communities, a federal structure, and the protection of minority rights. Since both sides accept the basic assumption that it is desirable for Jerusalem to remain physically undivided, current proposals combine aspects of vertical and horizontal partition. Of course, proposals that advocate doing away with the problem forcibly or removing Jerusalem from the control of both sides in the conflict (such as by internationalization) are not addressed here.

The difficulty resides not in the quality of the proposals but in their being posited as effective mechanisms for the solution of the conflict. Intercommunal conflicts are not crossword puzzles with only one solution, and a "solution-oriented" approach is not applicable in their case. What is needed is a "process-oriented" approach, which requires a constant effort to grapple with the exigencies of a changing reality, with no shortcuts via once-and-for-all solutions. This dynamic approach to problem solving is difficult for those who are used to analytical thinking based on theoretical models, but it is the one required by the complex situation whose improvement is being sought.

The process-oriented approach is solidly planted in the "mud" of reality; there is no previously determined final and definitive goal. On the contrary, the assumption is that the two parties have conflicting final goals, and that it is pointless to exert oneself in the pursuit of a common goal, except for the purpose of conducting the dialogue. Progress is measured not in terms of approaching some predetermined objective but by the mere fact of agreement, even on the pettiest of issues. Such agreement has value not only when it leads to a positive end, but also when it relates to objectives that either cannot be achieved within a given time frame, are impossible to achieve at all, or are achievable but impossible to implement. Does this analysis mean that, in the absence of a solution to the problem of Jerusalem, the city is doomed to be the site of continuing violent conflicts? Is there no value in the attempt to envision a more positive political future?

The process-oriented approach may indeed inspire a cautious optimism. Its being grounded in reality means that the debate will address various aspects of the actual situation such as those enumerated here. Paradoxically, the very intensity of the alienation and separation between Jewish and Arab Jerusalemites has acted as a motivating force behind the process leading to a political settlement. The Intifada stripped the Israelis of the last remnants of any illusions they may have harbored regarding "peaceful coexistence in the unified city." The violence, prolonged commercial strikes, and other manifestations of the collective rebellion of the residents of East Jerusalem against Israeli domination fractured the city's urban space along its ethnic fault line.

Israelis, fearing for their safety, ceased to visit the Arab neighborhoods and became accustomed to regarding any Arab who blundered into their domain with suspicion. The geography of fear became more powerful than the sacred geography of the unified city, with people on each side feeling the need for ethnic and physical separation from those on the other. This need superseded even the will to realize Israeli national aspirations for a unified Jerusalem and laid bare a fact that had been concealed beneath a thick layer of propaganda and wishful thinking: "Unified Jerusalem" was nothing but a forcibly imposed fiction.

The element of force in Israeli rule of East Jerusalem and the rest of the occupied territories increased greatly in response to Intifada incidents as the military and the police attempted to impose order. As the use of force grew, the illusion that there was any chance of a permanent settlement based on Israeli control of a unified Jerusalem, with religious and municipal autonomy for the Arabs, melted away. The violence was a slap in the face for peace-seeking liberals, who had sought in vain to reconcile opposing sentiments: to give free rein to their patriotic feelings as Israelis while giving some recognition to the legitimacy of the demands of the "non-Jewish population" for self-administration. Slogans extolling "tolerance" and "coexistence," which actually amounted to paternalism within the Israeli system, became farcical. There was no longer even any point in continuing to invest efforts in improving the living conditions of the Arabs, since these were only a way of proving that the Arabs were citizens of a unified city.

The desire to be rid of the Arabs, to create a separation between them and the Israelis, was the principal factor in launching the Israeli-Palestinian peace process and was the main force shaping the agreements on the interim status of the occupied territories. Jerusalem was explicitly excluded from this process, but the thrust toward separation was felt there as well and afforded the Israeli government a certain degree of flexibility on issues concerning the city, such as elections to the Palestinian National Authority (PNA). This impetus, if judiciously employed, could also be applied to the process toward a settlement regarding Jerusalem.

The borders drawn by fear and alienation blurred the artificial demarcation lines that divided the "unified city" from the West Bank. The blurring increased in the wake of the accelerated urbanization within the city's metropolitan area. This accelerated growth, part of it planned and part of it natural, created a huge area of continuous building stretching far beyond the municipal boundaries of Jerusalem. The

12. Ma'ale Adumim

Israelis erected enormous dormitory communities in the West Bank, and these settlement cities—Ma'ale Adumim, Giv'at Ze'ev, Efrat, and blocks of smaller settlements—became connected to the built-up area of Jerusalem itself, radiating from the urban center like tentacles.

The Palestinians, prevented from building inside Jerusalem, set up their own satellite towns adjacent to the Arab neighborhoods of the city. This suburban and urban sprawl extending from overgrown villages bordering Jerusalem (Azariyeh, Abu-Dis, Kafar Aqab, A-Ram, and others)—as far as Bethlehem, Beit Sahour, and Beit Jala in the south and Ramallah and el Bireh in the north—formed a solid urbanized area with Arab East Jerusalem at its hub.

This metropolitan expanse encompasses an immense area, just one-fifth of which falls within the municipal boundaries of Jerusalem (including the territory annexed in 1967). In 1995, nearly one million people inhabited this area, roughly half of them Jewish and half Arab. It is composed of ethnically homogeneous sections, bordering one another but isolated. This "tribal map" is amazing in the degree of difference between its Jewish and Arab areas. The Jewish neighborhoods are marked by comprehensive planning and enjoy highly developed services and a modern infrastructure. In the Arab sections, by contrast—and sometimes just across the road—sit haphazard collections of houses without even minimal infrastructural features such as sewer and water systems, proper access roads, or public buildings. Any human contact between these mutually alienated groups occurs not in the residential districts or on the borders between them, but in the center of the city, which for both communities serves as a focus for business, services, and entertainment. But the urban center is also divided and has been "off limits" to the great majority of West Bank Palestinians since early 1993. Thus, the model of human and functional separation affects the great majority of inhabitants in the entire area.

For many years, the Israeli regime attempted to emphasize the administrative distinction between "the sovereign Israeli territory" of East Jerusalem and the "administered territories," where military rule prevailed. Of course, the Jewish communities of the West Bank, known as "settlements," were outside the jurisdiction of the military government. They were annexed to Israel de facto; only the Arab sections suffered the depredations of the oppressive military regime, which denied residents their freedom of movement, expropriated their landholdings, and subjected them to a hostile bureaucracy. The Intifada succeeded in ousting the bureaucracy and even forced the withdrawal of the Israeli army from population centers to their fringes, where they concentrated on defending Jewish settlements and the access roads to them. The "shock committees" and "popular committees" controlled the Arab districts, where they built a strong territorial power base that gained legitimacy with the implementation of the political arrangements set out in the Oslo Accords. The consolidation of the process set in motion at Oslo and the inevitable dynamic arising from long-standing spatial and political separation are both strong forces furthering the process toward a settlement.

The majority of Israelis used to believe that East Jerusalem had become, from the point of view of "law, jurisdiction, and administration," an integral part of Israel. They could not have been more wrong. Granted, the political reality of East Jerusalem was entirely different compared with the eve of annexation, but it was not at all like that in Israel (even in Arab areas of the state). The Israelis who sought to impose their rule on East Jerusalem underestimated the collective strength of the Palestinian community, its staying power, and its resourcefulness. By waging a series of public, occasionally violent campaigns, the Palestinian community succeeded in thwarting Israeli measures designed to rob them of their collective heritage. The Israelis attempted to undermine the religious hierarchy, the education and health care systems, the trade unions, the independence of the Arab electric company, and freedom of the press. Their efforts in all these areas failed, and the institutions continued to function. The Intifada was evidence of the Palestinians' ability to mobilize the will of the community—and this will did not slacken despite great hardship, collective punishment by the Israelis, and a dramatic decrease in economic activity. At the opening stages of the Oslo process, the Palestinian community in Jerusalem was consolidated around its national, religious, and civil institutions.

In the period preceding the Intifada, a small number of Israelis thought that the Palestinians' success in maintaining their institutions and Israeli acquiescence with this outcome would form the cornerstone for a political settlement. They did not understand that pragmatic arrangements obtained as the result of a struggle for survival by a community whose legitimacy is not recognized by the authorities are not sufficient to serve as the basis for a lasting settlement. Only after these pragmatic arrangements are incorporated in a formal political agreement do they become meaningful.

The Declaration of Principles with the PLO, and its implementation in the form of the "Gaza and Jericho First" agreement and the redeployment of Israeli forces in the West Bank, acknowledged the legitimacy of the Palestinians as a national community and recognized the body providing the community's leadership. This recognition extended to that part of the Palestinian community living in East Jerusalem, and it was no longer possible to treat them as an amorphous population lacking a national identity. The transfer of civil powers to the PNA has had an immediate effect on the lives of the Palestinian residents of Jerusalem, who have become dependent on the decisions of the Authority in all areas related to civil powers—issuing of passports, religious jurisdiction, education, health care, the economy—anything not connected to territorial jurisdiction. The religious, civil, and national institutions that had been preserved were integrated into the governing apparatus of the PNA. The chair of the Supreme Muslim Council, who has responsibility for the Muslim holy places in Jerusalem, the religious court system, and the Waqf (religious endowment), was appointed minister of religion of the PNA. The Palestinian Ministry of Education was made responsible for curriculum, provision of textbooks, and teacher training for the municipal Arab public school system in Jerusalem. It became clear that Arab Jerusalem, which decades of Israeli rule had not succeeded in turning into another Israeli-Arab town like Nazareth, was fast becoming a territory partially controlled by an independent Palestinian ruling body recognized by Israel.

The redeployment arrangements for the West Bank, known as "Oslo 2," have made a significant contribution to this process, by granting the PNA a territorial foothold within the Jerusalem metropolitan area. The handing over of the cities Ramallah-al Bireh and Bethlehem-Beit Jala-Beit Sahour to Palestinian rule and the rural area to the east of the city's municipal boundaries to the PNA's civil authority produced what is almost a geographical bisection of the metropolitan area along ethnic lines. This partitioning has created the following areas of mono-ethnic rule: (1) the Jewish areas within the municipal boundaries of Jerusalem as well as the built-up areas of the urban "settlements" of Ma'ale Adumim, Efrat, Giv'at Ze'ev, and the P'sagot Bloc (to the northeast of Ramallah-el Bireh), which are fully under Israeli control; (2) areas transferred to the PNA; and (3) the Arab neighborhoods of East

Jerusalem (within its municipal boundaries), where Israeli rule is currently in force but where the Palestinians essentially enjoy communal independence.

The aptness of the preceding description of the status of the Arab neighborhoods of Jerusalem was reinforced by the outcome of the general elections to the PNA. As constituents of an electoral district encompassing the whole of metropolitan Jerusalem, the Palestinian residents of Jerusalem participated both as voters and as candidates. The representatives elected from Jerusalem duly joined the Authority, whose territorial jurisdiction did not include Jerusalem. However, by the very fact of their being elected and their representing Jerusalem residents, they have forged a strong link between the PNA and the Arab areas of East Jerusalem. The general elections also accelerated preparations for the establishment of an unofficial Arab city council, which is endeavoring to take on municipal functions in the Arab areas that have been neglected for years by the Israeli municipal council.

One interesting fact that came to light during the election campaign is that many Palestinian Jerusalemites were hesitant to participate in the elections for fear of endangering their rights as residents of Israel. These rights include national insurance and other forms of social insurance as well as, of particular import, an Israeli identity card allowing full freedom of movement. Others, especially candidates and those elected to the Authority, those involved in the media, and academics, while publicly condemning the Israeli system, in private greatly appreciated the security it granted them. The more apparent the arbitrariness of Palestinian rule and the lack of scrupulousness regarding civil rights in the Palestinian territories become, the greater the perceived advantage of living outside these areas. East Jerusalem's being a "gray area" is thus useful to the Palestinians as well as to the Israelis, who continue to be able to designate it Israeli territory.

The emerging pattern is, then, as follows: A metropolitan area encompassing some half-million dunams (125,000 acres), where demographic parity between Israelis and Palestinians prevails, is divided into two relatively equal parts. In areas adjacent to the municipal boundaries of Jerusalem that are under the jurisdiction of the PNA, Palestinian law, judicial process, and administration are in force, with one of these areas (Bethlehem, Azariyeh, or Ramallah) to be designated the Authority's administrative center and seat of the elected council. The residents of the Arab neighborhoods of Jerusalem are subject to the authority of the PNA in all areas concerning personal matters and communal needs. Municipal services in these neighborhoods will be provided through the cooperative efforts of the unofficial East Jerusalem municipal council and the neighboring Palestinian town councils. Muslim holy places, religious courts, and the Waqf will be, as they are now, autonomous and subject to the PNA.

The efficient functioning of this metropolitan area as an indivisible physical, urban, and economic unit will require Israeli-Palestinian cooperation and coordination in all areas of service delivery—roads, sewers and garbage disposal, water, electricity—as well as in the areas of ecology and the economy. Whatever the political leanings of the mayors of the Jewish settlement towns (members of parties opposed to the Oslo Accords), they will have no choice but to work in conjunction with the Palestinian civil authorities whose territories they abut. If they are wise enough to set up local coordinating bodies, a pattern of binational municipal government will develop that should evolve into a model for a metropolitan authority. If coordination is not achieved at the local level, it will have to be enforced at the level of central government—between Israel and the PNA as laid out down in the Oslo 2 Accords and annexes.

The model referred to here is not some theoretical scheme but rather the culmination of a mutually agreed-upon process that has in large part already been completed. The Oslo Accords created a dynamic sufficiently powerful to move this process forward, and if it continues without interference, to enable the eventual achievement of a more precisely defined arrangement, one that may rightly be called "the final settlement."

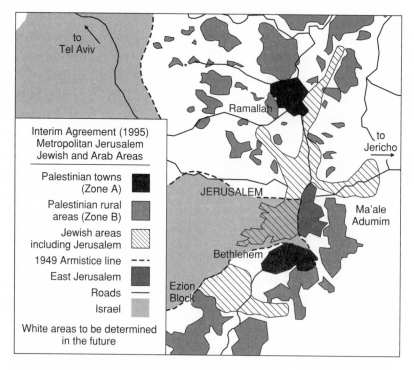

MAP 6.   Metropolitan Jerusalem, 1995

The so-called Oslo process was successful because its initiators took a process-oriented approach. Opponents of the process, both Israeli and Palestinian, denounced it as a betrayal of their national interests. For its Palestinian detractors, the Oslo Accords meant that the Jewish West Bank settlements would remain in place and the Arabs of East Jerusalem would continue to suffer under the yoke of the Israeli occupation. For its Israeli opponents, the accords meant that Israel had sold out "unified Jerusalem." Even the planners of the "perfect solution" were not satisfied. They would have liked to cram reality into neater molds. Thus, they obstinately persisted in searching for the exact answer to the problems of "sovereignty," "the holy places," and "urban administration." The political upheaval caused by the Israeli general election held in May 1996 boded ill for the future of the process-oriented approach. The winner, Prime Minister Benjamin Netanyahu, made the issue of Jerusalem a central theme of his election campaign and denounced his opponent Shimon Peres, saying that he "intends to divide Jerusalem." Netanyahu vowed to "ensure that Jerusalem is not negotiable," and to present an inflexible stance in the "final status" negotiations with the Palestinians.

The published "guidelines" of the new right-wing government have threatened to eliminate the constructive ambiguity and pragmatic style that have been essential to the success of the Oslo process. Yet, Prime Minister Netanyahu is unable to impose unilateral arrangements on the Palestinians, whose political independence in the framework of the PNA has become an irreversible fact. The alternative to the Oslo process is a renewal of the confrontation, renewed violence, and an international crisis. The risks of a renewed conflict are well known to Netanyahu. Therefore, it is likely that his approach will be more pragmatic than was indicated by his election sloganeering. What became clear beyond any doubt after the election was that the "solution-oriented approach," born out of the optimism of Oslo, had suffered a serious blow. The enigma of Jerusalem remains.

CHAPTER EIGHT

SEASHELLS ON THE JERUSALEM SHORE

Our walk through the shadows and twisted alleyways of the earthly Jerusalem has done little to reinforce the hope that this conflict-riven city will attain peace and tranquillity any-time soon. Perhaps the city of the dead, so detached from mundane conflicts, can offer us a more tranquil panorama. Perhaps the cemeter-ies of Jerusalem, where the personal and collective fates of all who have lived and fought one another merge, may provide an understanding of the eternal nature of the Holy City, and offer some consolation.

Disappointment with the living is not without justification in the context of Jerusalem, nor is turning to the dead. In this city the dead are mightier than the living. The myths of the ancient forefathers are the essence of local politics, and on the shoulders of the living the her-itage of past generations weighs as heavily as their tombstones.

We would like to believe that the cemetery is a tranquil refuge through whose gates the hatreds and violent confrontations of the liv-ing may not gain entry. This is, after all, the resting place of people no longer involved in religious, cultural, or national quarrels. We hope that our visit to the community of the dead might allow us to reflect on the

collective human condition from a safe distance. Unfortunately, however, in the atmosphere of Jerusalem this is but a pious hope. The city of
the dead is a reflection of that of the living, and the tensions of the latter are projected onto the former. The living do not allow the dead to
rest in peace, but recruit them to their petty struggles. The visitor,
impelled by the impulses of the living, transforms the visit to the graves
into a ritual act. Indeed, the cult of the fallen martyrs of the wars
between the Sons of Light and the Sons of Darkness is a central motif in
the lives of Jerusalemites. Herman Melville, author of *Moby Dick*, visited
Jerusalem in the mid-nineteenth century, and commented in his diary:
"Jerusalem is besieged by an army of the dead. . . . I wander among the
tombstones until I begin to regard myself as one possessed." (*Journal of
a Visit to Europe and the Levant* [Princeton, 1955], 144–45).

And indeed, Jerusalem's necropolis surrounds the city of the living
on all sides. It encompasses two dozen cemeteries: public and private,
large and small, in use and abandoned; of Jews, Karaites, Muslims, and
more than twenty Christian sects. The compulsive exclusivism so characteristic of Jerusalem's history and of its neighborhoods—so alienated
from one another—is also reflected in the city's concept of eternity. The
other monotheistic religions adopted the Jewish belief that humankind
will be gathered in Jerusalem on the Day of Judgment. But each
Jerusalemite awaits that day in a segregated plot fortified by stone walls,
within whose precincts no alien foot may tread. The living have for
some reason decided that the repose of the departed will be disturbed,
and their prospects for redemption diminished, if they are buried beside
members of another religion.

"For dust thou art and unto dust shalt thou return," and "dust to
dust," intone the ministers of all the religions in a variety of languages
and to various melodies. However, in Jerusalem death is not the "great
equalizer" but the great divider. Nowhere does blind fanaticism rule
with greater force than in the city of the dead. The nationalist zeal and
militant tribalism rampant in the city of the living are as nothing in
comparison to the cruel coercion that rules the graveyards. Men and

women who lived their entire lives in intimate partnership are forced to come to terms not only with bereavement, but with the inevitability of being buried separately merely because one of them belongs to the "wrong" faith. The granting and withholding of the right of burial is a device that the sectarian religious establishment has often employed in the past, and does not hesitate to use in the present.

The Greek Orthodox hierarchy enjoyed preferential treatment under the Ottomans, since this denomination was regarded as being both indigenous and loyal in contrast to the Catholic community, which was considered an agent of Christian Europe. Thus, the Greek Orthodox claims to ownership of most of the Christian holy places in Jerusalem were officially recognized. The Orthodox also received preference, virtually amounting to exclusivity, in the allocation of Christian burial grounds.

When the first Protestant missionaries arrived in Jerusalem, in the 1820s and 1830s, the Orthodox priests agreed to bury those who died in Jerusalem in their cemetery on Mount Zion. However, when the numbers began to swell, they reneged. Edward Robinson, a pioneer in the historical geography of the holy land, recounts that during his sojourn in Jerusalem in 1839, the Orthodox suddenly decided to prohibit Protestant burials, even though one person's grave stood ready and waiting. "On a strong representation of the case to the heads of the Greek convent, the burial was allowed to take place with the express understanding that a like permission would never more be given" (*Biblical Researches* [London, 1841], 1:228–29). Consequently, the American Protestants bought a small plot of ground near King David's tomb on Mount Zion, but the Ottoman authorities withheld approval of the purchase for months because "they were concerned that it might not be fitting that bodies of Christians be buried so close to David's tomb."

The Protestants themselves did not display excessive tolerance toward Lutheran sects that were not part of the establishment. Late in the 1870s, a large group of Germans arrived in Jerusalem from Wurtemburg, led by Cristoph Hoffmann. The group, which was at first called "God's People," and later "The German Templars," believed that the gathering of tens of thousands of Christian believers in Jerusalem was the only remedy for the ills of the world. This sect had adopted a form of ritual different from that accepted by the Lutheran church and was consequently expelled. For some years they buried their dead in the Anglican-Lutheran cemetery, but in 1877 this was prohibited, "since their worship was no longer Christian." The Templars established their own burial ground adjacent to the southern Jerusalem neighborhood they inhabited.

Prohibition of the burial of Jews who succumbed to Christian missionarism was the Jewish community's principal weapon against conversion attempts. These missionary efforts were carried out by Anglican priests who believed that the return of the Jews to their ancient homeland and their conversion to Christianity would hasten the second coming of Christ. They established hospitals and workshops in Jerusalem, seeking to attract Jews through provision of medical treatment and vocational training. The Jewish community authorities were infuriated by these efforts. They excommunicated, ostracized, and persecuted not only those Jews who showed an interest in Christianity, but even the sick and unfortunate Jews who had had no choice but to avail themselves of the mission's health or welfare services. The rabbis of Jerusalem decreed that anyone accepting help from the mission doctors "shall not be given a Jewish burial."

In her book *Jerusalem*, Nobel Prize-winning Swedish author Selma Lagerloff describes how an old Jewish woman fell and broke her leg in the street in front of a hospital run by the British Missionary Society. She was taken to the hospital and died there two days later. After her death, the English asked the head of the Jewish community to have the deceased taken for burial. The Jews refused, and the English had no choice but to bury her themselves. The Jews did nothing to interfere with their work, but the following night, they opened the grave and pitched the coffin out. The English reburied the woman, but the next night she was again tossed out of her grave. A member of the Swedish-American community passed by while six men were busy exhuming the body, and exchanged blows with them. "'God help us!' he shouted, 'How can anyone thus persecute a person after death?'"

It is not only in the older cemeteries that signs of religious fanaticism are evident; the past 150 years have not produced a more tolerant atmosphere in the city of the dead. In the Greek Orthodox cemetery on Mount Zion there are separate sections for Rumanians, Serbs, and Russians (all members of the same religious community) alongside sections for local Arabs and Greek priests. Here the visitor comes across the gravestones of Christian men and women who married Jews but did not convert. Their relatives were thus forced to bury them far from their spouses and the rest of the Jewish community to which they had linked their fate. In this cemetery, too, is the grave of an Israeli soldier, buried here because his mother had never converted to Judaism.

The problem of the burial of mixed couples became acute in the late 1980s, when approximately a quarter of the tremendous number of immigrants arriving in Israel from the former Soviet Union were non-Jews married to Jews, and the religious authorities refused to bury them with their spouses. The relatives suffered unbearably, as they were compelled to drag themselves from town to town—with the coffin—until they found a member of the clergy willing to perform the burial. The government finally established secular cemeteries, but even these are situated far from Jerusalem.

In one of the Christian cemeteries lies John Grauel, a hero in the saga of the Exodus, the famous "illegal" immigrant ship that set sail from France in 1946, attempted to run the British blockade of the Palestine coast, and was seized and returned to Europe. This American pastor had volunteered to serve on the ship's crew, took part in the violent clashes with the British on board the Exodus, and maintained close connections with Israel for the rest of his life. Prime Minister Golda Meir assured Grauel that he would be permitted to be buried in the

Israeli military cemetery on Mount Herzl. However, upon his death it became clear that he could not be interred in a Jewish military cemetery. Nevertheless, his gravestone bears the emblem of the Israeli army. At least this final honor was not denied him.

Jerusalem's necropolis is not only the battlefield of various regimes and religious sects; in Jerusalem a violent campaign is being waged between the dead and the living, or more precisely between those who have appointed themselves the guardians of those who have "returned to dust" and have no means of defending themselves, and the public officials who are striving to provide for the needs of the living. This scenario has become routine: bulldozers working on a site destined for the construction of homes or roads uncover ancient burial caves; ultra-orthodox Jews, who closely monitor all building activity in the city, alert their friends and interfere with the work; a violent confrontation ensues, culminating in a compromise with political overtones; the work is halted and the authorities consent to change their plans in conformity with the demands of the ultra-orthodox at a considerable cost to the public. The burial caves are resealed, and if they have been damaged beyond repair, the ultra-orthodox gather up the bones and give them a Jewish burial.

These almost daily confrontations are often supplemented by violence in print. When the archeologist who excavated the City of David—and who had been accused of desecrating Jewish graves—passed away, the ultra-orthodox posted large public notices on walls throughout the city expressing their joy over the demise of this "despicable person," who had died, they claimed, after being cursed by the rabbis. Nor are secular circles lacking in strong sentiments. The struggle of the ultra-orthodox against the desecration of the burial caves is depicted as "a civil war over the control of Jerusalem, a Jewish Intifada." The ultra-orthodox are described as the partners of Israel's worst enemies, a "Jewish *Hamas*," no less.

This confrontation, between the needs of the dwellers in the lands of the living and the repose of those who have returned to dust, can be explained in terms of a concept peculiar to Judaism, which decrees the absolute and eternal separation between the city of the dead and the city of the living. Judaism regards the cemetery as the home of the dead, where they await resurrection (hence the Hebrew term, "house of eternity"). Its site is therefore appropriated and totally removed from the authority of the living and eternally consecrated to the dead. The living are absolutely forbidden to make use of the cemetery, its land, or anything connected with it: "One does not graze animals there, one does not divert water through it, one does not gather weeds there, or if one does, burns them on the spot." Since the dead cannot defend themselves against those endangering their chances of resurrection "at the end of days," the rabbis impose explicit and severe prohibitions on the living, lest they disturb the repose of the dead. Those who are zealously scrupulous in their observance of these prohibitions fear that unless they prevent harm to the departed, they themselves will be harmed and their prospects for resurrection endangered.

Thus, the Jewish way of perceiving cemeteries differs from that of the Muslims and Christians who do not regard them as places of perpetual holiness, nor envision graves as the "eternal homes" of the dead. For the latter two alteration of land usage is permissible (within certain limitations), as are the collection of the bones of the dead after a certain period of time and their reburial. The Jewish concept applies, of course, only to Jewish dead and does not extend to the dead in general. The self-styled defenders of the dead, who are so concerned for every bone of anyone they identify as Jewish, (often insisting that clearly non-Jewish burial places are Jewish, to be on the safe side), are not willing to lift a finger in the case of the dead of other religions. Graves that were part of the large Mamilla Muslim cemetery in central West Jerusalem were destroyed in the course of road-widening and in the construction of a public park. The protests of the Muslim clergy were ignored. Preservation of the dignity of the dead, like that of the living, is a matter of religious affiliation.

Many cemeteries have been desecrated or destroyed in the course of the numerous wars over Jerusalem, but the most extensive acts of destruction and vandalism were perpetrated between 1948 and 1967 in the Jewish cemetery on the Mount of Olives. For hundreds of years this was the only Jewish burial ground in Jerusalem, its sanctity arising from the fact that it overlooks the site of the Temple, where the dead are to be resurrected on the Day of Judgment. The cemetery is second in sanctity only to the Western Wall, by virtue of its location and the tens of thousands of dead buried on its grounds: it has been referred to as "God's footrest." However, its close proximity to areas inhabited by Arabs has meant that every time intercommunal riots broke out between Jews and Arabs, Arabs would attack Jewish funerals and desecrate graves. These incidents reached a peak in December 1947 with the commencement of the incidents leading to the 1948 war, and in February 1948, Jews were prevented from continuing further interment on the mount.

During the nineteen years that the area remained under Arab control, tombstones were uprooted, people trespassed on the cemetery grounds, and roads were built through them. The full extent of the destruction became evident only after the 1967 war. Approximately 40,000 of the 50,000 tombstones had been desecrated. A commission appointed to investigate the state of the cemetery itemized the typical acts of destruction: three roads and a parking lot were built on cemetery land; some of the land was plowed; fences were destroyed; gravestones were scattered about or employed in the construction of buildings, military camps, paths, stairs, and fences.

The rehabilitation of the cemetery was an extensive operation, lasting some twenty years, in which an enormous amount of money was invested. Just as the acts of vandalism had been motivated by nationalist sentiments, the cemetery's rehabilitation was a reflection of aspirations to establish a Jewish Israeli presence in East Jerusalem, an expression of the city's reunification, and yet another example of how the city of the dead mirrors that of the living. The Muslim cemeteries in the western (Jewish) half of the city—Mamilla, Ein Kerem, Malha, and others—did not merit rehabilitation, and this too is a reflection of the reality prevalent in the land of the living: their rehabilitation would have been seen as acknowledging Arab political claims to West Jerusalem.

Evidence of the violent political conflict can be seen throughout the city of the dead on the Mount of Olives, but such conflict is not limited to that site. Elsewhere, military cemeteries, special plots set aside for the burial of civilian victims of political violence and intercommunal disturbances, memorial stones and plaques in squares and on street corners—all of these places constitute a sad reminder of the intensity of the struggle over Jerusalem and of its many victims.

On forty occasions since historians began chronicling the story of Jerusalem, the city has been subjected to siege and warfare. The cemeteries and memorials commemorate only a tiny minority of the many multitudes who fought over the Holy City and met their death. The warriors' graves that are visible are from recent generations. But where are the burial places of King David's soldiers; of Sennacherib and Nebuchadnezzar's troops; of Judah the Maccabi, Vespasian and Titus, and Jonathan of Gush Halav; of Caliph 'Omar and Godfrey of Bouillon; of Suleiman the Magnificent and Muhammad Ali? The only representatives of the distant empires that battled over the Holy City are the British and German soldiers who fought here during the First World War. All the other warriors buried here were members of the communities whose home is Jerusalem, though among the Jews and Arabs rest a handful of British who got caught in the inter-ethnic crossfire and were killed because they tried to mediate between the combatants or because each of the warring communities, in its turn, regarded them as foreign occupiers.

Anyone wishing to fully understand the tragedy of the Jewish-Arab intercommunal conflict must visit two graves, distant from each other, one in West Jerusalem and the other in the East. The tragic encounter between their occupants could only have taken place in the Holy City, and epitomizes the entire conflict.

In the Israeli military cemetery on Mount Herzl in West Jerusalem, beside the graves of three unknown soldiers, lies that of Sergeant Major

Meir Karmiol. Born in Germany in 1923, Karmiol fled with his family to Poland when Hitler came to power, and from there immigrated to Palestine. With the outbreak of the Second World War, he joined the British police and was employed guarding military airbases. In addition to his police service, Karmiol was a member of the Jewish underground military organization the *Hagana* and was a boxing champion. At the beginning of the 1948 war, he joined a militia brigade composed of Jerusalem residents and participated in all its military actions.

Early in April 1948, Meir Karmiol took part in the capture of Mount Kastel, a hill overlooking the main road connecting Tel Aviv and Jerusalem that was situated so that whoever controlled it dominated the western approaches to Jerusalem. The Jewish fighters succeeded in driving the Arabs out, thereby breaking the siege of Jerusalem. The Arabs attempted to retake the hill. During one of the Arab counterattacks, Meir Karmiol discerned a figure approaching his position in the darkness; he called out in English, "Who's there?" and the response came back in Arabic, "It's us, friends." Karmiol fired a round from his submachine gun, and the Arab fell on his face. Karmiol disarmed the dead man, and removed his documents and a miniature *Qur'an* he was carrying. The young Jewish immigrant did not know that his bullets had cut down the beloved commander of the Arab forces and member of a leading family in the Palestinian national struggle. Several hours later, during another Arab counterattack, Karmiol stayed behind to help a wounded comrade, and while doing so he too was hit by a burst of fire, and killed. He left no family.

On the Temple Mount, in one of the rooms of the fourteenth-century western patio, the graves of 'Abd al-Qader al-Husseini and his father Mousa Kazzim Pasha lie side by side. Mousa Kazzim (1850–1934) was briefly mayor of Jerusalem (see Chapter 4). The senior al-Husseini was of the old generation of leaders who believed in nonviolent struggle against British rule. 'Abd al-Qader rebelled against the pacifism of his elders, believing that only through armed struggle would it be possible to eliminate Zionism and oust the British occupiers. He lead a

13. Israeli military cemetery

guerrilla band in 1936–37 and was twice wounded in battles with the British army. With the conclusion of the Arab Revolt in 1939, he went into exile in Iraq and Saudi Arabia, returning to Palestine in 1947. He revived his guerrilla organization and commanded the Jerusalem sector. After his death at Kastel, he was given a funeral the likes of which Jerusalem had never known. His coffin was borne above the heads of the tens of thousands of people who lined the funeral route from outside the city all the way to the mosques on the Temple Mount. "With his death, Palestine was lost," declared the mourners.

The son of 'Abd al-Qader, Faisal Husseini, is following in his father's footsteps as a Palestinian leader, although with a gentleness reminiscent of his grandfather. Much bloodshed separates the grandchildren of 'Abd al-Qader and those of the generation of Israelis who fought in 1948, and rivers of blood continue to flow toward both the Jewish and Arab cemeteries even as efforts are made to close the account and bridge the abyss.

The Jewish people's commemoration of their war dead is organized and institutionalized, as befits a nation dwelling in its sovereign state. Its fallen are buried with full military honors in the carefully tended graves of the military cemetery, a moving memorial and concrete expression of the nation's mourning on Mount Herzl in Jerusalem. More than 4,000 people are interred there, the overwhelming majority of them young men. This is the final resting place of those soldiers who fought in the Israeli army when it was founded in 1948, as well as of those who fell in the Second World War and in the struggle against the British. High retaining walls and lush vegetation divide the sections of the graveyard into relatively small units, where the dead are buried according to the battlefields where they fell. A special section is devoted to the memory of the fallen whose place of burial is not known. Monuments have been erected to the memory of those who were buried abroad or who drowned at sea while on active duty.

The graves themselves are raised flowerbeds planted with fragrant evergreen rosemary. The cypress, pines, and cedars of Lebanon crowning the green burial plots represent the merger of lost youth with the cosmic and ever-renewing cycle of nature. The symbolism of a grave in the form of a bed of flowers—drinking in the vigor of youth, as it were, and immortalizing it in the blossoms—blends with that of the planted tree, itself an Israeli national symbol. Day after day, grief-stricken fathers and mothers visit this cemetery of children, and lay wreaths on the graves. As far as they are concerned, the price of this city has been paid in full.

The concrete expressions of Arab mourning for the fallen of their national struggle are for the most part intermingled with those of persons who passed away in the general stream of human fate. Having no state, the Arabs have no military cemeteries of their own. The graves of those who were killed during acts of rebellion and struggle against the Israeli regime lie scattered throughout Muslim civilian cemeteries. The authorities often do not permit Jerusalem Arabs killed in violent incidents to be buried in the city's cemeteries for fear that the funeral might turn into a violent nationalist demonstration. Therefore there is a special "terrorists' graveyard" in the Jordan Rift Valley, where dozens of Palestinians are buried in numbered, but otherwise unmarked graves.

Many Palestinian fighters are buried in the Muslim cemetery near the Gate of Mercy on the eastern slopes of the Temple Mount. There, among the graves of simple families and the mausoleums of the well-connected, one can find the graves of those who fell in 1947–49 and 1967, of PLO fighters who fell in the Lebanon war (1982) and of those killed in terrorist incidents and the Intifada. The Palestinians honor the memory of their war dead with a ceremony beside the Monument to the Fallen of 1967, which is not far from the cemetery. The story of this monument illustrates the fact that in Jerusalem, death does not wipe out blood debts, and the dead enemy is no less threatening than the living one. The sentiment that death is the common fate of mortals is not shared by those who feel they are engaged in a struggle for survival.

In June 1967, only a few hours after the sounds of the battle for Jerusalem faded into silence, mounds of small stones began to spring up in various spots throughout the city—improvised monuments erected by members of Israeli units that had fought in Jerusalem in memory of their fallen comrades. These monuments were duly replaced by permanent memorials that were placed in the heart of the Arab neighborhoods where the battles had taken place. The visible memorialization of the Israeli soldiers caused the Arabs also to seek a way of commemorating their fallen. These were private initiatives, since the Arabs had no public agency left operating that was capable of taking on this task. Soon the eastern part of the city was dotted with some two dozen monuments, half of them Jewish and half Arab. Most were situated opposite each other, for the soldiers of both sides had fallen at the sites of the same battles.

The Israeli authorities sought to arrange for the erection of permanent Arab monuments and the removal of the improvised ones. In negotiations with the Mufti, head of the Muslim religious community, it was agreed that four monuments would be built. When work was begun on the first and it was reported in the Hebrew press, a major storm erupted. Most of the Jewish public regarded the granting of permission to establish memorials to fallen Arabs as "rewarding those who set out to annihilate us." One of the opponents of the memorial drew an interesting comparison, asking, "Would it have occurred to the relatives of Nazi pilots killed in the London blitz to demand the erection of memorials in the heart of Hyde Park?"

There were also prominent supporters of the project. David Ben-Gurion wrote: "The soldier in the Arab Legion did his duty to his people by fighting, and he should be honored with the erection of a monument to his memory. . . . If his parents so desire, they are entitled to this." However, the voices of the supporters were weaker than the shouts of the opponents. People viewed their situation as a war for survival, and they were incapable of seeing their dead enemies as human beings who did their duty and fell defending what was dear to them. The commemoration of the fallen Arabs was perceived as a threat, and their memorial ceremonies were seen as an incitement to violence. Indeed, these ceremonies often have become occasions not for preaching peace on earth but for converting the dead into silent partners in the cry for revenge.

The Jerusalem cemeteries memorialize not only the victims of direct combat, but victims of other forms of violence as well: those who were uprooted from their homes or who fled in fear from war, that is, the refugees. Grave plots not belonging to Jerusalemites are located in the cemetery east of the Old City walls. In its easternmost section—the lowest part, and the farthest from the mosques on the Temple Mount— are the graves of refugees from the Jerusalem area villages that were conquered by the Israelis in 1948 and totally destroyed. The names of the deceased and the villages of origin are painted on simple monuments. Here lie the dead who were born in towns where not one stone remains on top of another, the names of which have even been struck from the official maps. Two generations since the last of the refugees left them, grandchildren proudly refer to those places as home. Palestinian research institutes in Jerusalem create paper memorials to these villages. In thick volumes they chronicle them and gather every shred of information on their inhabitants. In the spring of 1995, a Palestinian research team discovered a mass grave containing fifty-two skeletons of residents of the village of Abu Shusha, midway between Tel Aviv and Jerusalem.

The Arab place-names that have disappeared from the map also appear on the tombstones of the Israeli soldiers who fell during their conquest in 1948. The sight of these graves evokes the despairing reflection that the real geography of this land is interred in its cemeteries, Jewish and Arab alike.

Our description of the city of the dead as a haven for refugees fleeing for their lives does not end here; the Jewish cemeteries also record the geography of the Jewish diaspora. On thousands of graves, on the Mount of Olives in the east and the Mount of Eternal Rest in the west, a distant place of birth is recorded. Names of far-flung Jewish communities that no longer exist, many having been destroyed during the holocaust, from Yemen to northern Russia, from India, China, and especially from Poland and the "pale of settlement," are carved on the graves. One wishing to comprehend the full magnitude of the tragedy can visit the Valley of the Destroyed Communities at the Yad Vashem holocaust memorial and compare the place-names on the individual graves with those on the collective memorial plaques. Only a small minority of the inhabitants of these towns and villages escaped the fate of the six million Jews who perished in the holocaust, whose last resting place is unknown.

The refugees from the holocaust who gathered in Jerusalem lie not far from refugees of another holocaust, that of the Armenians. A few thousand of the approximately one million Armenians who had lived for generations in Asiatic Turkey and were murdered or perished on death marches during the First World War managed to evade their Turkish persecutors and reach Jerusalem. The city's ancient Armenian community took them in and they became another beautiful piece of the mosaic of Jerusalem. On April 24 every year, the entire Armenian community gathers beside the obelisk commemorating the contribution of Armenian soldiers to the victory over the Ottoman Empire in the First World War. This is the date when, in 1915, the Turkish authorities imprisoned, exiled, or murdered all of the political and religious leaders of the Istanbul Armenian community, thereby signaling the beginning of the Armenian holocaust.

The Jerusalem calendar is full to bursting with memorial days. The cult of the dead results in the departed having more influence on the living than do the deeds of the living themselves. Yet confronting the martyrs of both sides brings precisely the opposite feeling into focus. Wandering through the cemeteries acts as a counterbalance to demonic stereotypes. The brief biographical details engraved on the tombstones, and even the names themselves, pluck the dead as it were from the pages of a history conscripted to serve the cause, and plants them in a different, neutral, and human soil.

It suddenly becomes clear that the lives and deeds, struggles and deaths of the residents of the cemetery have no meaning in the absence of their "shadow selves"—their sworn enemies. Here is the grave of a man you knew as a bloodthirsty enemy who was cruel and barbaric, but a brief perusal of the biographical lexicon reveals that this man completed law school, translated poetry, and fought for the values in which he believed. He was undoubtedly an enemy, but his life story causes you to reflect that in your tribe's cemetery lies the mirror image of this man, who also studied, loved, and devoted himself to the ideals he believed in. In these rare moments of compassion one can place a hand upon the enemy's grave and feel the blood ties that unite all Jerusalemites and make them such intimate enemies.

The clamor of the disputes between the national collectives drowns out the voices of other communities that also sought dominion in Jerusalem, but heavenly rather than earthly dominion. The members of the religions of Moses and Muhammad converted their religious aspirations to national ones, also embodying, of course, the longing for divine salvation. Members of the third monotheistic religion, the Christians, also sought their salvation in Jerusalem. However, with one exception—the Crusader period (and perhaps also during the British Mandate)—these yearnings were not translated into attempts to establish earthly authority or massive colonization of the city. The legions of the Christian colonial powers and their diplomatic and religious emissaries did, however, seek to annex the Holy City to their empires, or at least to attain positions of decisive political influence via their religious activities. However, these aspirations were not accompanied by the creation of demographic "facts," and it is only the presence of communities that have sunk roots in a place that can, when all is said and done, establish a claim to material proprietorship. This does not mean that some Christian groups did not settle in Jerusalem and attempt to establish communities there.

Two Christian communities, the American-Swedish colony and the German Templars, are commemorated by the buildings they erected in the city, which have long since been emptied of their original inhabitants. Nowadays, human contact with these communities can only be accomplished by a visit to their cemeteries, where tales are told of lives of great hopes and faded dreams. In themselves, they were no more than a footnote in the chronicles of the city, and their religious beliefs and way of life became thorns in the flesh of the mainstream Christian sects. However, their history also reveals the universal aspect of the Holy City, which is all too often overwhelmed in the tumult of the Jewish-Arab conflict.

The American connection with Jerusalem began in 1820, with the arrival in the city of Levi Parsons, a 21-year-old missionary from New England. He and his friend Plini Fisk were sent to establish a mission in the Holy City. Their attempt failed, and their successors, too, encountered a wall of hostility on the part of the Ottoman authorities and the Christian religious establishment. The Americans retreated from Jerusalem and based their activities in Beirut, where their religious and educational institutions—first and foremost the famous American

University—flourished. A few isolated American missionaries continued limited activities in Jerusalem, and some of them died there and
were buried in a small cemetery (previously mentioned) that they had
established on Mount Zion.

In the summer of 1881, a group of Americans led by Horatio Spafford
and his wife Ann arrived in Jerusalem. This group believed that deeds of
charity and mercy would hasten the second coming of Christ. They did
not engage in missionary activity, but instead promoted artisanship and
advancements in agriculture, and offered vocational training and education to the city's inhabitants. Their distinctive manner of prayer and
their semi-collective lifestyle aroused the suspicion of the Christian
churches as well as the hostility of the American consuls, most of whom
were connected with the Protestant establishment in America.

The "American Colony" was joined in the 1890s by a group of
Swedish-Americans, followed by Swedes from Dalarna, northwest of
Stockholm. Unlike similar groups of Americans, who had tried to establish themselves in Palestine and failed, the members of the American
Colony succeeded in putting down roots in Jerusalem and became an
important factor in its economic and social development. Their most
well-known undertaking was the American Colony Hotel, a fine building in East Jerusalem's prestigious Sheikh Jarah neighborhood, which
they purchased from a local dignitary. The hotel is the last remnant
(apart from a children's clinic in the Old City) of a community that, at
its peak, numbered 150. The leader of the American Colony, Horatio
Spafford, died in 1886 and was buried in the old cemetery on Mount
Zion; in the course of time another ten members of the group were
interred there—both Americans and Swedes.

The hostility of the American missionaries and of American consul,
Selah Merrill (himself a member of the religious missionary establishment in Andover, Massachussets) toward the members of the American
Colony was reflected in the way they treated the graves of the colony's
dead. In 1897, missionaries in Beirut sold the cemetery to German
monks who were planning to build a church on the adjacent plot of

land. With the knowledge of the American consul, the dead from the colony were removed from their graves in a disorderly manner, put into packing crates, and thrown into a pit beside the wall of the Anglican-Lutheran cemetery on the hillside. The people of the colony knew nothing of the transfer of the bodies beforehand, and only after intervention by the British consul were they permitted to open the burial pit. Therein they found fifteen crates containing the bones of twenty-five dead, including those of missionaries who had died before the arrival of the colonists. The colony's leader, Spafford, was the only one whose body it was possible to identify, because of a missing tooth; however, he too shared his crate with another body.

The dead Americans' troubles were not over yet. In 1906, a second attempt was made to exhume their bones, but was forestalled by the intervention of the German and Swedish consuls. Eventually the colony established its own cemetery, on the summit of Mount Scopus. Selma Lagerloff, who visited the American community in Jerusalem in 1900, described the incident of the grave desecrations in her book, and quoted the colonists' defiant words regarding their late leader: "We believed in him, and he brought us to a land where we are more despised than dogs, and to a city that has killed us with its cruelty."

The German Templars arrived in Jerusalem in 1877 and established a neighborhood for themselves in the southern part of the city. Far from the Old City walls, it was a replica of a Swabian village, with fifty-two buildings including a school, a meeting hall, and a church. Its straight streets and its rustic houses, clad in greenery with gigantic pines towering over them, have retained their old-fashioned beauty, and today the German Colony is one of the most desirable residential neighborhoods in Jerusalem. Not one of the original settlers is, of course, living there. Only the colony's small cemetery remains as a record of the saga of three generations that began with messianic hopes and ended in disgrace and expulsion.

"Gathering the people of God unto Jerusalem" and establishing a community living in the spirit of the Old and New Testaments which would "inherit the holy land and thus proclaim redemption" were the noble ideas that brought German peasants to settle in this land, and they melted like snowflakes when they touched the ground of reality. The spirit that had animated the missionaries evaporated, and their messianic faith was replaced by material concerns. After one generation a new philosophy already prevailed: their mission was no longer the exaltation of man in God's congregation, but the amelioration of economic conditions in the holy land.

And indeed they proved greatly successful at this task. The Templar community—with villages and neighborhoods in Jerusalem, Jaffa, and Haifa—was undoubtedly one of the most important agents of material progress in late nineteenth century Palestine. The Germans accelerated development in agriculture, in industry and transportation, and in commerce and tourism. German coachmen driving German carriages built in German workshops conveyed thousands of tourists to German hotels whose water pumps and plumbing accessories had been produced in German factories, and which served food from German farms.

The Germans' contribution to the economic development of the Jewish community was considerable, and their material achievements served as a model for the development of the Zionist settlement enterprise. However, this contribution could not obscure the decline of their pious, humanist culture and the ascendancy of German nationalistic sentiments among the second- and third-generation Templars.

Monuments to Templars who died in the ranks of the German army during the First and Second World Wars bear witness to the colonists' support for the imperialistic adventures of Kaiser Wilhelm II and the crimes of the Nazi regime. In the Templar cemetery in Jerusalem, there stands a monument to forty-seven Palestinian Germans who were killed in the First World War on the battlefields of Flanders, the Somme, Messines, and Verdun. A more recent memorial commemorates "more than 450 dead and those who fell in 1914–18 and 1939–45." This is where all the dead of the Templar communities outside Jerusalem are interred, their bodies having been moved here in the 1950s. The initiators of the memorial clearly chose this vague wording for the inscription with only one aim in mind; to downplay the role of the Templars in the Second World War and their participation in the Nazi movement.

Sixty-three Templars were killed in the Second World War, fighting in the ranks of the German army and the S.S. Their names appear only in a forgotten memorial booklet. But the Nazi connections of the descendants of the "people of God" were open and well known. In 1937, 700 men and women out of a total Templar population of 2,000 were members of the Nazi party. They paid for this dearly: with the outbreak of the war, the Templars were arrested and placed in British internment camps. Although they enjoyed comfortable conditions there, at the wars' end they were expelled from the country, some to Australia and some back to Germany. The last Templar in Jerusalem, architect and carpenter Hermann Immberger, a member of the Nazi party, was expelled from Jerusalem by Israel in 1950. The graves of sixteen members of the Immberger family, including five children under a year-and-a-half old, remain orphaned as it were in the German Colony cemetery. These graves bring to mind the many noble hopes shattered on the rocks of Jerusalem. How then should the people buried there be remembered? By how they set out or by how they ended up?

Pilgrimages to Jerusalem for the purpose of settling there and establishing religious communities did not, of course, begin only in the mid-nineteenth century, neither were they limited to Americans, Swedes, and Germans. There have been Christian communities in Jerusalem ever since St. James the Great established the Jewish-Christian community after the crucifixion of Jesus. The changing number of Christians in Jerusalem serves as a reliable indication of the prevailing security conditions in the city and of the arbitrariness of the authorities. This is clear when Christian population figures over the course of the past two centuries are examined.

In 1800, approximately 3,000 Christians lived in Jerusalem, roughly one-third of the city's population. Seventy years later, their numbers had reached 5,250 (about one-quarter of the population). Following the

British conquest Christians numbered 14,700, and at the end of the Mandatory period their numbers reached an all-time high of 31,000 souls (about 19 percent of Jerusalem's population). The 1947–48 fighting wreaked havoc on the Christian community, and nearly half of its members left the city. At the commencement of the Israeli occupation in 1967, 11,000 Christians remained in Jerusalem, constituting about 4.2 percent of the population of the reunified city. The intercommunal tensions that erupted during the Intifada resulted in Christian emigration from the city that equaled the birthrate; during this period the size of the community did not grow, and its proportion in the general population fell, reaching 2.5 percent in the mid-nineties. Even this minute figure was only reached because of the inclusion of Christian members of the families of Jewish immigrants from the former Soviet Union. Most members of the Christian community are local Arabs, almost equally divided between Catholics and Greek Orthodox. Among the non-Arab sects, the Armenians, numbering fewer than 2,000, are worthy of note.

Christian leaders, and especially the Vatican, have always understood the importance of having a strong Christian community in the Holy City. Anxiety regarding the diminishing relative size of the Christian population of the city was one of the factors guiding the Church leaders, whose concern is apparent in the following admonition: "The holy places must be houses of prayer and worship full of people, and not empty museums and graveyards." Yet inter-religious and inter-national rivalries hampered their efforts to act on this concern. Instead of cooperating to frustrate the authorities' schemes and to foster ecumenical unity as a defense against the destructive influences of the Jewish-Arab conflict, the heads of the various sects fought each other.

Not until the 1970s and eighties did the heads of some of the Christian communities begin to cooperate. This ecumenical spirit was largely the outcome of the Arabization of the church hierarchies, leading to the placing of Arab priests at the head of the local Catholic and Anglican churches (The Greek Orthodox were a notable exception to this process and will be discussed separately). National allegiance proved stronger than dogmatic schism. This held no guarantee that the process of demographic attrition would be arrested or reversed, but the lesson had been well learned: everyone was the loser in intra-Christian rivalry. Indeed, evidences of Christian failure are clearly discernible along Jerusalem's skyline and in its cemeteries. The "flocks" of all the competing denominations voted with their feet, leaving only their dead behind in the Catholic, Protestant, and Greek Orthodox cemeteries. As Herman Melville wrote in his *Journal*, "I stroll to Mount Zion, along the terraced walks and survey the tombstones of the hostile Armenians, Latins, Greeks, all sleeping together" (146).

On the summit of Mount Zion, opposite the Old City walls, sits the Greek Orthodox cemetery, in which the members of all the Orthodox communities were buried—Russians, Serbs, Rumanians and, of course, members of the local Arab community and the Greek hierarchy. The tension between the foreign priesthood and the local community is reflected in the placement of the gravestones whose inscriptions are in Greek in comparison with those whose inscriptions are in Arabic; the graves of the church fathers occupy one side of the cemetery. In addition to their ancient titles—resurrections of fifth and sixth century A.D. Byzantine appellations—the birthplaces of these priests are engraved on their stones: Asia Minor, Greece and the Greek Islands, Cyprus. The privilege of sacred service in senior posts is reserved for men of Hellenic origin.

This discrimination infuriated the members of the community, all of whom were Arab. The lay Arab community watched these foreigners doing as they pleased with the vast property holdings of the church, and were enraged by the fact that practically nothing was being done for their welfare or to improve their children's education. The more Palestinian nationalist feelings grew, the more their resentment increased.

Not that the Palestinian members of the Greek Orthodox community were ignorant or lacking in influence. On the contrary, a visit to the other side of the Orthodox cemetery reveals the Arabic-inscribed tombstones of some of the most highly-educated, wealthy, and able members of Jerusalem's Palestinian community. The great majority of these families have vanished from the city's human landscape; a sad loss for Jerusalem.

Just over the fence lies the Armenian cemetery, in which are buried members of this united community that has not ceased to feel the pain of exile. One tombstone bears a drawing of Mount Ararat, proud symbol of this ancient people. On another is written, "Here lies Gnevod from Lake Van, a lover of letters." When old Armenians die, a little sack of soil from their ancient homeland is placed under their heads.

The old Catholic cemetery is wedged into the grounds of the Armenian cemetery. This was the first graveyard where Christians of European origins, referred to as "Franks," were buried. It has been closed for years, having been replaced by a large cemetery on the hillside. All that remains in the old one are a few graves that were dug before the close of the nineteenth century. The graves of monks, priests, and pilgrims from the sixteenth through nineteenth centuries have been removed and the bones placed in a large ossuary. Monumental tombstones, belonging to the Irish Dead Sea scholar Christopher Costigan as well as Catholic consuls and famous monks, are imbedded in the cemetery wall. Costigan's mother engraved the following on his: "O son, may the celestial Zion receive you—where there is no death, no mourning, no suffering, but where eternal joy reigns."

On the slope below lies the Protestant cemetery. The lives and deaths of its residents are bound together by a connecting thread—the story of the appearance of Europeans in Jerusalem, their attempts to gain a foothold in the city, and their disappearance from its landscape amidst waves of Arab and Jewish nationalism. On the western side of the cemetery lie the dead of the nineteenth and early twentieth centuries, members of communities that populated the Ottoman city: English and German bishops, missionaries, Jewish and Arab converts, architects and builders, merchants and bankers, doctors, tailors, and pilgrims. In the center are buried German soldiers and airmen who fell in the First World War, having failed to prevent the conquest of Ottoman

Jerusalem by a Christian power. And in the eastern and northern sections of the cemetery lie the dead of the British Colony (1918–48), the officials, policemen, officers, and their families, members of a people that endeavored to rule the conflict-torn holy land and found themselves in the line of fire from both sides. In one section lie the policemen and officers killed in the Arab Revolt of 1936–39, while the members of the British forces killed in the Jewish Revolt of 1944–47 are buried in a separate area. On many of the graves, the words "gave his life for this land" are inscribed.

The tranquillity in which Mount Zion is wrapped does not succeed in silencing the tumult of quarrels, rivalries, and confrontations rising from the graves of the dead interred in this holy ground. Nor does tranquillity reign within the precincts of the Jewish cemetery on the Mount of Olives or the Muslim cemetery on the slopes of the Temple Mount. And perhaps the absence of eternal tranquillity is an outcome of the fact that in Jerusalem death is a temporary state, because so many people believe that the day is not distant when the dead shall rise, and the resurrection of the dead will take place in that city. The Jerusalem-born Arab historian, al-Muqadassi, wrote in A.D. 985: "and as to Jerusalem being the most spacious of cities; why, since all created things are to assemble there on the Day of Judgment what place on earth can be more extensive than this?"

The Muslims adopted many traditions concerning the sacredness of Jerusalem whose roots were in Judaism; among these was the belief that the resurrection of the dead and the "Last Judgment" would take place there. Jerusalem is designated as the site of the Last Judgment in the prophetic books of Zechariah and Joel. Zechariah prophesies: "Behold the day of the Lord cometh. . . . For I will gather all nations against Jerusalem to battle. . . . And his feet shall stand in that day upon the Mount of Olives, which is before Jerusalem on the east, and the Mount of Olives shall cleave in the midst thereof toward the east and toward the west, and there shall be a very great valley. . . ." (Zech. 14:1–8). And the Prophet Joel states: "Let the heathen be wakened, and come up to

14.   Mount of Olives and the Valley of Jehoshaphat

the valley of Jehoshaphat: for there will I sit to judge all the heathen round about. . . . Multitudes, multitudes in the valley of decision: for the day of the Lord is near in the valley of decision. The sun and the moon shall be darkened, and the stars shall withdraw their shining. The Lord also shall roar from Zion, and utter his voice from Jerusalem; and the heavens and the earth shall shake. . . ." (Joel 3:12–16). And the following verses from the *Qur'an* describe the scene: "On the day the trumpet sounds its first and second blast, all hearts shall be filled with terror, and all eyes shall stare with awe. They say 'We are turned to hollow bones, shall we be restored to life? A fruitless transformation!' But with one blast they shall return to the earth's surface [*a-sahira*]" (Sura 79; 6–14).

An ancient tradition identifies *a-sahira* with the upper reaches of the Kidron Valley, that is, in the Valley of Jehoshaphat mentioned by the Prophet Joel, which is located to the southwest of the Mount of Olives. Hence the Jewish and Muslim cemeteries were situated on either slope of the Valley of Jehoshaphat, since the dead who are buried there will be the first to face judgment on the resurrection day. "The righteous will burst forth and surface in Jerusalem," states Jewish tradition, adding that "on that day, when the dead shall rise, they shall immediately bow down the place of the Shechinah," that is, the Temple Mount which stands opposite the Mount of Olives. A Persian traveler wrote (1047): "When you have passed out of the noble sanctuary there lies before you a great level plain, called *a-sahira*, which it is said, will be the place of the resurrection, where all mankind shall be gathered together. For this reason men from all parts of the world come hither and make their sojourn in the holy city till death overtakes them, in order that when the day fixed by God—be he praised and exalted—shall arrive, they may thus lie in their graves, ready and present at the appointed place" (*Palestine Under the Moslems*, 219).

Muslim tradition says that on the Day of Judgment a bridge will span the Valley of Jehoshaphat between the Temple Mount and the Mount of Olives, which the resurrected will cross on their way to be judged. Those buried in Jerusalem will be the first to be resurrected. But what of all those buried outside the holy land? They will have to tunnel underground like rats "until they come to the Mount of Olives that is in Jerusalem—upon which the Lord stands—and it will open for them and they will emerge from it." So the Jewish belief is phrased as well, adding that even before the resurrection there are "many advantages to burial in Jerusalem: the dead there do not suffer from the vigorous beatings the angels inflict on the bodies of the dead, maggots and worms will not devour their flesh, and the 'ascent of the soul' from Jerusalem is directly through the gateway to heaven."

The Muslims also took an interest in the fate of the dead prior to the day of their resurrection. The entranceway to hell (Gehenna/Gehinom; the Hinom Valley)—not only that to paradise—is in Jerusalem. From the entrance to Gehenna, south of the Valley of Jehoshaphat, "according to the testimony of local people, you may hear the cries of those in hell, which come up from below," wrote the Persian traveler, "however I myself went there to listen, but heard nothing" (Ibid., 220). Muslim belief states that every person's death is predetermined. But what of those who are alive on the Day of Judgment? They (except for a few important saints) will die when the trumpet sounds, and will be resurrected immediately with all of humankind.

Christian tradition too shares these beliefs regarding the resurrection and Day of Judgment, but does not specify the exact locations where these events will take place. However, it is no coincidence that the site of the Ascension of Jesus is the summit of the Mount of Olives. There he parted from his disciples: "And it came to pass, while he blessed them, he was parted from them, and carried up into heaven" (Luke 24:51).

For hundreds of years, elderly Jews have gathered in Jerusalem in order to die and be buried there. A Christian traveler recounted that "prosperous Jews write in their wills that after their death their bodies are to be taken from the Christian countries and buried in Jerusalem." Another stated, "From all ends of the earth they go up to Jerusalem with wondrous sacred awe before its holiness and with an unbelievable desire to be buried with their ancestors." Small bags of earth from the Mount of Olives have been taken to all parts of the diaspora and laid by the headrests of the dead, so that they may gain holiness from the holy land.

Jews and Muslims came to Jerusalem to be buried in its soil; Christians sent their hearts. The Scottish poet king Robert de Bruce had vowed to take part in the crusades for the deliverance of Jerusalem. Before he could fulfill his vow he fell ill, and prior to his death he requested of his friend, Sir James Douglas: "Since my body cannot go nor achieve that my heart's desire, I will send the heart instead of the body to accomplish mine vow instead of myself. . . . ye take my heart . . . and embalm it. . . . and present my heart to the Holy Sepulchre." And Sir Douglas did as he was requested, but on his way to the holy land, with the heart preserved safely in a silver case, he stopped in Spain to fight the Moors and was killed. The heart was returned to Scotland and buried there. An inscription immortalizing de Bruce's pious wish was placed in St. Andrew's Church in Jerusalem on the six-hundredth anniversary of the king's death. John Patrick Crichton Stuart, a descendent of de Bruce, decided to fulfill his relative's wish by proxy, and ordered his own heart buried in Jerusalem. Members of his family transported it and buried it on the Mount of Olives in 1901.

Why is it that the traditions of all the religions come together only at the End of Days? Why is it that the love of Jerusalem and the reverence for its holiness, shared by all the religious communities, do not become a unifying force in this world, but instead a force for conflict and divisiveness? Serbian author Milorad Pavic explains the power of hatred among neighbors and envy among kin, no doubt from his experience in his own country, which is riven by ethnic and religious conflict: "And there, at the junction of these three borders are confronted the three worlds of the dead . . . the Christian hades with Lucifer's throne . . . the Muslim underworld with Iblis' kingdom of icy torment, and Geburah's territory to the left of the Temple, where the Hebrew gods of evil, greed and hunger sit. . . . These three underworlds do not interfere with one another; their common borders are drawn by an iron plow, and no one is allowed to cross them. . . . Take this as a powerful and ultimate warning, my lord, as the greatest word of wisdom. Have nothing to do with things that involve the three worlds of Islam, Christianity, and Judaism here on earth, so that we may have nothing to do with their underworlds. For those who hate one another are not the problem in this world. They always resemble one another . . . it is those who actually differ among themselves who pose the greatest danger. They long to meet one another because their differences do not bother them. And they are the worst" (*Dictionary of the Khazars* [London: Penguin, 1989], 52–53).

We have not found tranquillity in Jerusalem's city of the dead, but perhaps we have found consolation there. All this city's dead loved her in their own ways. They all sought a safe haven, a new land, a new life—they all strove to build the celestial Zion. They all were borne on waves of hope and they all descended to the depths of despair. Now their tombstones are turning white on her soil, like seashells on the shore, but hope did not perish with them. Perhaps this accumulation of hopes and desires buried in the graveyards of Jerusalem may nurture faith that peace and reconciliation can prevail, even in this world. There is no doubt that the dead, had they mouths to speak, would wish to pass this message on to the living. For when all is said and done, their lives and their deaths bear witness to the fact that in the struggle over Jerusalem there are no victors and no vanquished.

INDEX

Compositor: Publication Services
Text: 10/15 Janson
Display: Syntax Bold
Printer: Bookcrafters
Binder: Bookcrafters